TALES FROM
HARROW
→ FAIR FOLK ←
COUNTY

TALES FROM

HARROW

◆ FAIR FOLK ◆

COUNTY

Created by
CULLEN BUNN
TYLER CROOK

President and Publisher
MIKE RICHARDSON

Editor
DANIEL CHABON

Assistant Editor
CHUCK HOWITT

Assistant Editor
KONNER KNUDSEN

Designer
KEITH WOOD

Digital Art Technician
JOSIE CHRISTENSEN

NEIL HANKERSON Executive Vice President · TOM WEDDLE Chief Financial Officer · DALE LaFOUNTAIN Chief Information Officer

TIM WIESCH Vice President of Licensing · MATT PARKINSON Vice President of Marketing

VANESSA TODD-HOLMES Vice President of Production and Scheduling · MARK BERNARDI Vice President of Book Trade and Digital Sales

RANDY LAHRMAN Vice President of Product Development · KEN LIZZI General Counsel · DAVE MARSHALL Editor in Chief

DAVEY ESTRADA Editorial Director · CHRIS WARNER Senior Books Editor · CARY GRAZZINI Director of Specialty Projects

LIA RIBACCHI Art Director · MATT DRYER Director of Digital Art and Prepress · MICHAEL GOMBOS Senior Director of Licensed Publications

KARI YADRO Director of Custom Programs · KARI TORSON Director of International Licensing

Published by Dark Horse Books
A division of Dark Horse Comics LLC
10956 SE Main Street
Milwaukie, OR 97222

First edition: March 2022
Ebook ISBN 978-1-50672-262-7
Trade Paperback ISBN 978-1-50672-261-0

Comic Shop Locator Service: comicshoplocator.com

Tales from Harrow County Volume 2: Fair Folk

This volume collects Tales from Harrow County: Fair Folk #1–#4.

10 9 8 7 6 5 4 3 2 1
Printed in China

DarkHorse.com

Library of Congress Cataloging-in-Publication Data

Names: Bunn, Cullen, author. | Schnall, Emily, artist. | Crook, Tyler, letterer.

Title: Tales from Harrow County : fair folk / script, Cullen Bunn ; art, Emily Schnall ; lettering, Tyler Crook.

Description: First edition. | Milwaukie, OR : Dark Horse Books, 2022. | "This volume collects Tales from Harrow County: Fair Folk #1-#4." | Summary: "Fresh off the loss of her goblin friend to a strange portal, Bernice must weigh her responsibilities as protector of Harrow County with her desire to get her companion back safe and sound"-- Provided by publisher.

Identifiers: LCCN 2021041718 (print) | LCCN 2021041719 (ebook) | ISBN 9781506722610 (trade paperback) | ISBN 9781506722627 (ebook)

Subjects: LCGFT: Paranormal comics. | Horror comics.

Classification: LCC PN6728.H369 B88 2022 (print) | LCC PN6728.H369 (ebook) | DDC 741.5/973--dc23

LC record available at https://lccn.loc.gov/2021041718
LC ebook record available at https://lccn.loc.gov/2021041719

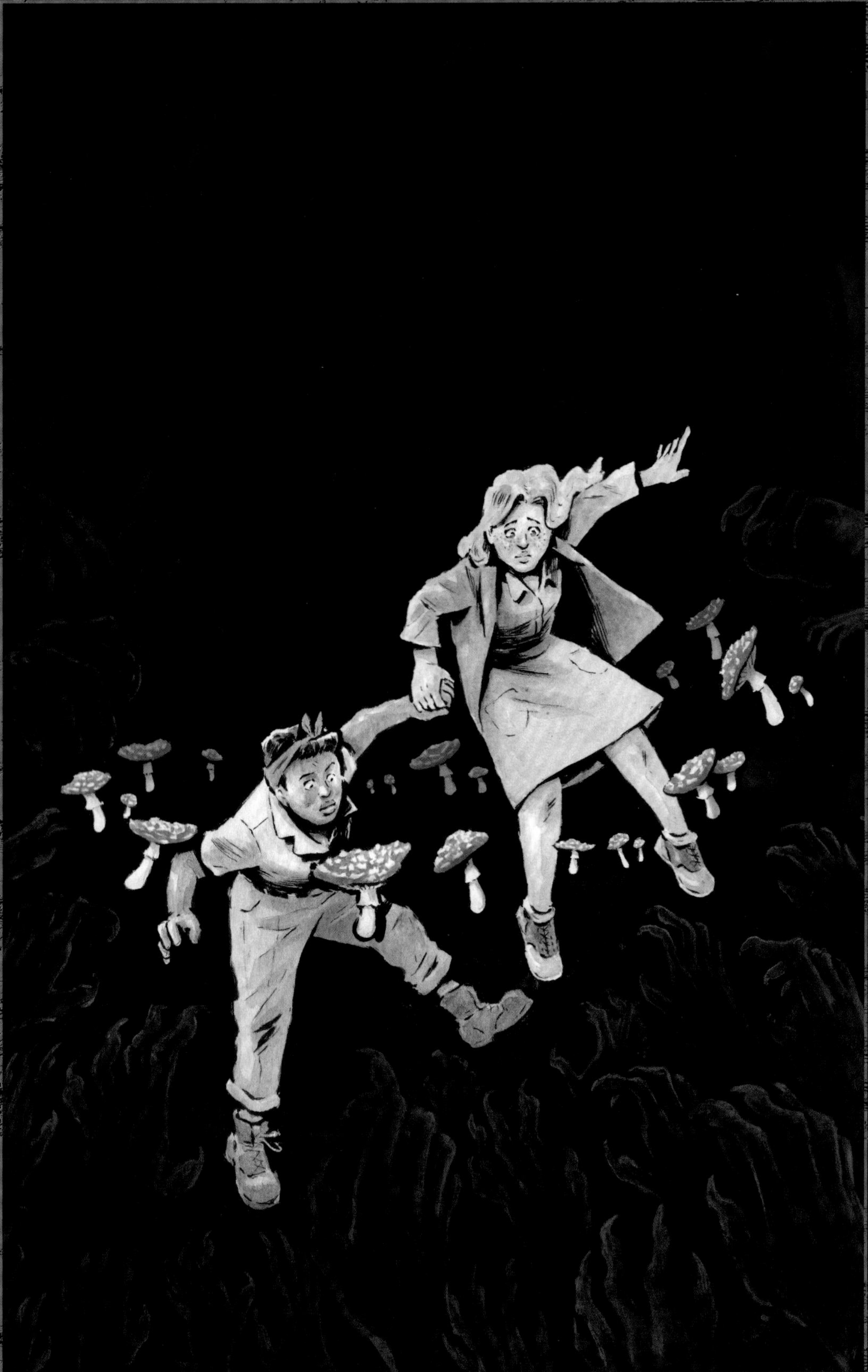

ONE

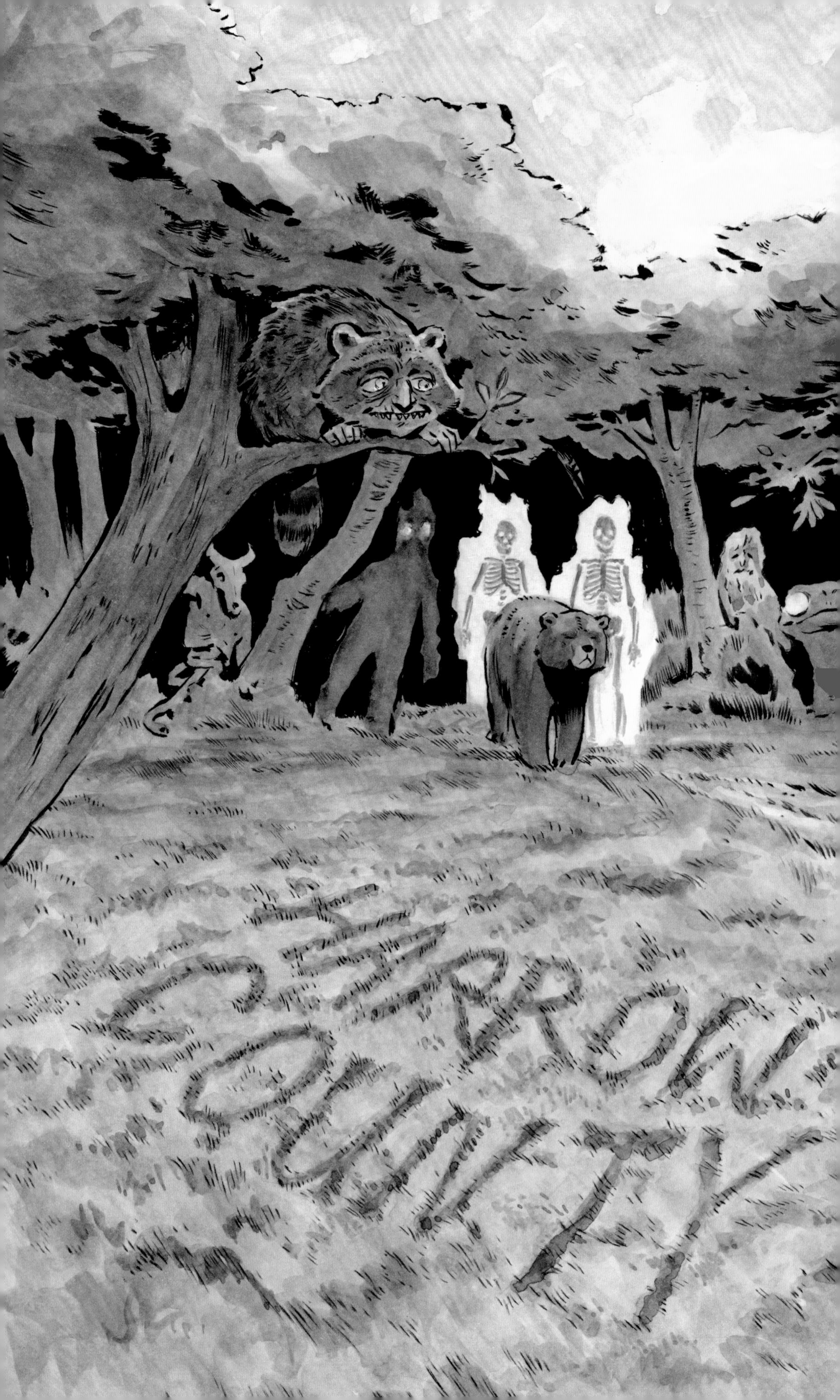
COUNTY

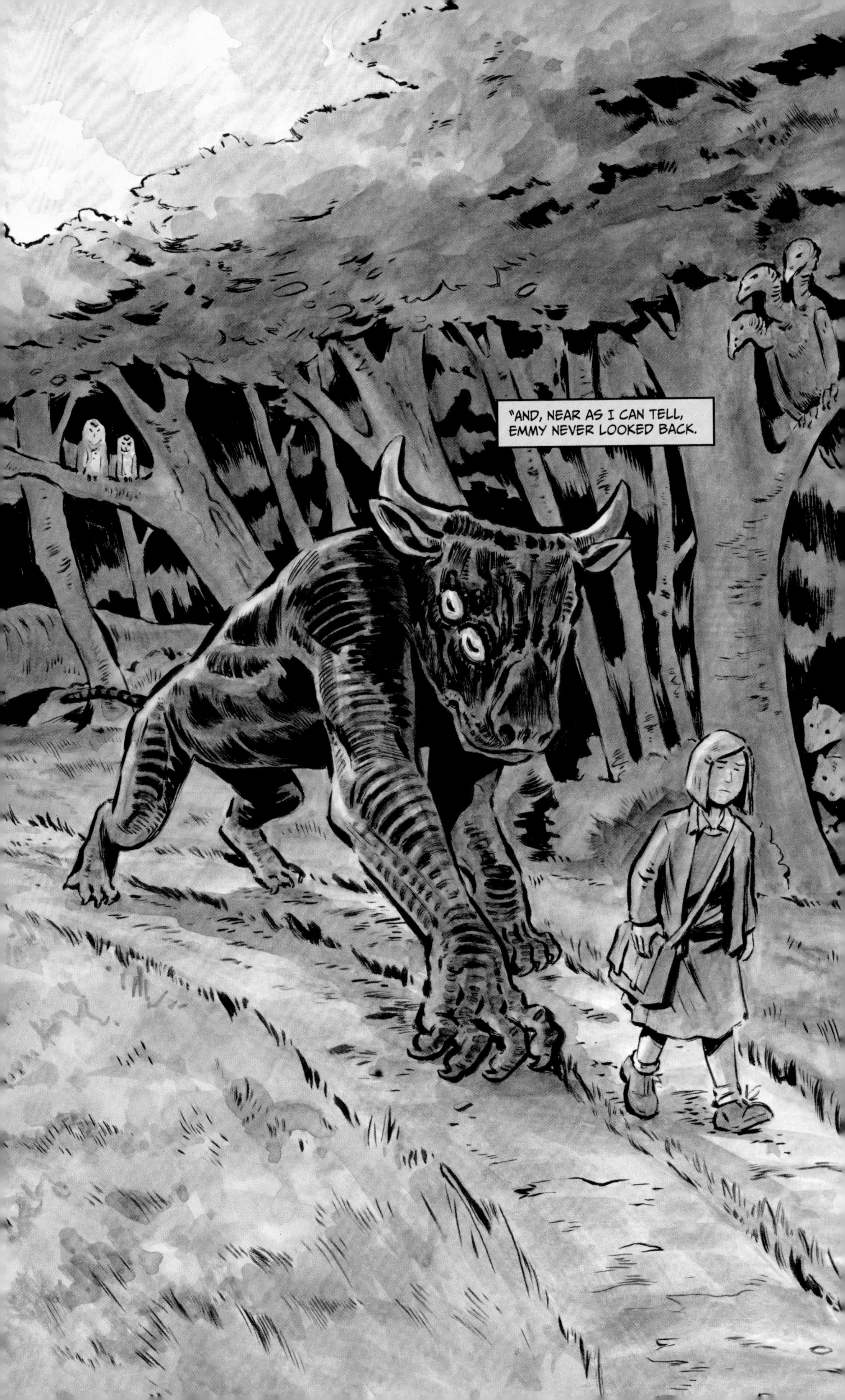
"AND, NEAR AS I CAN TELL, EMMY NEVER LOOKED BACK.

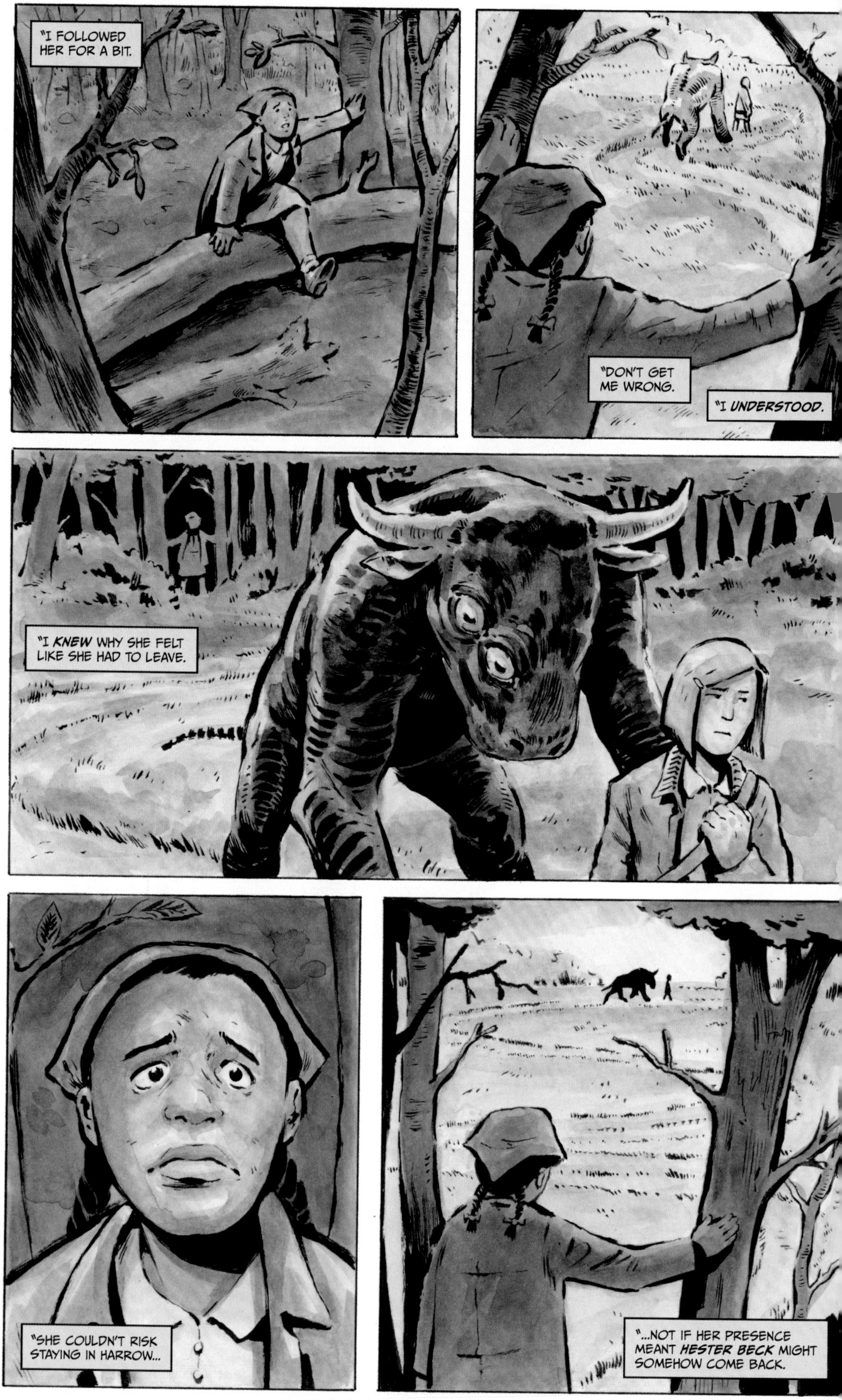
"I FOLLOWED HER FOR A BIT.
"DON'T GET ME WRONG.
"I UNDERSTOOD.
"I KNEW WHY SHE FELT LIKE SHE HAD TO LEAVE.
"SHE COULDN'T RISK STAYING IN HARROW...
"...NOT IF HER PRESENCE MEANT HESTER BECK MIGHT SOMEHOW COME BACK.

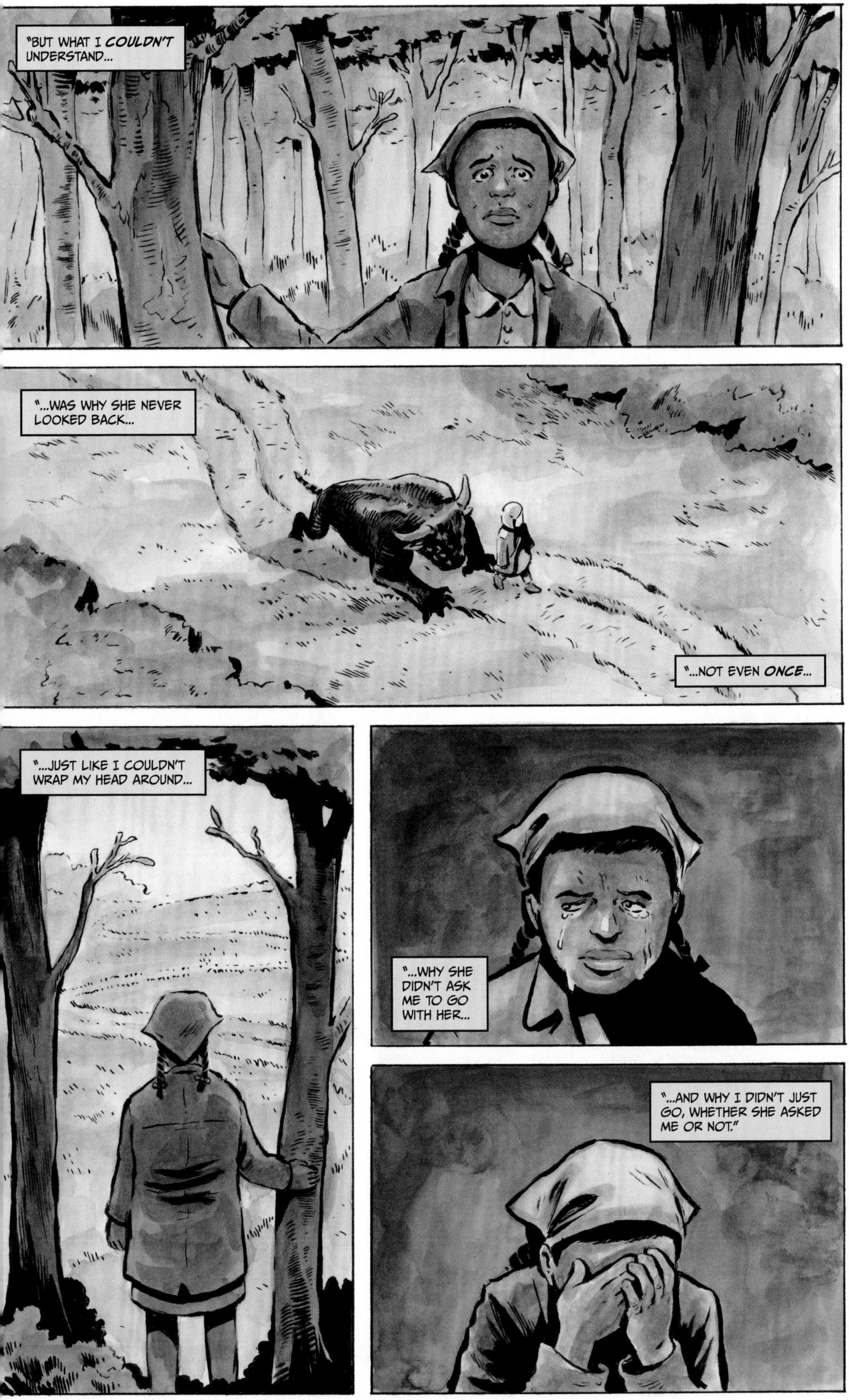
"BUT WHAT I COULDN'T UNDERSTAND...
"...WAS WHY SHE NEVER LOOKED BACK...
"...NOT EVEN ONCE...
"...JUST LIKE I COULDN'T WRAP MY HEAD AROUND...
"...WHY SHE DIDN'T ASK ME TO GO WITH HER...
"...AND WHY I DIDN'T JUST GO, WHETHER SHE ASKED ME OR NOT."

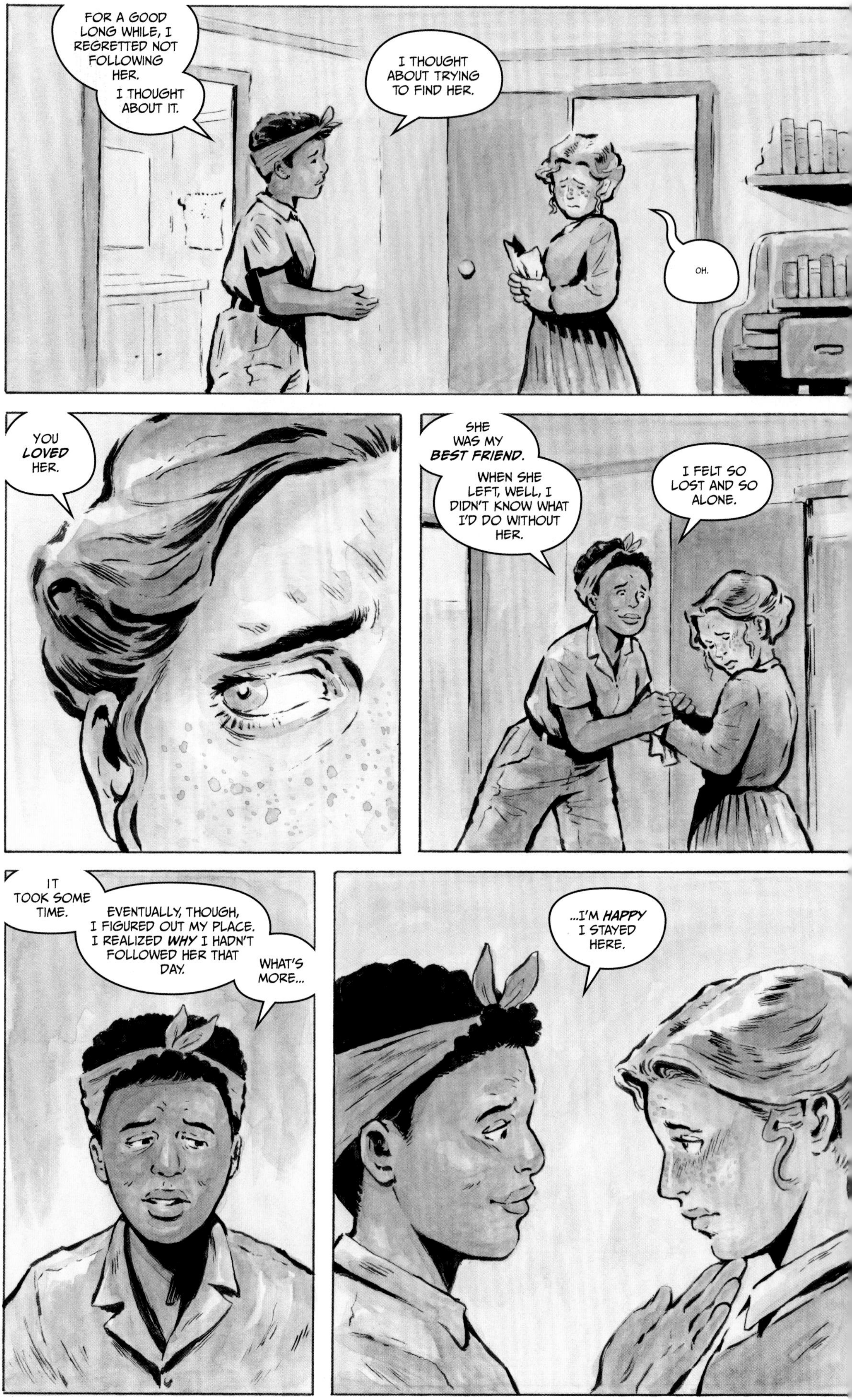

FOR A GOOD LONG WHILE, I REGRETTED NOT FOLLOWING HER.
I THOUGHT ABOUT IT.
I THOUGHT ABOUT TRYING TO FIND HER.
OH.
YOU *LOVED* HER.
SHE WAS MY *BEST FRIEND.*
WHEN SHE LEFT, WELL, I DIDN'T KNOW WHAT I'D DO WITHOUT HER.
I FELT SO LOST AND SO ALONE.
IT TOOK SOME TIME.
EVENTUALLY, THOUGH, I FIGURED OUT MY PLACE. I REALIZED *WHY* I HADN'T FOLLOWED HER THAT DAY.
WHAT'S MORE...
...I'M *HAPPY* I STAYED HERE.

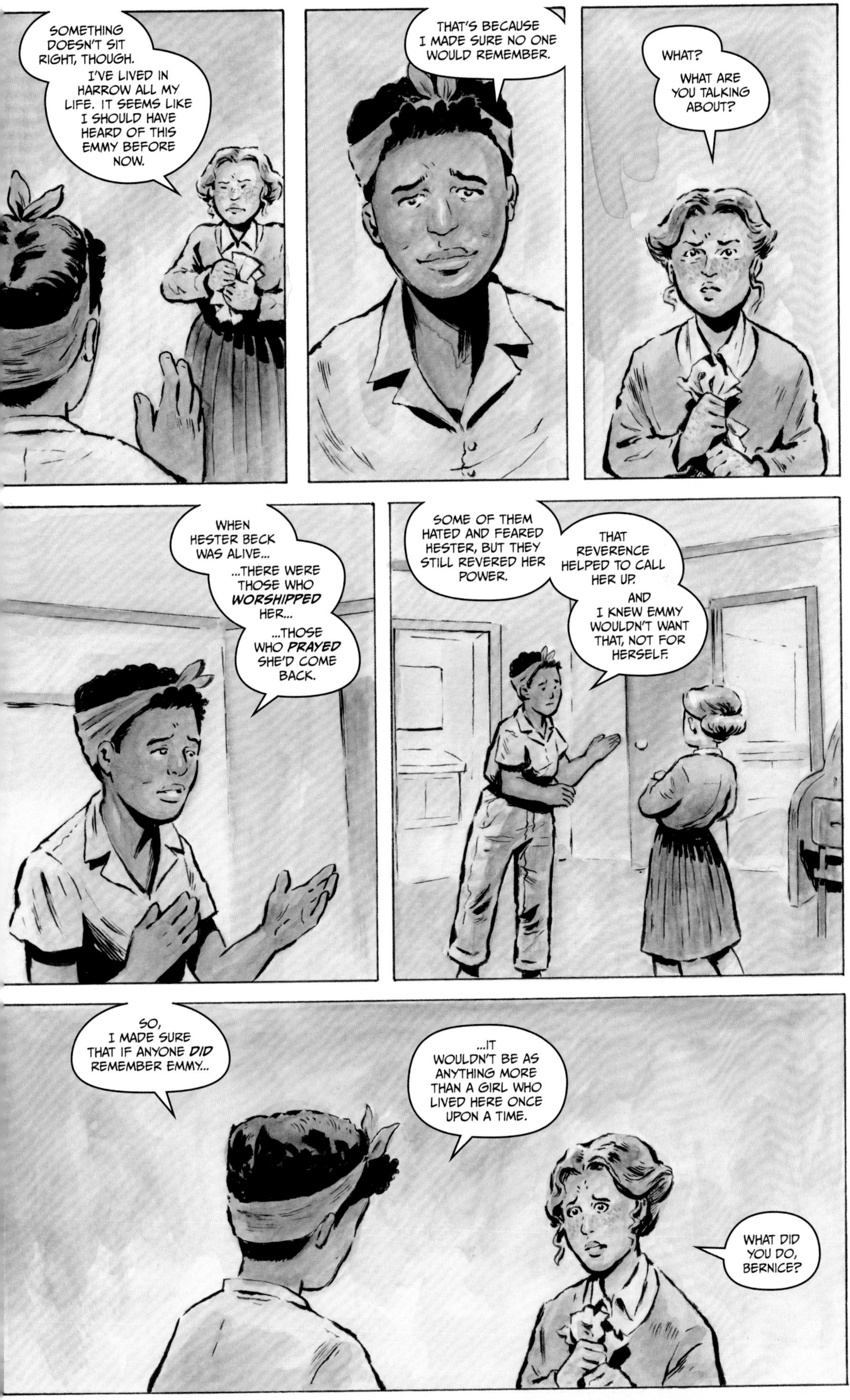
SOMETHING DOESN'T SIT RIGHT, THOUGH.
I'VE LIVED IN HARROW ALL MY LIFE. IT SEEMS LIKE I SHOULD HAVE HEARD OF THIS EMMY BEFORE NOW.
THAT'S BECAUSE I MADE SURE NO ONE WOULD REMEMBER.
WHAT?
WHAT ARE YOU TALKING ABOUT?
WHEN HESTER BECK WAS ALIVE...
...THERE WERE THOSE WHO WORSHIPPED HER...
...THOSE WHO PRAYED SHE'D COME BACK.
SOME OF THEM HATED AND FEARED HESTER, BUT THEY STILL REVERED HER POWER.
THAT REVERENCE HELPED TO CALL HER UP.
AND I KNEW EMMY WOULDN'T WANT THAT, NOT FOR HERSELF.
SO, I MADE SURE THAT IF ANYONE DID REMEMBER EMMY...
...IT WOULDN'T BE AS ANYTHING MORE THAN A GIRL WHO LIVED HERE ONCE UPON A TIME.
WHAT DID YOU DO, BERNICE?

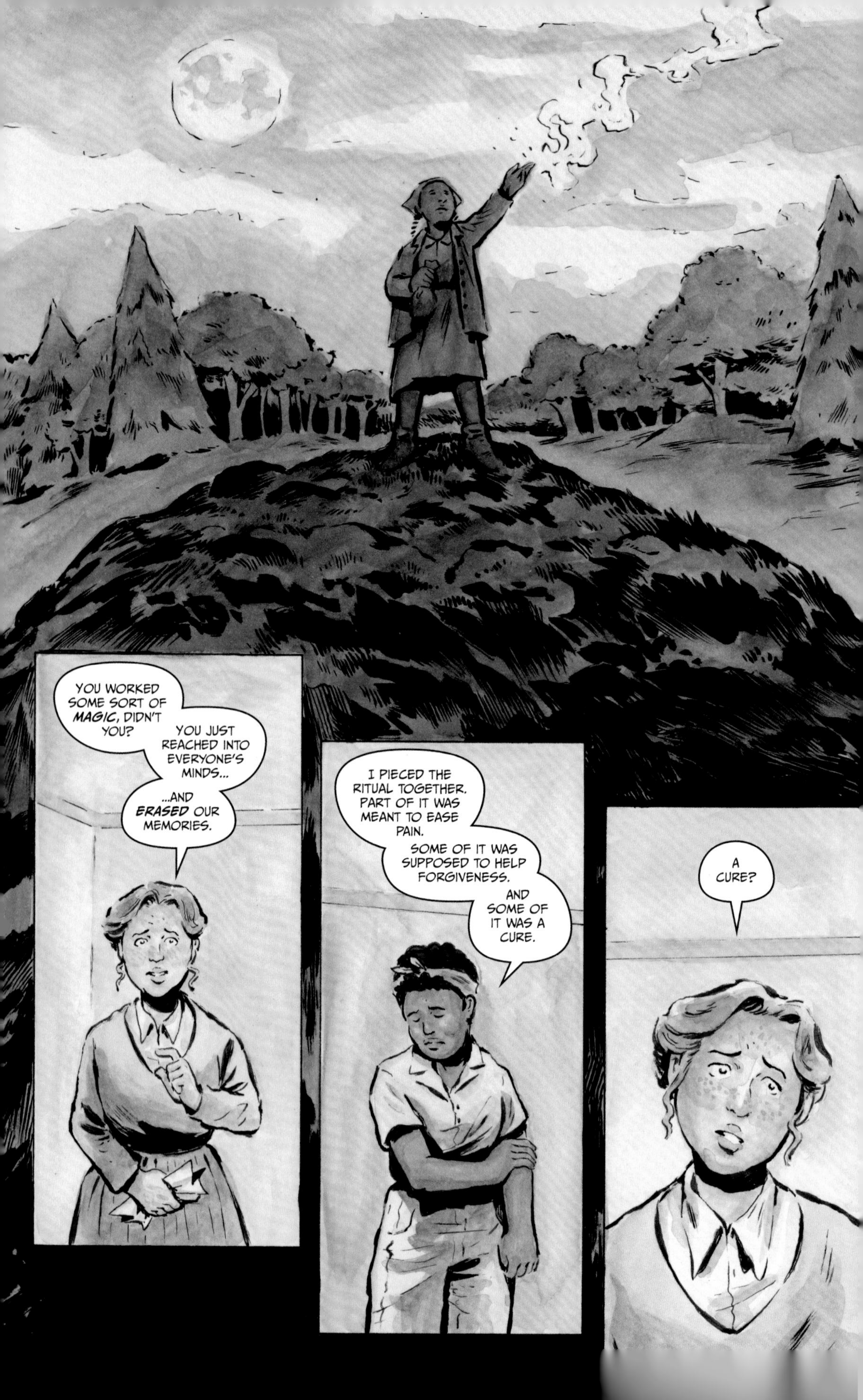
YOU WORKED SOME SORT OF MAGIC, DIDN'T YOU?
YOU JUST REACHED INTO EVERYONE'S MINDS...
...AND ERASED OUR MEMORIES.
I PIECED THE RITUAL TOGETHER. PART OF IT WAS MEANT TO EASE PAIN.
SOME OF IT WAS SUPPOSED TO HELP FORGIVENESS.
AND SOME OF IT WAS A CURE.
A CURE?

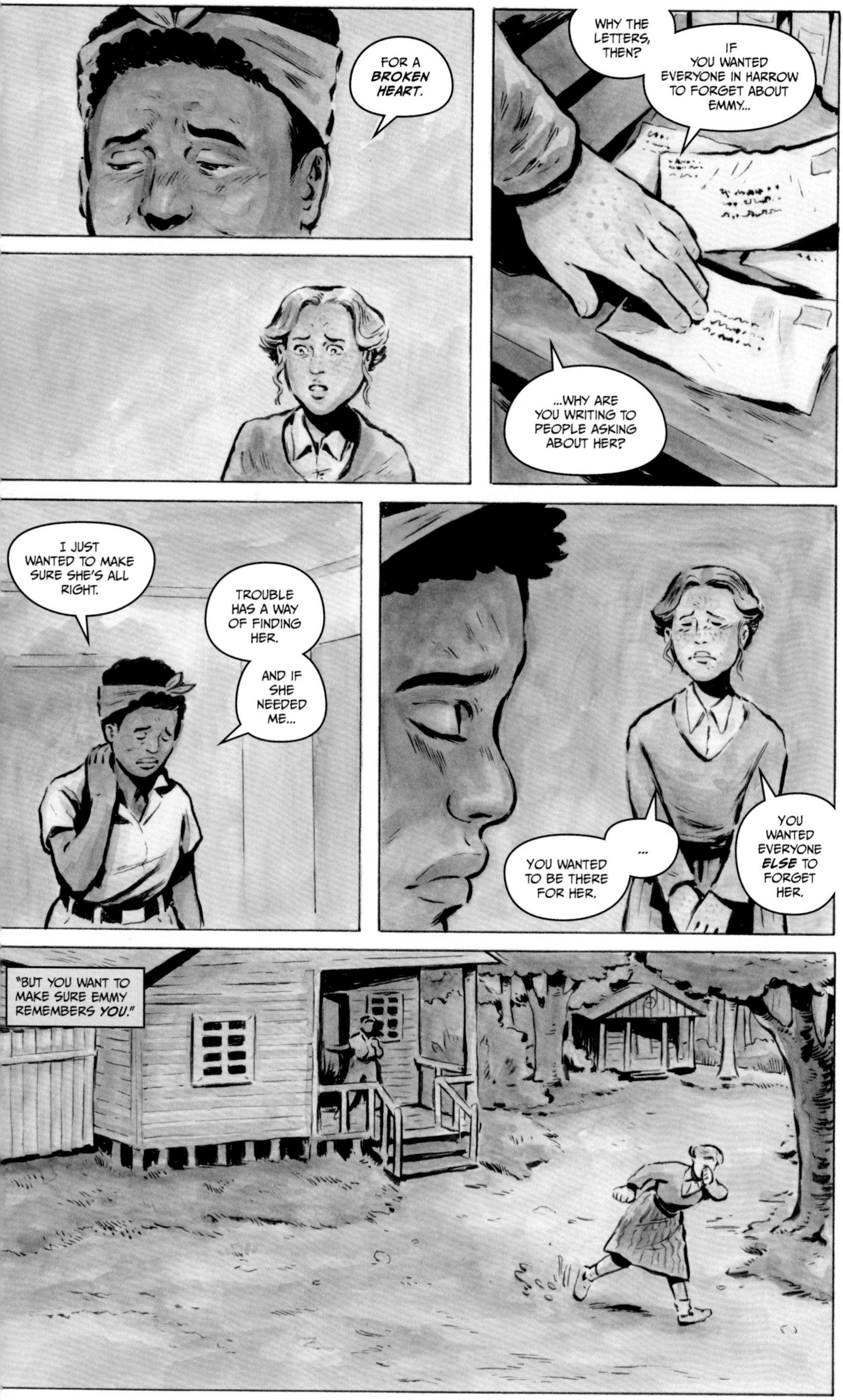
FOR A *BROKEN HEART.*
WHY THE LETTERS, THEN?
IF YOU WANTED EVERYONE IN HARROW TO FORGET ABOUT EMMY...
...WHY ARE YOU WRITING TO PEOPLE ASKING ABOUT HER?
I JUST WANTED TO MAKE SURE SHE'S ALL RIGHT.
TROUBLE HAS A WAY OF FINDING HER.
AND IF SHE NEEDED ME...
...
YOU WANTED TO BE THERE FOR HER.
YOU WANTED EVERYONE *ELSE* TO FORGET HER.
"BUT YOU WANT TO MAKE SURE EMMY REMEMBERS *YOU.*"

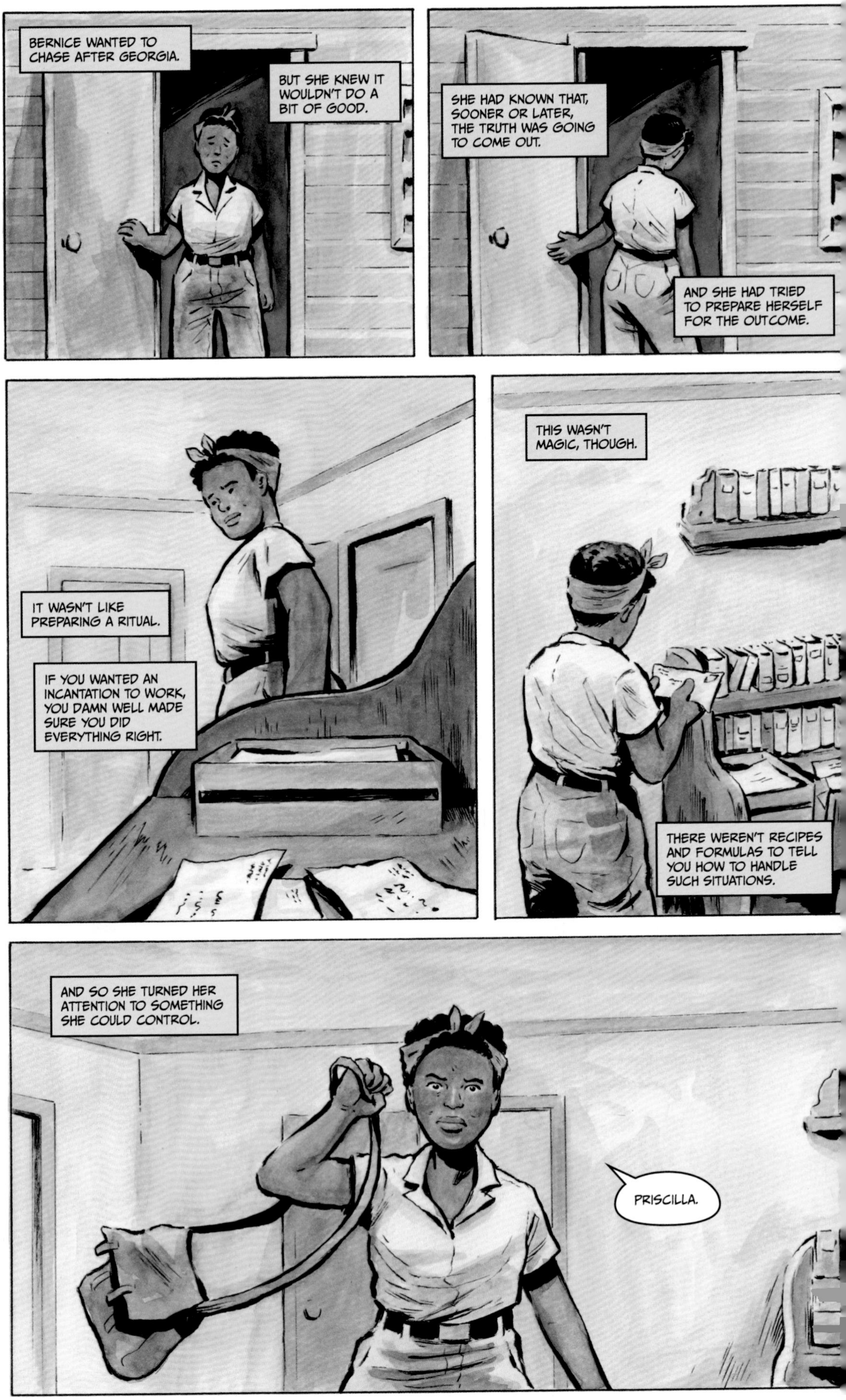
BERNICE WANTED TO CHASE AFTER GEORGIA.
BUT SHE KNEW IT WOULDN'T DO A BIT OF GOOD.
SHE HAD KNOWN THAT, SOONER OR LATER, THE TRUTH WAS GOING TO COME OUT.
AND SHE HAD TRIED TO PREPARE HERSELF FOR THE OUTCOME.
IT WASN'T LIKE PREPARING A RITUAL.
IF YOU WANTED AN INCANTATION TO WORK, YOU DAMN WELL MADE SURE YOU DID EVERYTHING RIGHT.
THIS WASN'T MAGIC, THOUGH.
THERE WEREN'T RECIPES AND FORMULAS TO TELL YOU HOW TO HANDLE SUCH SITUATIONS.
AND SO SHE TURNED HER ATTENTION TO SOMETHING SHE COULD CONTROL.
PRISCILLA.

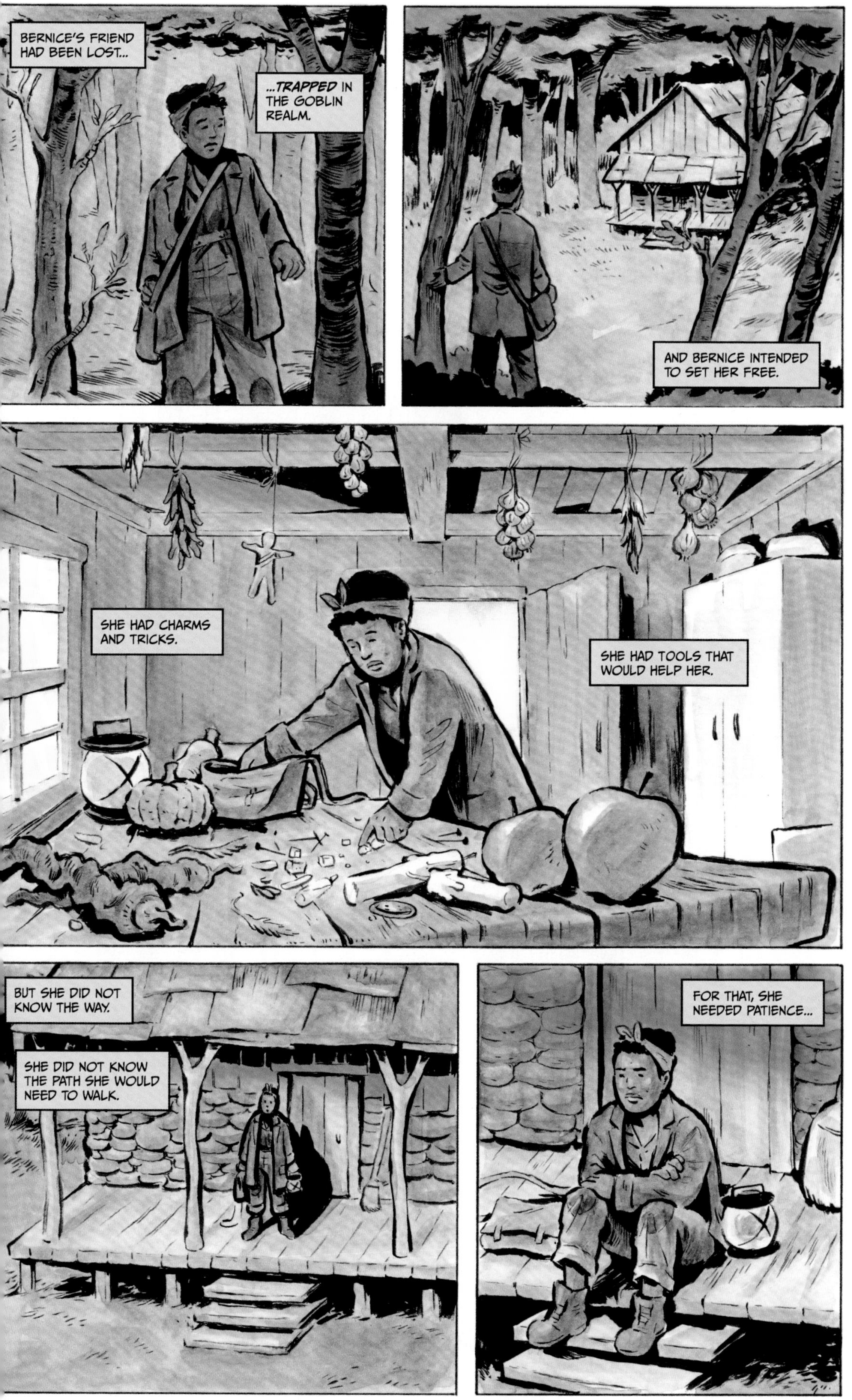

BERNICE'S FRIEND HAD BEEN LOST...
...*TRAPPED* IN THE GOBLIN REALM.
AND BERNICE INTENDED TO SET HER FREE.
SHE HAD CHARMS AND TRICKS.
SHE HAD TOOLS THAT WOULD HELP HER.
BUT SHE DID NOT KNOW THE WAY.
SHE DID NOT KNOW THE PATH SHE WOULD NEED TO WALK.
FOR THAT, SHE NEEDED PATIENCE...

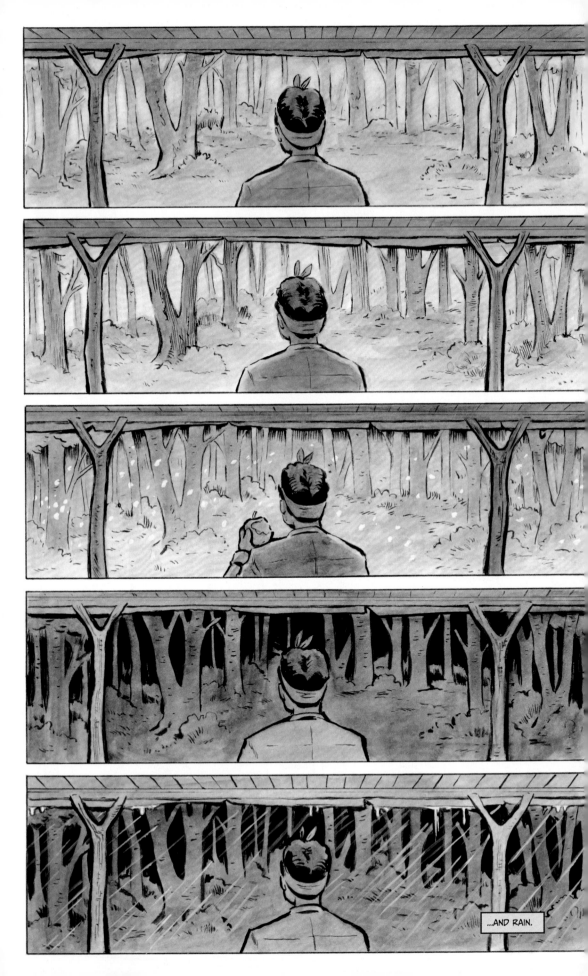

...AND RAIN.

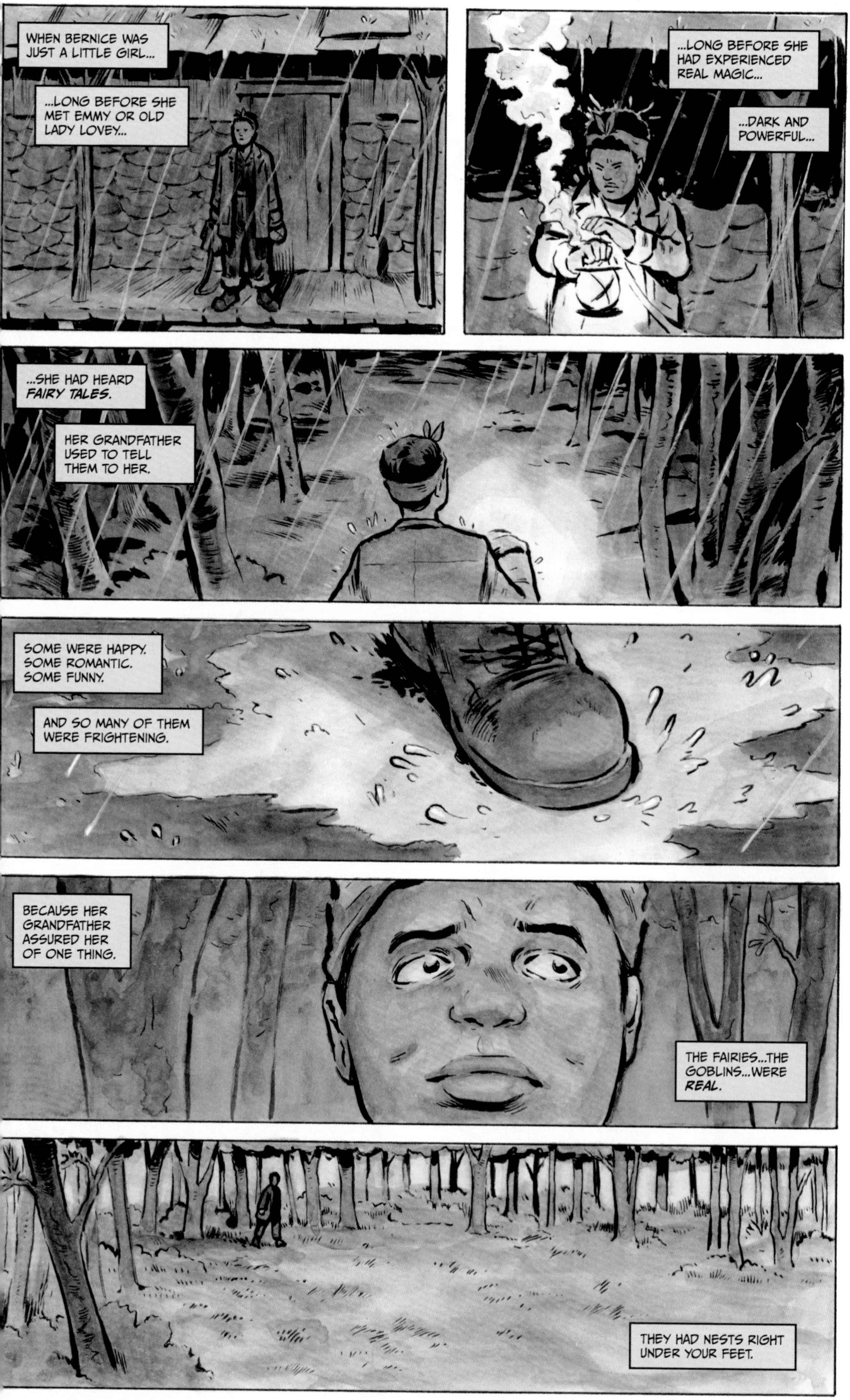
WHEN BERNICE WAS JUST A LITTLE GIRL...
...LONG BEFORE SHE MET EMMY OR OLD LADY LOVEY...
...LONG BEFORE SHE HAD EXPERIENCED REAL MAGIC...
...DARK AND POWERFUL...
...SHE HAD HEARD *FAIRY TALES*.
HER GRANDFATHER USED TO TELL THEM TO HER.
SOME WERE HAPPY. SOME ROMANTIC. SOME FUNNY.
AND SO MANY OF THEM WERE FRIGHTENING.
BECAUSE HER GRANDFATHER ASSURED HER OF ONE THING.
THE FAIRIES...THE GOBLINS...WERE *REAL*.
THEY HAD NESTS RIGHT UNDER YOUR FEET.

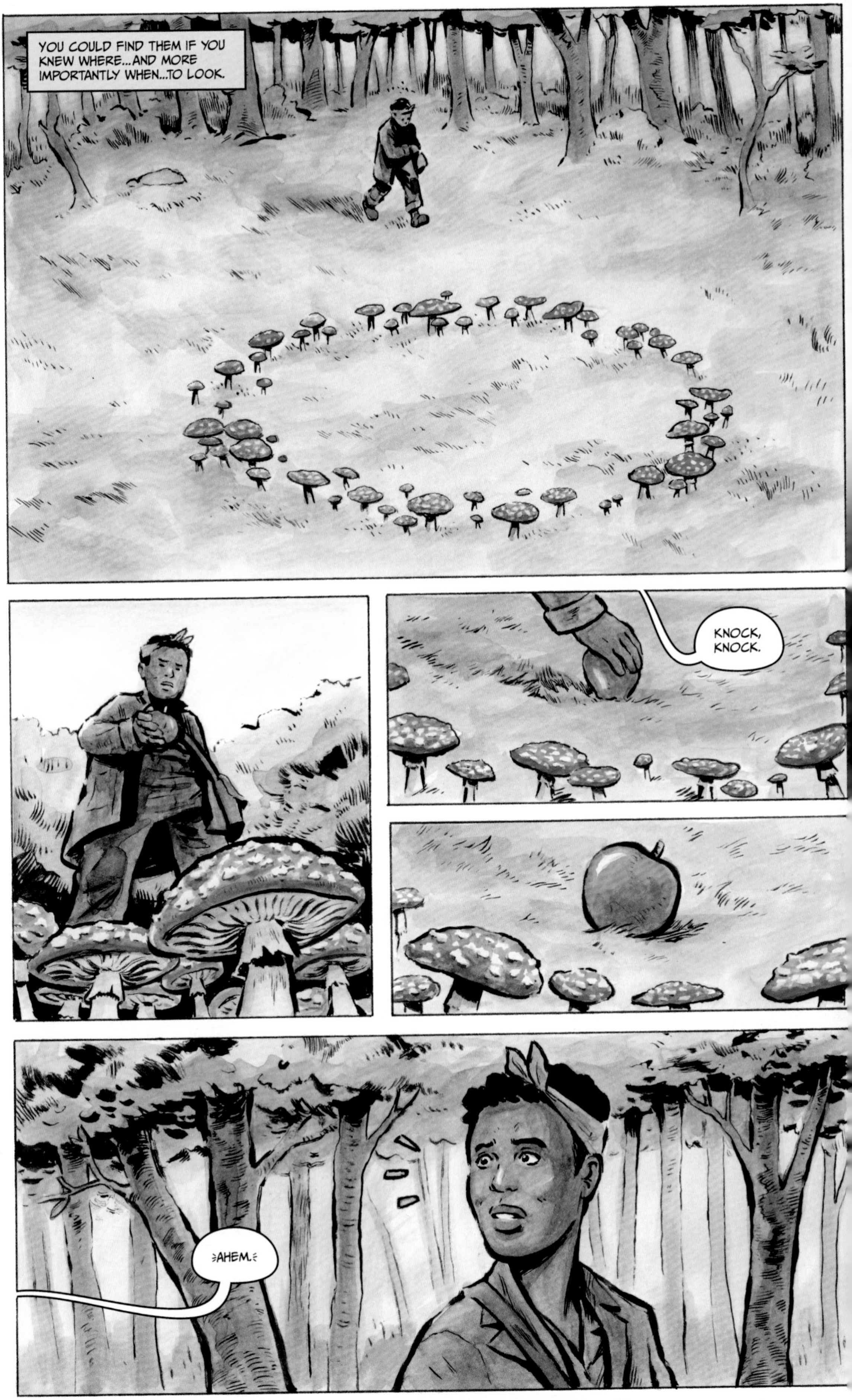
YOU COULD FIND THEM IF YOU KNEW WHERE...AND MORE IMPORTANTLY WHEN...TO LOOK.
KNOCK, KNOCK.
AHEM.

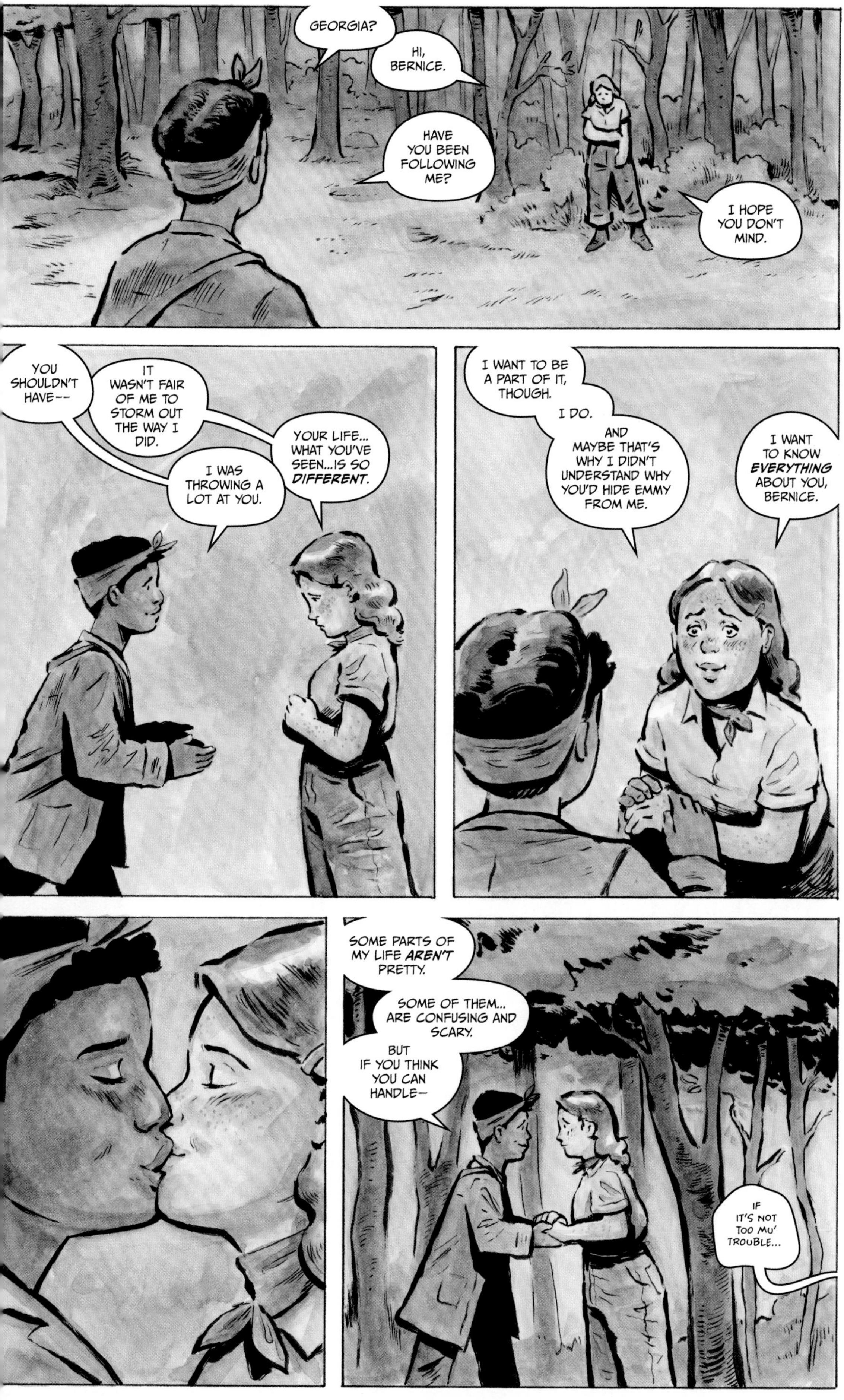
GEORGIA?
HI, BERNICE.
HAVE YOU BEEN FOLLOWING ME?
I HOPE YOU DON'T MIND.
YOU SHOULDN'T HAVE--
IT WASN'T FAIR OF ME TO STORM OUT THE WAY I DID.
I WAS THROWING A LOT AT YOU.
YOUR LIFE... WHAT YOU'VE SEEN...IS SO *DIFFERENT*.
I WANT TO BE A PART OF IT, THOUGH.
I DO.
AND MAYBE THAT'S WHY I DIDN'T UNDERSTAND WHY YOU'D HIDE EMMY FROM ME.
I WANT TO KNOW ***EVERYTHING*** ABOUT YOU, BERNICE.
SOME PARTS OF MY LIFE ***AREN'T*** PRETTY.
SOME OF THEM... ARE CONFUSING AND SCARY.
BUT IF YOU THINK YOU CAN HANDLE--
IF IT'S NOT TOO MU' TROUBLE...

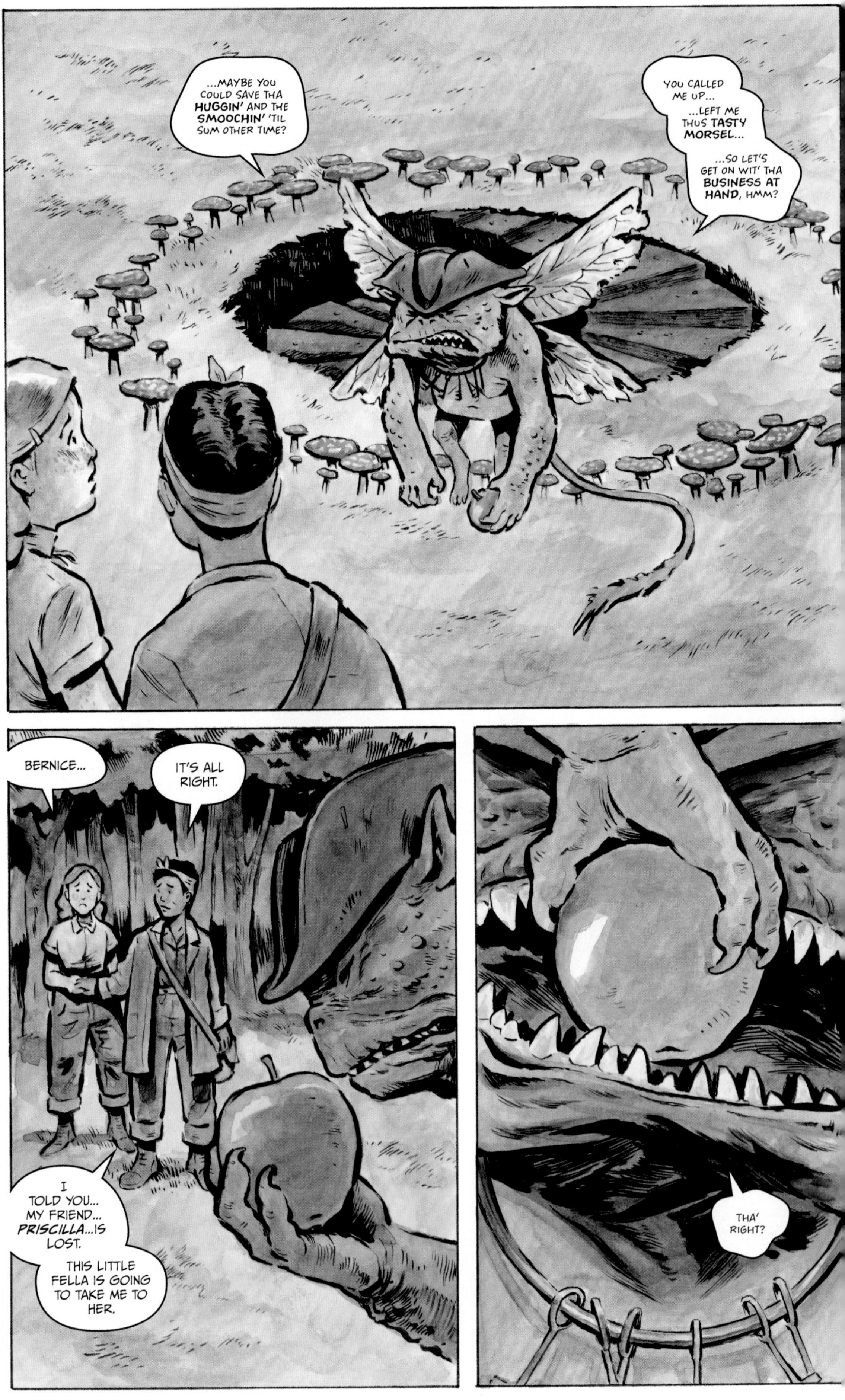

...MAYBE YOU COULD SAVE THA HUGGIN' AND THE SMOOCHIN' 'TIL SUM OTHER TIME?
YOU CALLED ME UP...
...LEFT ME THUS TASTY MORSEL...
...SO LET'S GET ON WIT' THA BUSINESS AT HAND, HMM?
BERNICE...
IT'S ALL RIGHT.
I TOLD YOU... MY FRIEND... PRISCILLA...IS LOST.
THIS LITTLE FELLA IS GOING TO TAKE ME TO HER.
THA' RIGHT?

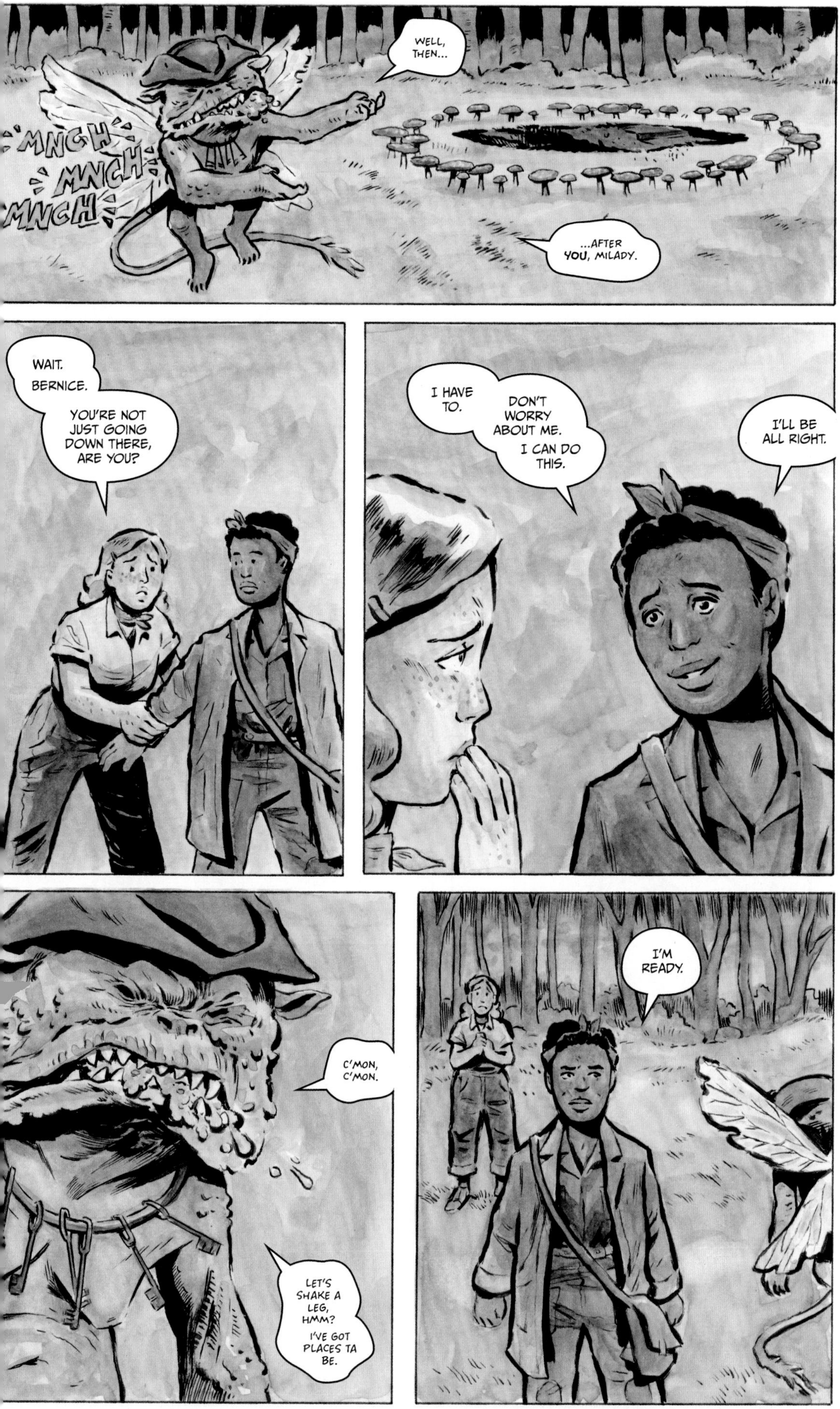
WELL, THEN...
MNCH MNCH MNCH
...AFTER YOU, MILADY.
WAIT.
BERNICE.
YOU'RE NOT JUST GOING DOWN THERE, ARE YOU?
I HAVE TO.
DON'T WORRY ABOUT ME.
I CAN DO THIS.
I'LL BE ALL RIGHT.
C'MON, C'MON.
LET'S SHAKE A LEG, HMM?
I'VE GOT PLACES TA BE.
I'M READY.

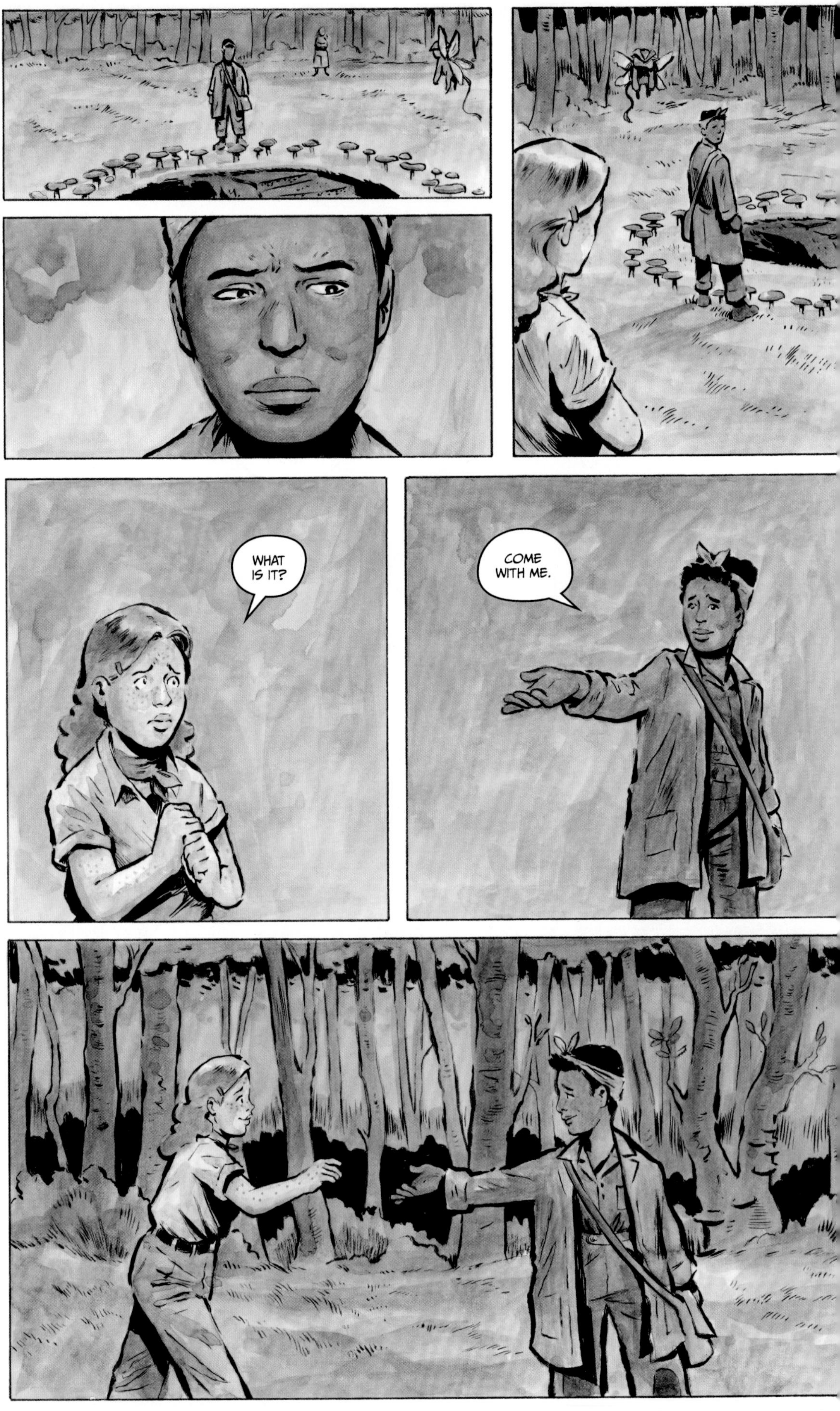
WHAT IS IT?
COME WITH ME.

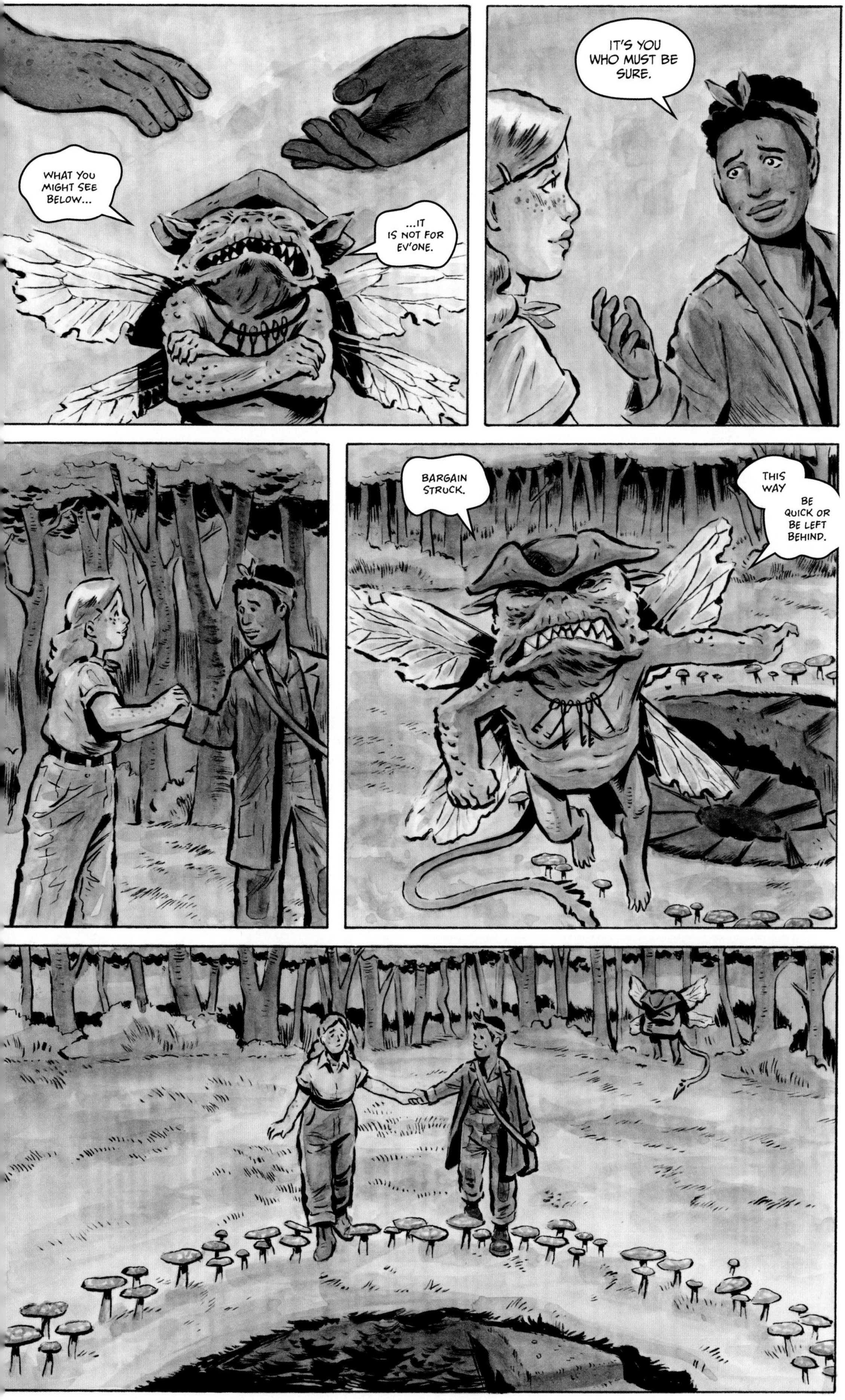
WHAT YOU MIGHT SEE BELOW...
...IT IS NOT FOR EV'ONE.
IT'S YOU WHO MUST BE SURE.
BARGAIN STRUCK.
THIS WAY
BE QUICK OR BE LEFT BEHIND.

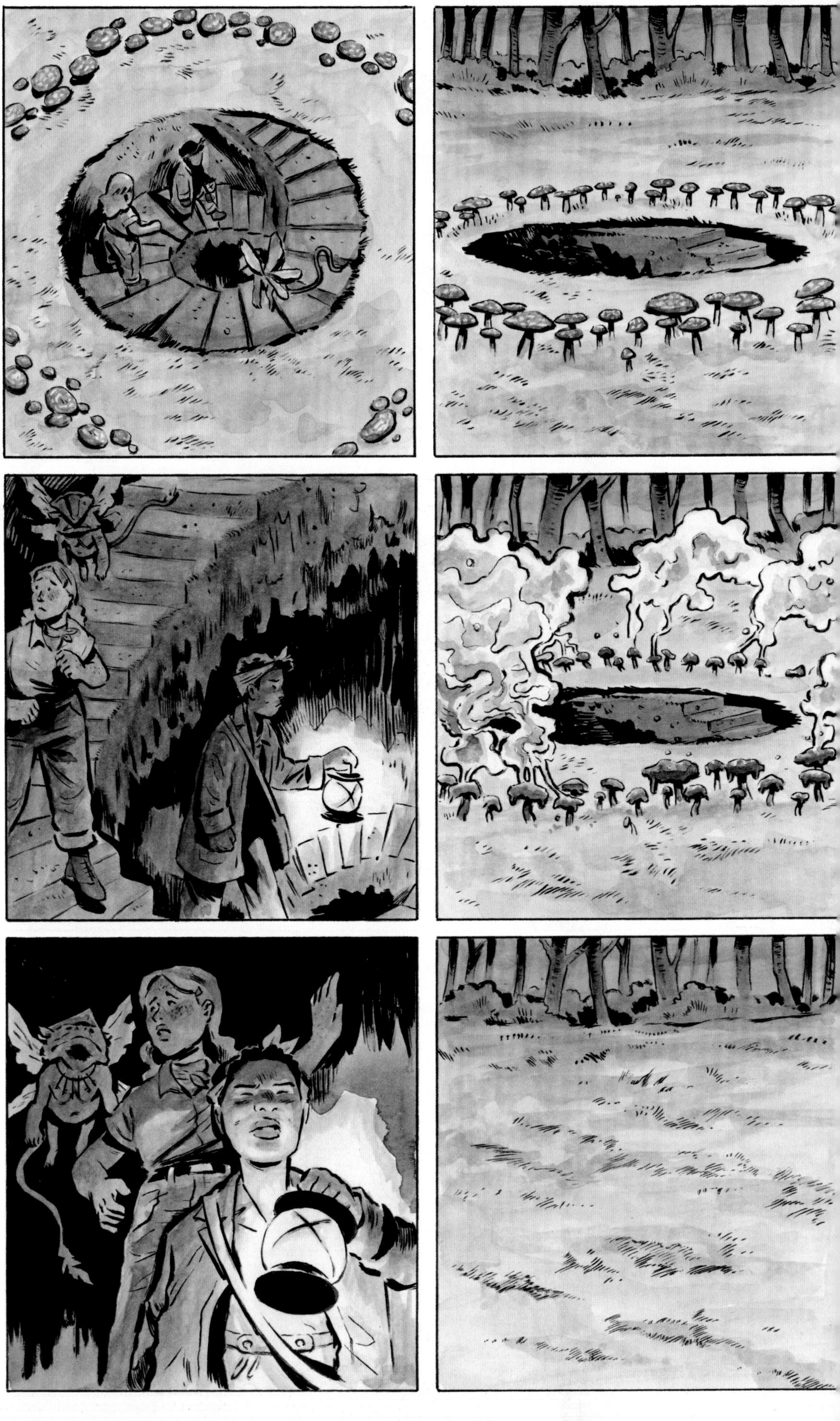

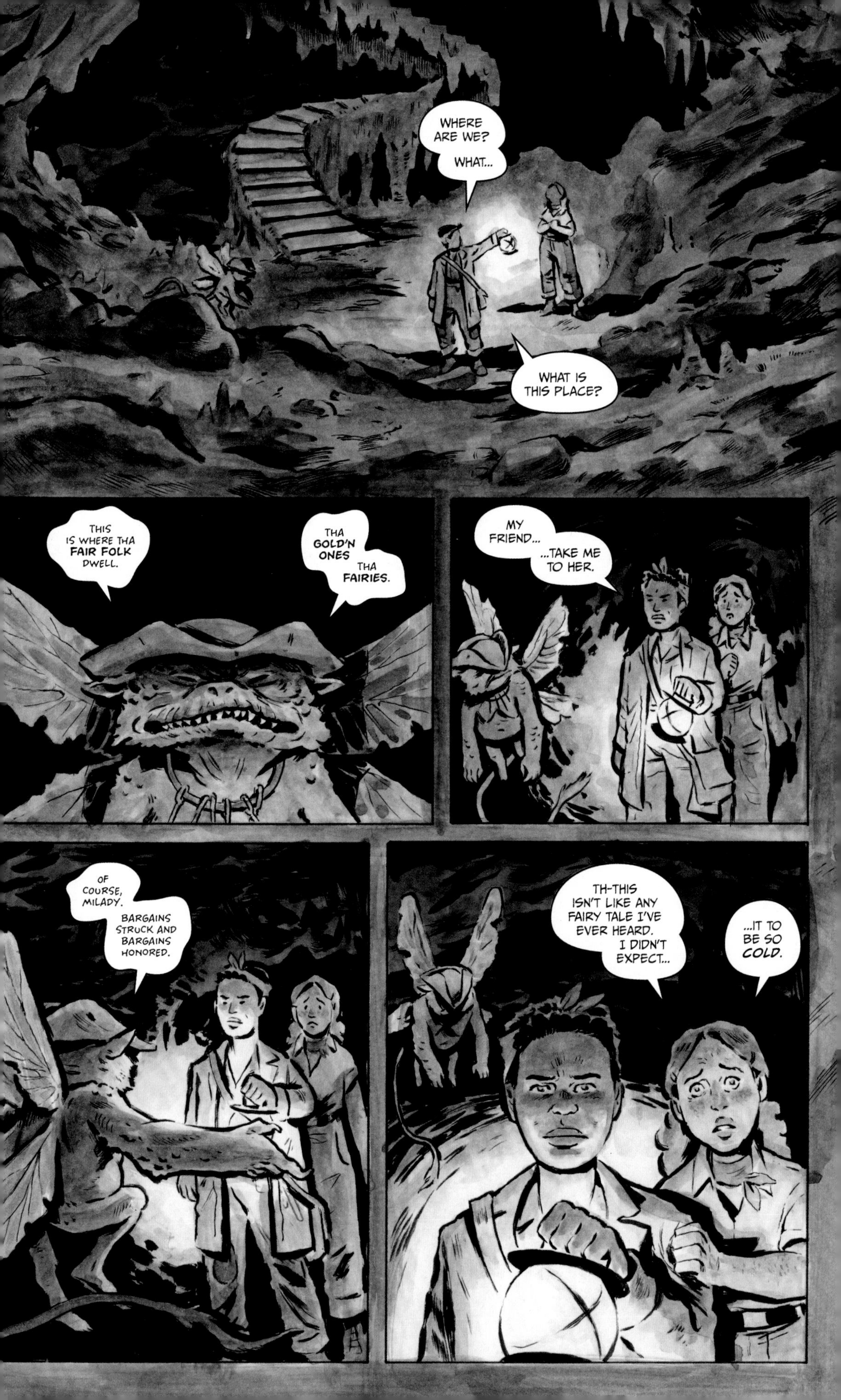

WHERE ARE WE?
WHAT...
WHAT IS THIS PLACE?
THIS IS WHERE THA FAIR FOLK DWELL.
THA GOLD'N ONES THA FAIRIES.
MY FRIEND...
...TAKE ME TO HER.
OF COURSE, MILADY.
BARGAINS STRUCK AND BARGAINS HONORED.
TH-THIS ISN'T LIKE ANY FAIRY TALE I'VE EVER HEARD.
I DIDN'T EXPECT...
...IT TO BE SO COLD.

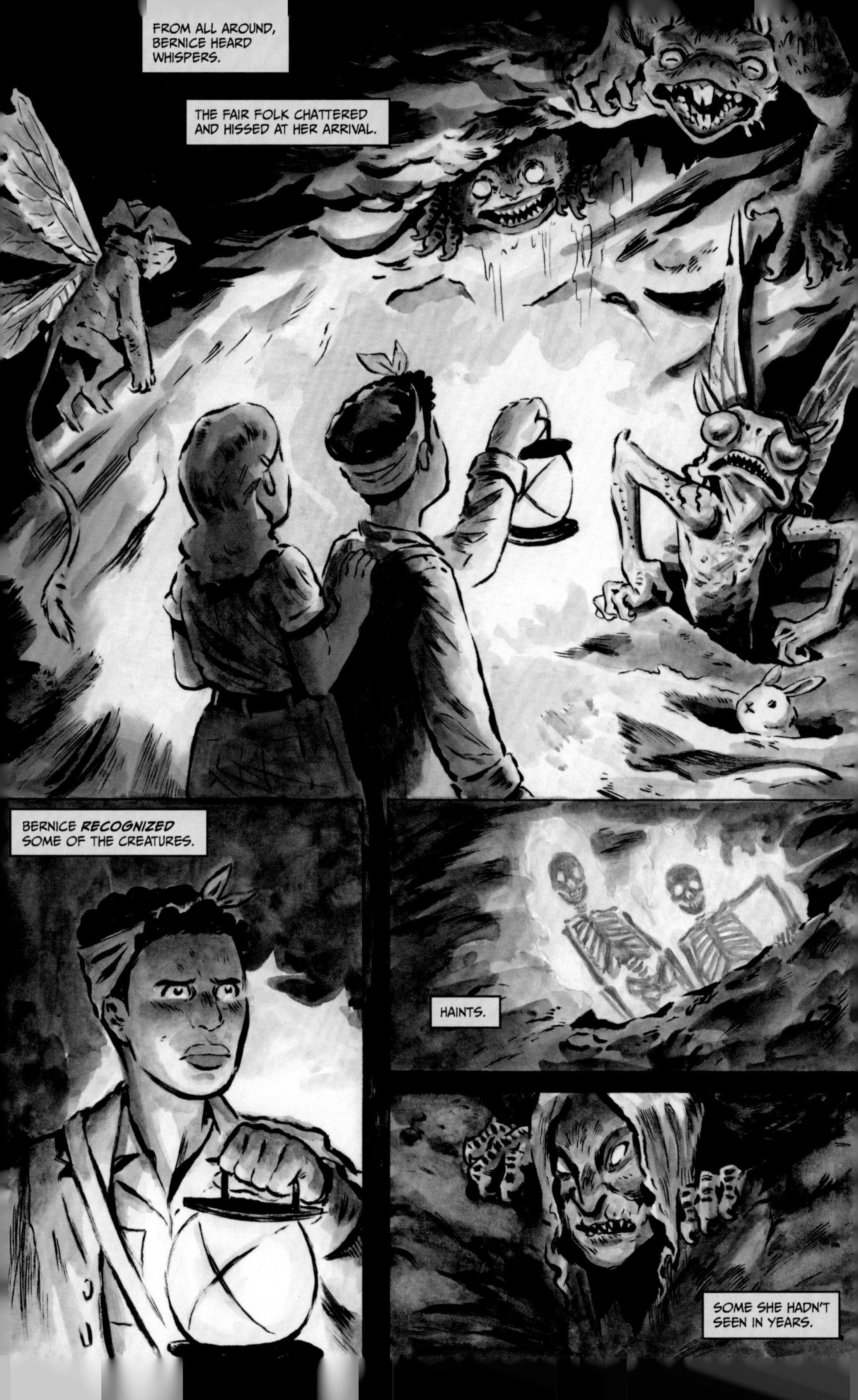
FROM ALL AROUND, BERNICE HEARD WHISPERS.
THE FAIR FOLK CHATTERED AND HISSED AT HER ARRIVAL.
BERNICE *RECOGNIZED* SOME OF THE CREATURES.
HAINTS.
SOME SHE HADN'T SEEN IN YEARS.

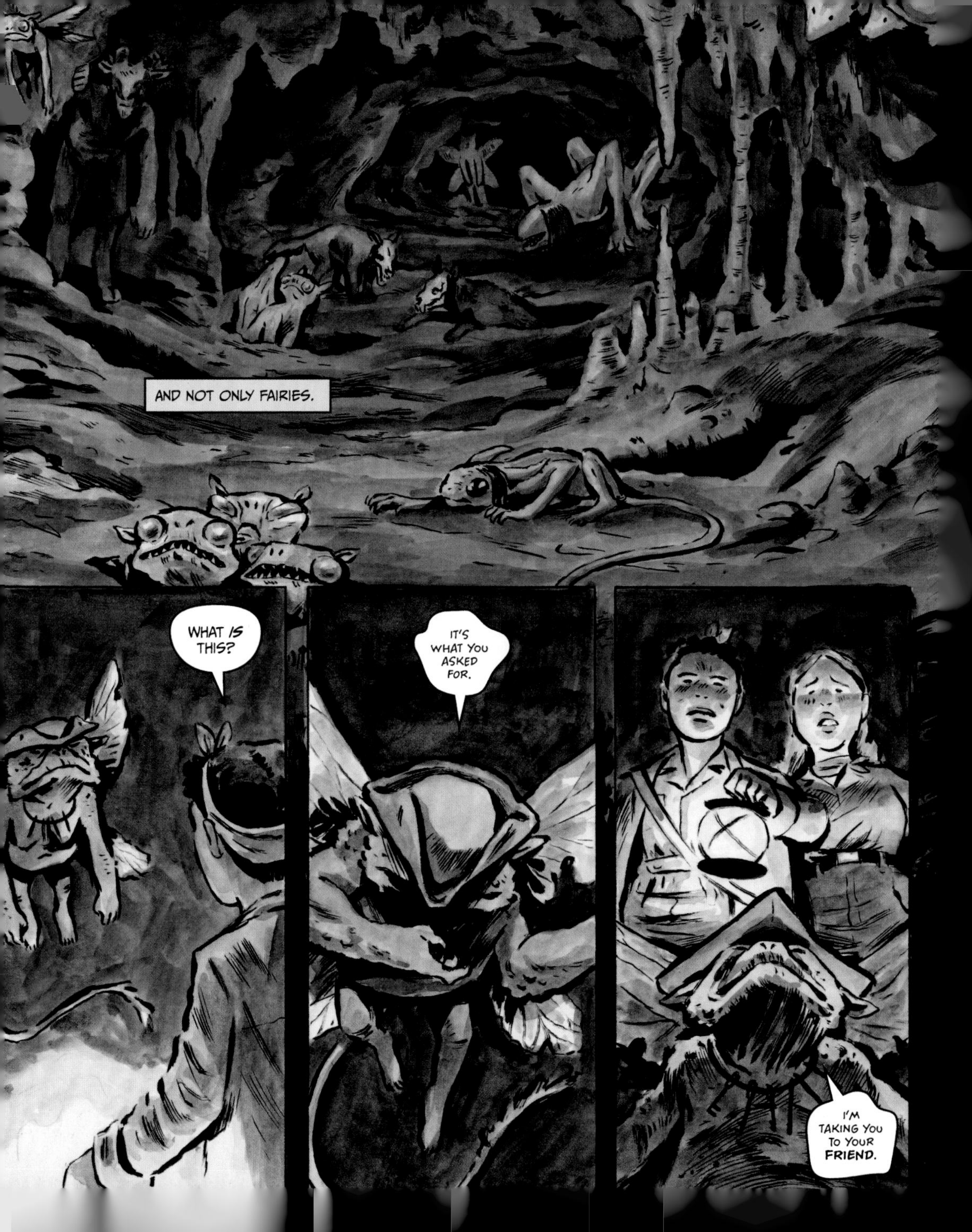
AND NOT ONLY FAIRIES.
WHAT *IS* THIS?
IT'S WHAT YOU ASKED FOR.
I'M TAKING YOU TO YOUR **FRIEND**.

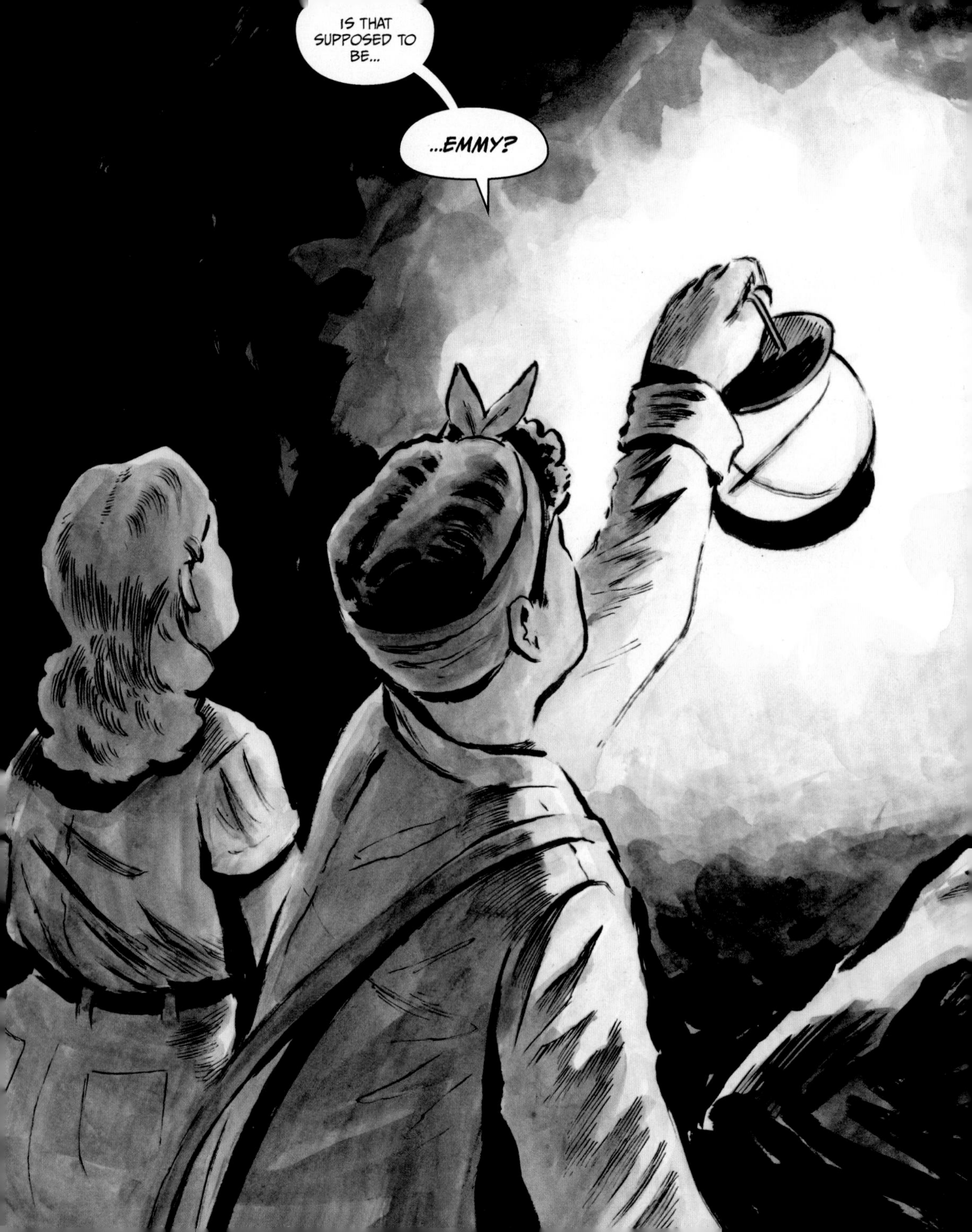
IS THAT SUPPOSED TO BE...
...EMMY?

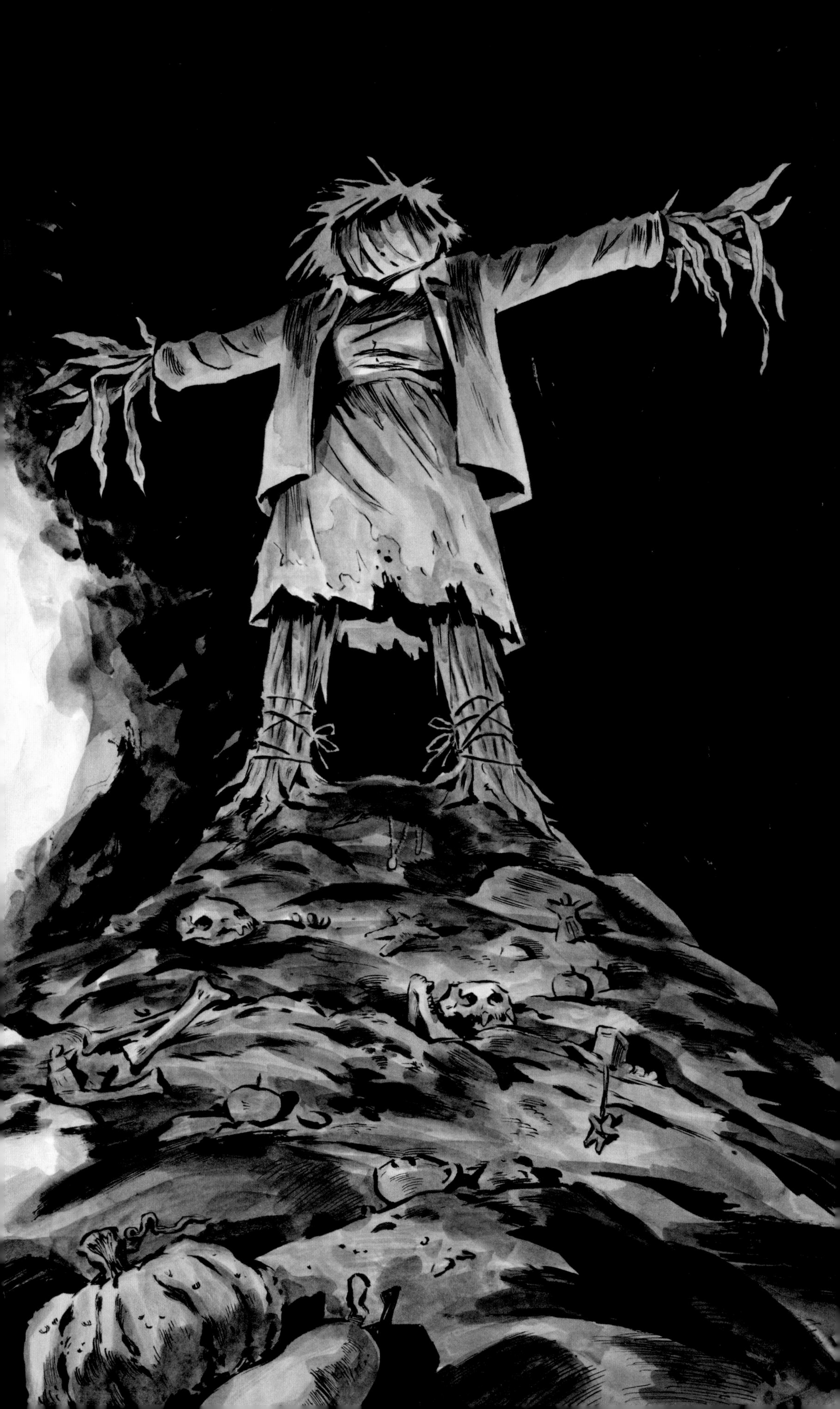

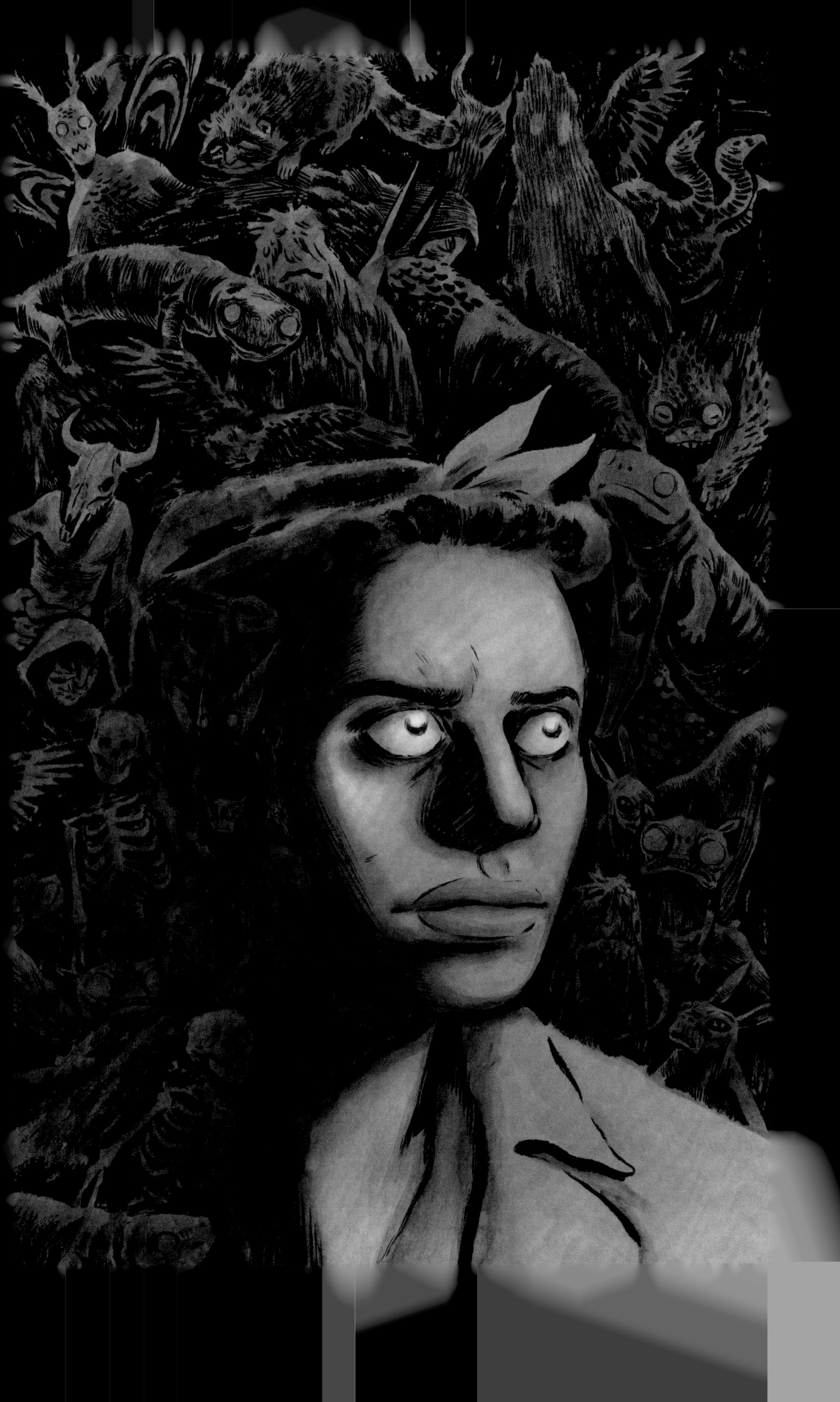

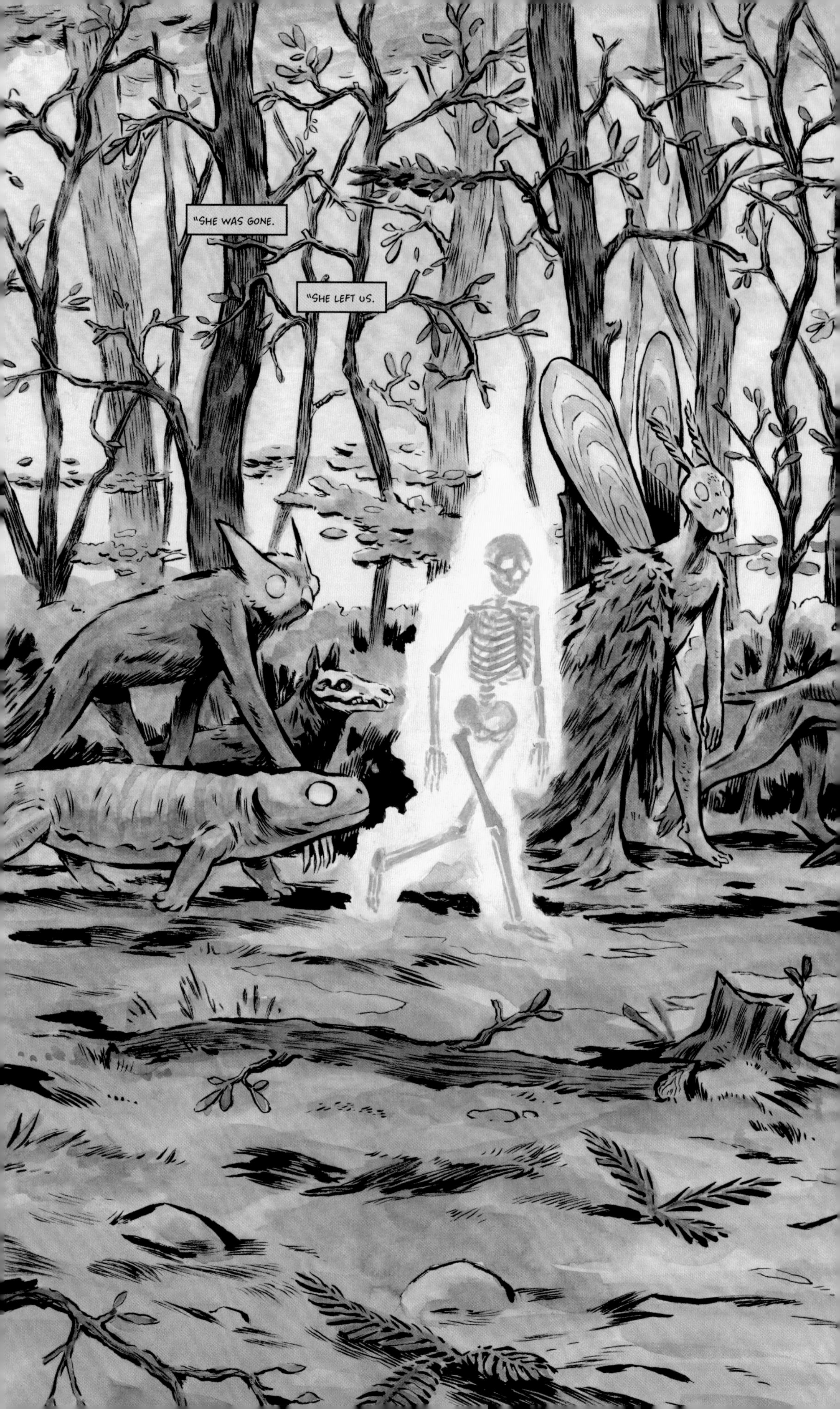
"SHE WAS GONE.
"SHE LEFT US.

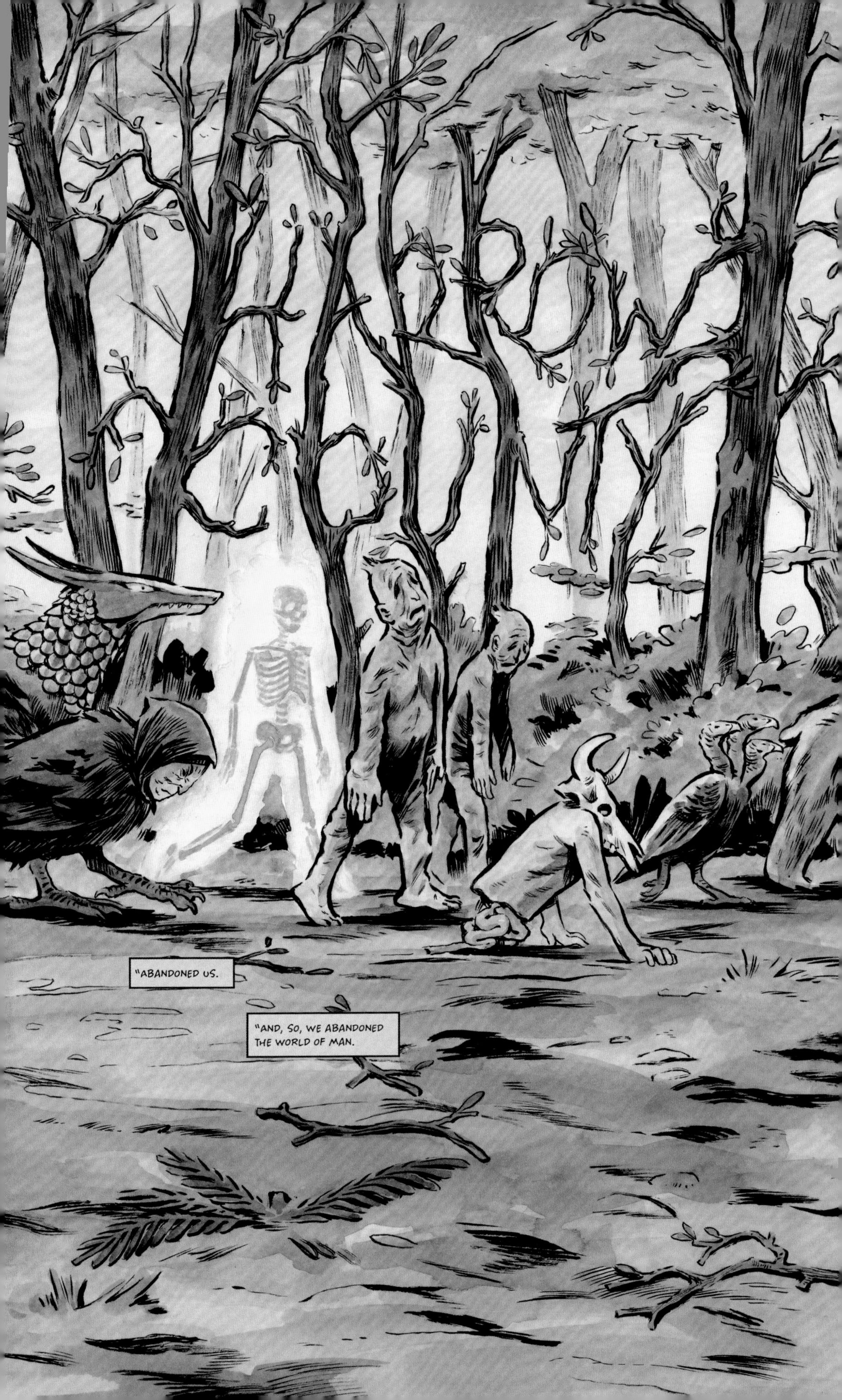
"ABANDONED US.
"AND, SO, WE ABANDONED THE WORLD OF MAN.

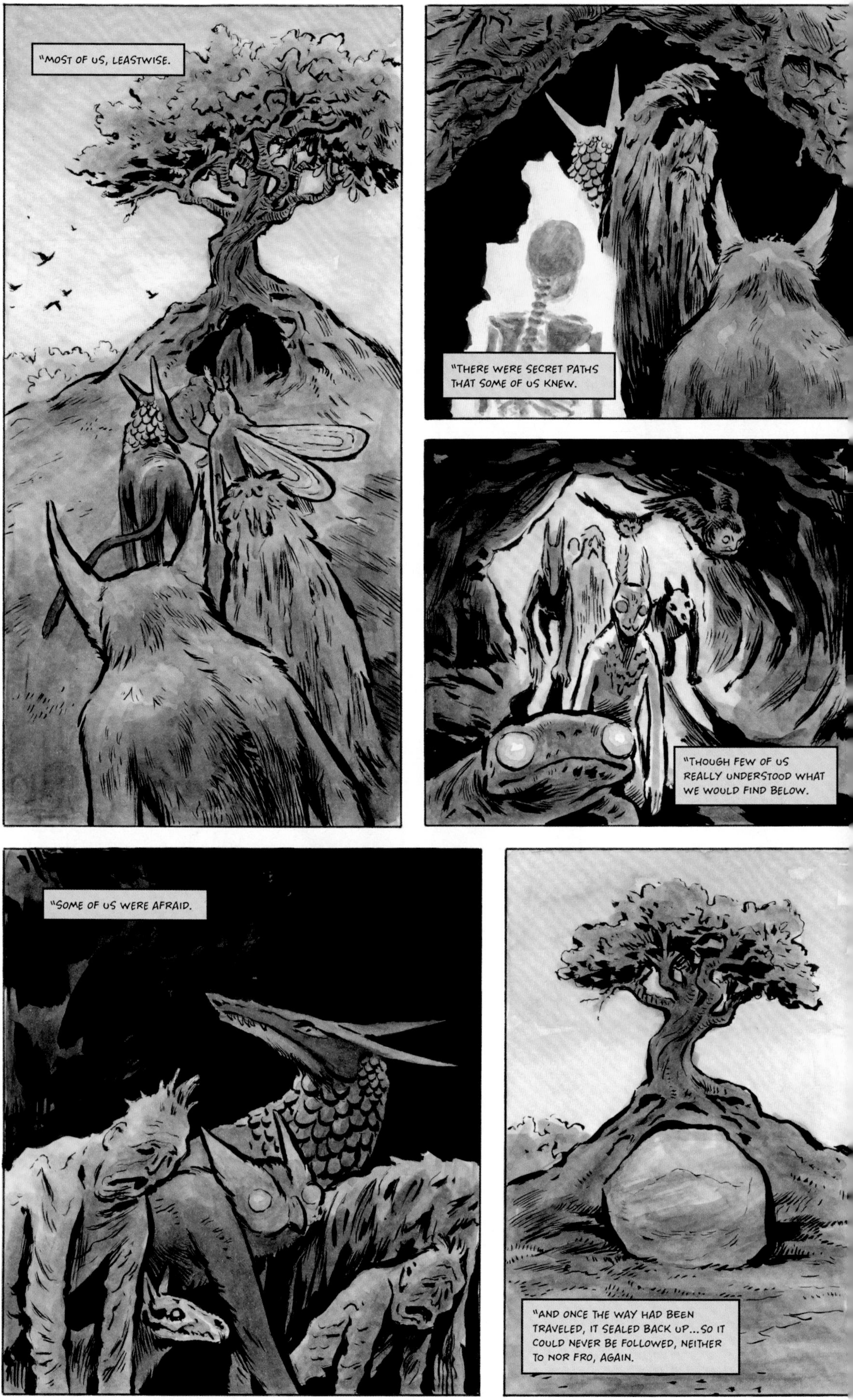
"MOST OF US, LEASTWISE.
"THERE WERE SECRET PATHS THAT SOME OF US KNEW.
"THOUGH FEW OF US REALLY UNDERSTOOD WHAT WE WOULD FIND BELOW.
"SOME OF US WERE AFRAID.
"AND ONCE THE WAY HAD BEEN TRAVELED, IT SEALED BACK UP...SO IT COULD NEVER BE FOLLOWED, NEITHER TO NOR FRO, AGAIN.

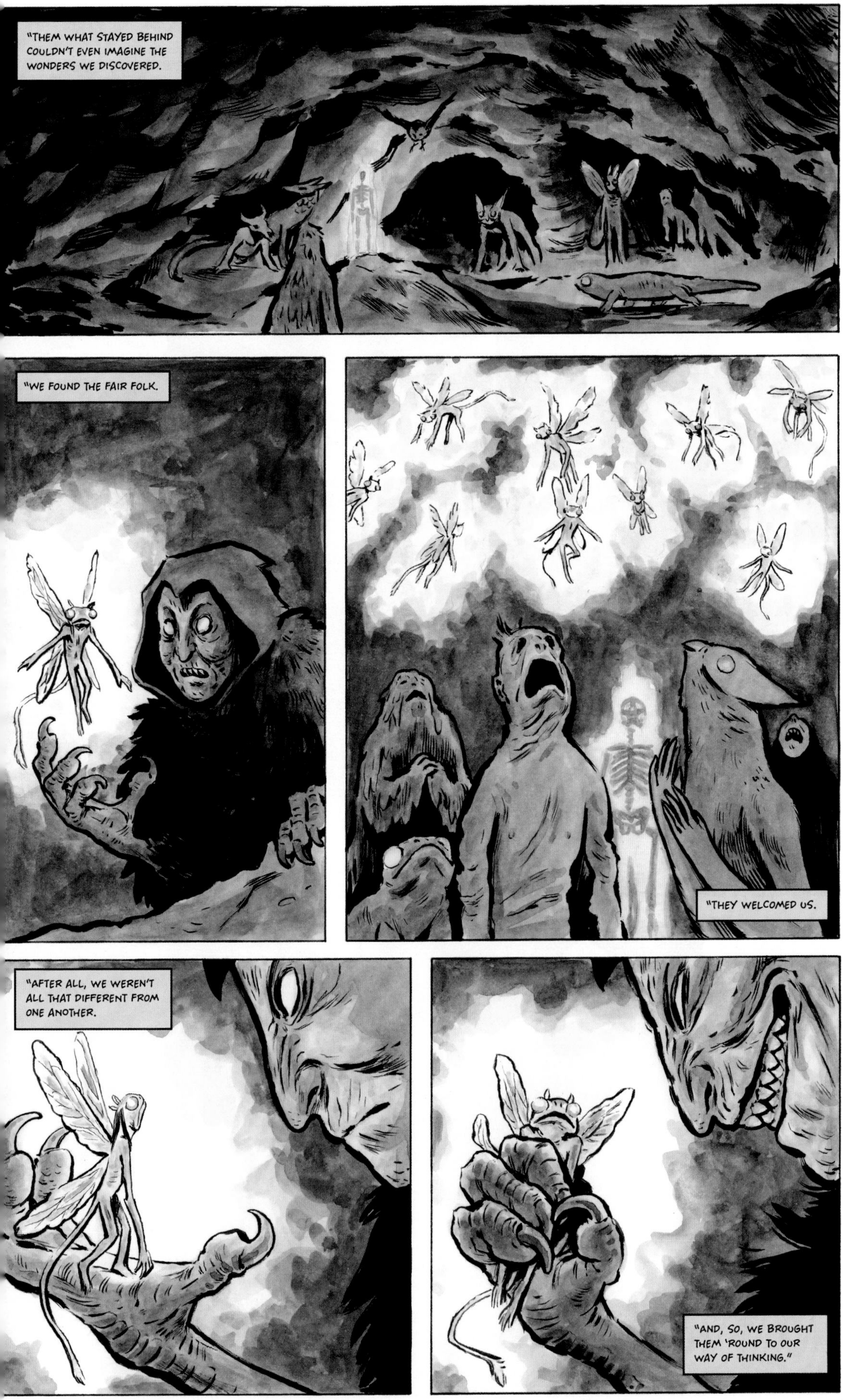
"THEM WHAT STAYED BEHIND COULDN'T EVEN IMAGINE THE WONDERS WE DISCOVERED.
"WE FOUND THE FAIR FOLK.
"THEY WELCOMED US.
"AFTER ALL, WE WEREN'T ALL THAT DIFFERENT FROM ONE ANOTHER.
"AND, SO, WE BROUGHT THEM 'ROUND TO OUR WAY OF THINKING."

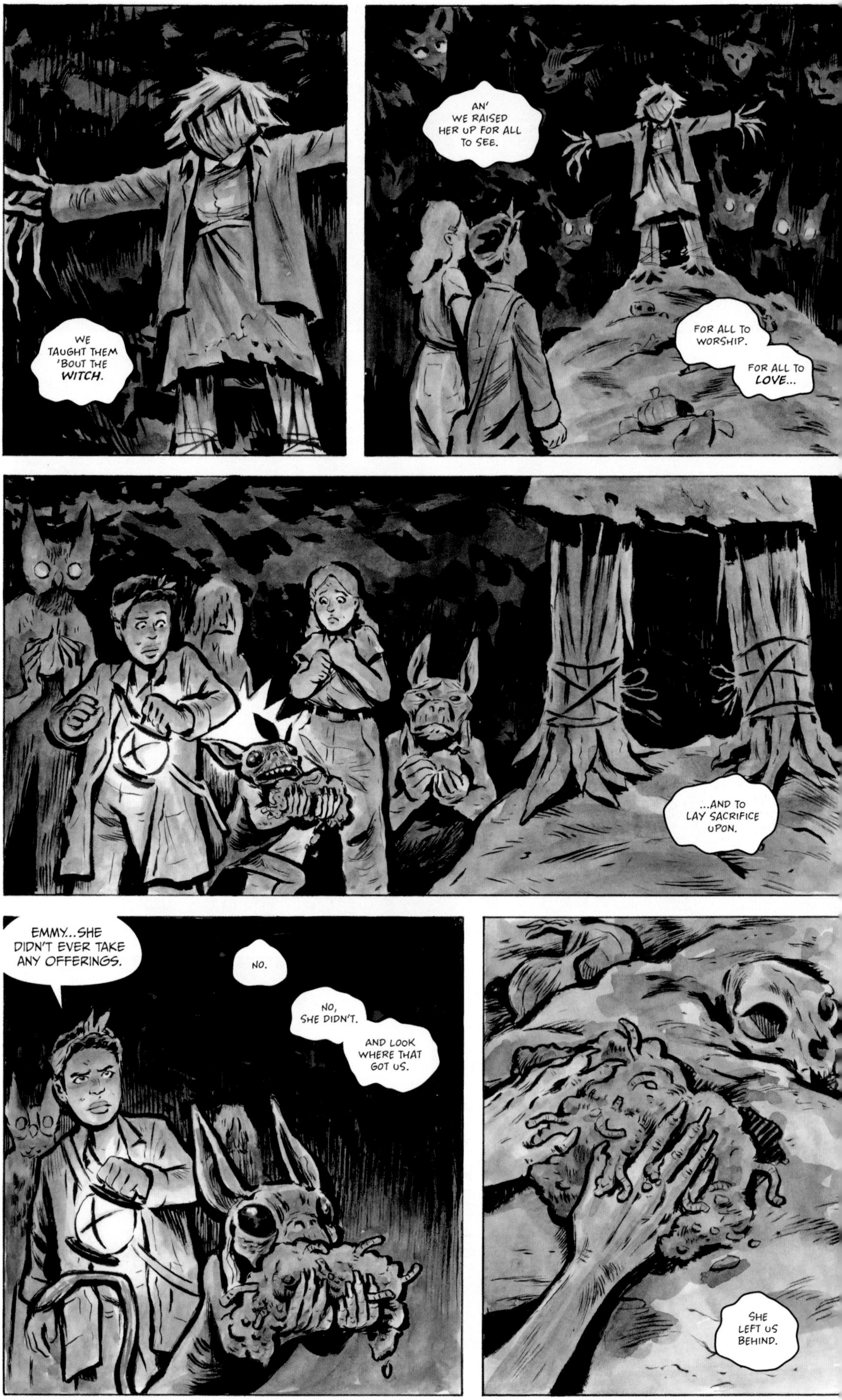
WE TAUGHT THEM 'BOUT THE WITCH.
AN' WE RAISED HER UP FOR ALL TO SEE.
FOR ALL TO WORSHIP.
FOR ALL TO LOVE...
...AND TO LAY SACRIFICE UPON.
EMMY...SHE DIDN'T EVER TAKE ANY OFFERINGS.
NO.
NO, SHE DIDN'T.
AND LOOK WHERE THAT GOT US.
SHE LEFT US BEHIND.

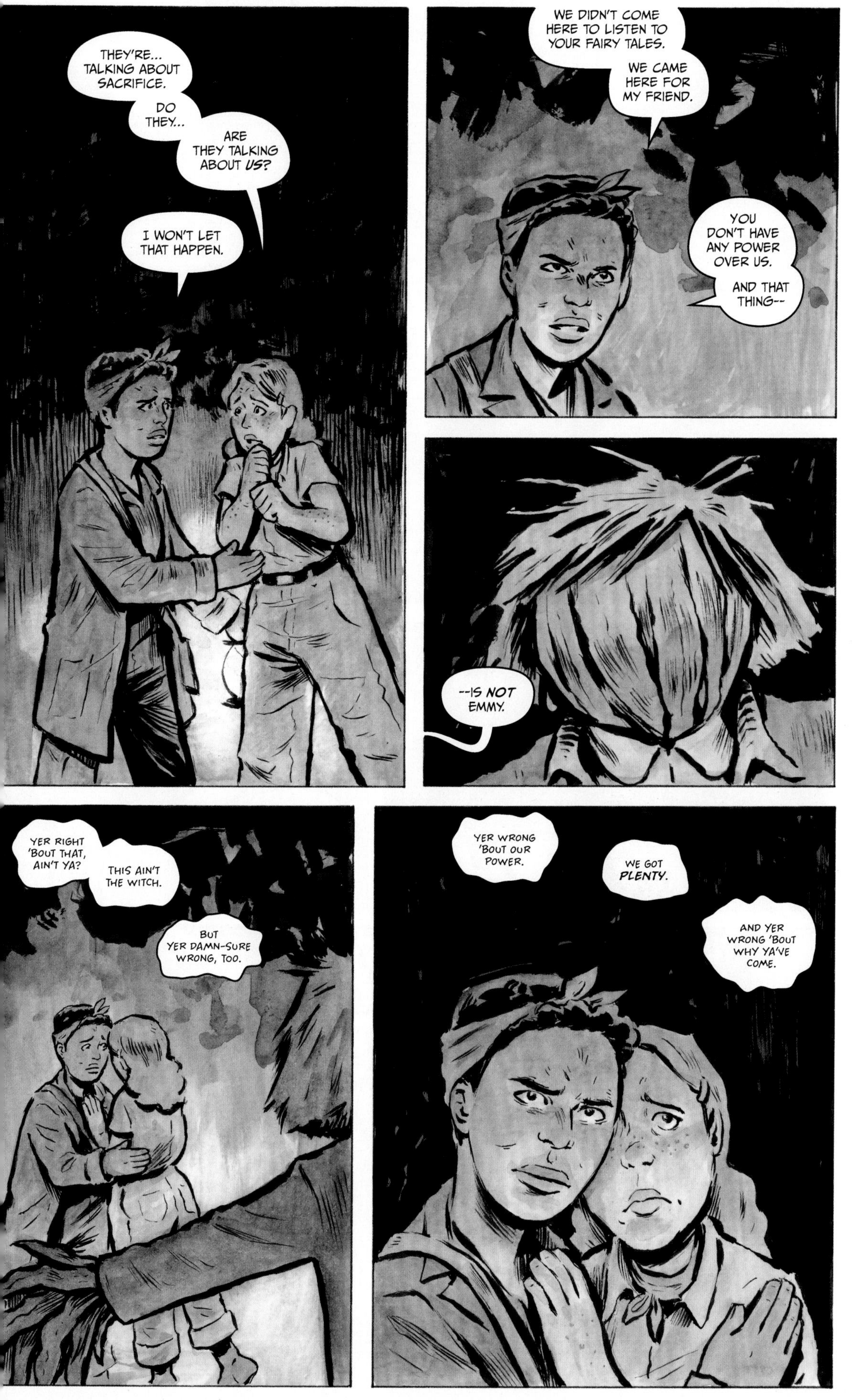
THEY'RE... TALKING ABOUT SACRIFICE.
DO THEY...
ARE THEY TALKING ABOUT *US?*
I WON'T LET THAT HAPPEN.
WE DIDN'T COME HERE TO LISTEN TO YOUR FAIRY TALES.
WE CAME HERE FOR MY FRIEND.
YOU DON'T HAVE ANY POWER OVER US.
AND THAT THING--
--IS *NOT* EMMY.
YER RIGHT 'BOUT THAT, AIN'T YA?
THIS AIN'T THE WITCH.
BUT YER DAMN-SURE WRONG, TOO.
YER WRONG 'BOUT OUR POWER.
WE GOT *PLENTY*.
AND YER WRONG 'BOUT WHY YA'VE COME.

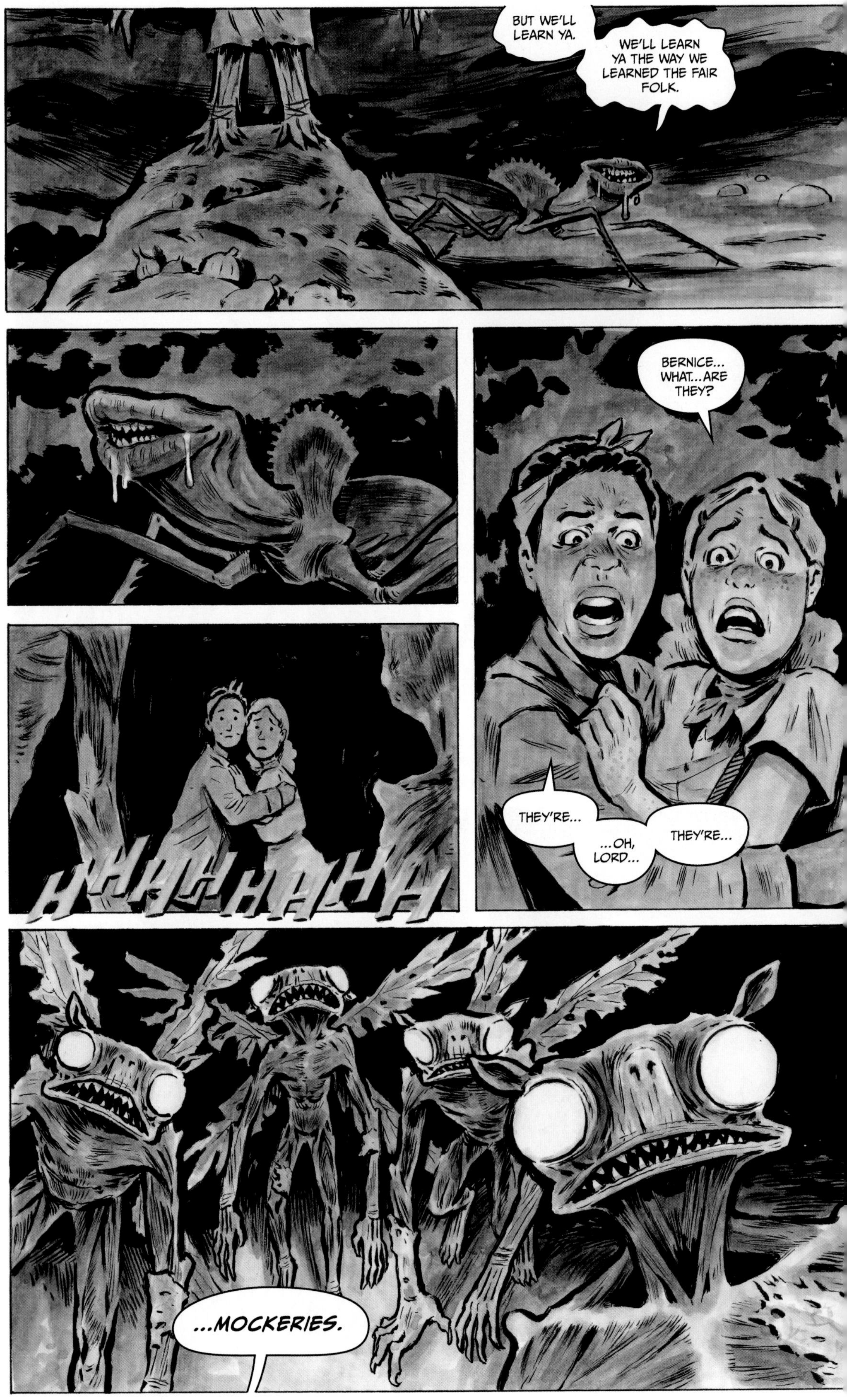
BUT WE'LL LEARN YA.
WE'LL LEARN YA THE WAY WE LEARNED THE FAIR FOLK.
BERNICE... WHAT...ARE THEY?
HAHAHAHAHAHA
THEY'RE...
...OH, LORD...
THEY'RE...
...MOCKERIES.

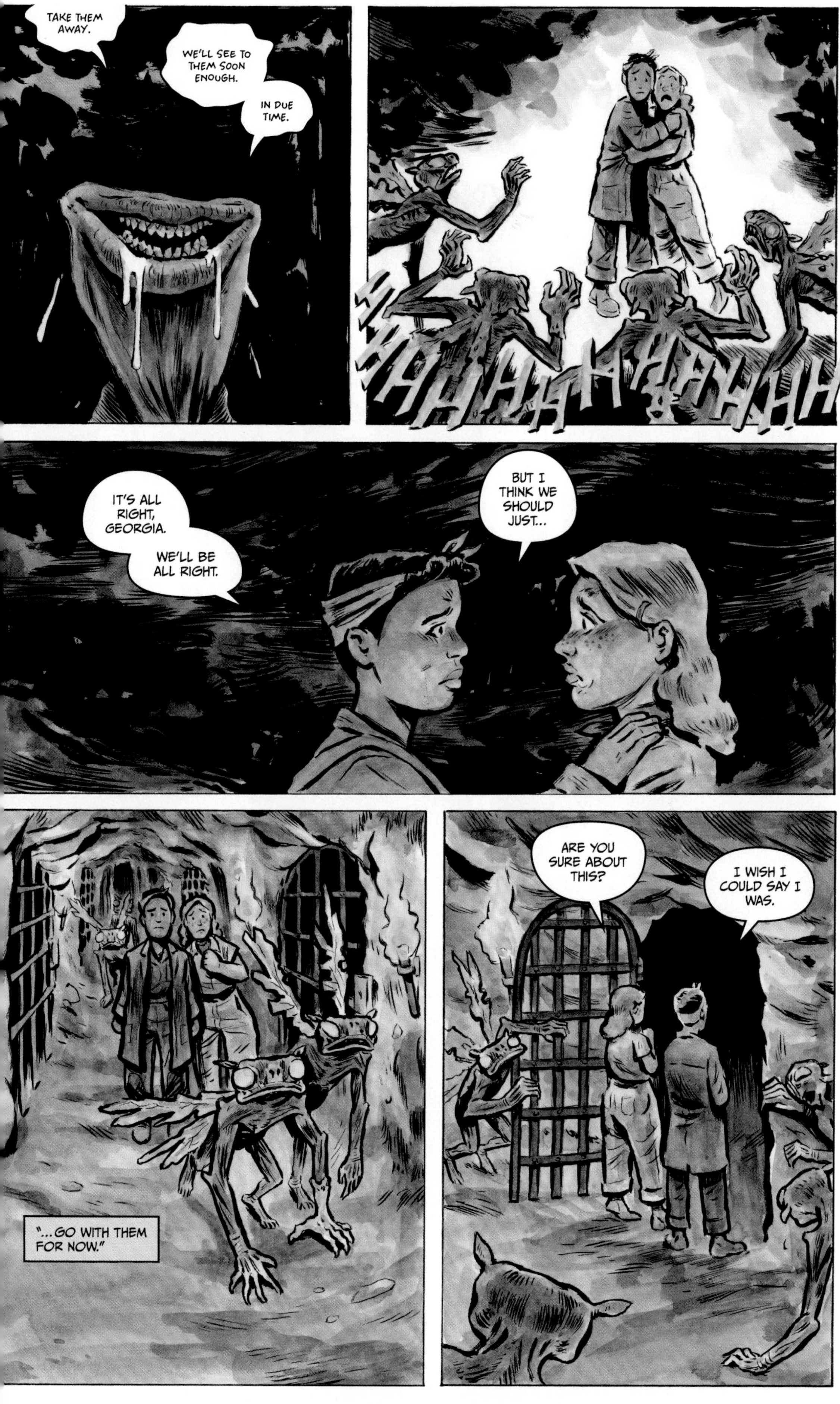
TAKE THEM AWAY.
WE'LL SEE TO THEM SOON ENOUGH.
IN DUE TIME.
HHHAAAHHHHAAAHHHH
IT'S ALL RIGHT, GEORGIA.
WE'LL BE ALL RIGHT.
BUT I THINK WE SHOULD JUST...
"...GO WITH THEM FOR NOW."
ARE YOU SURE ABOUT THIS?
I WISH I COULD SAY I WAS.

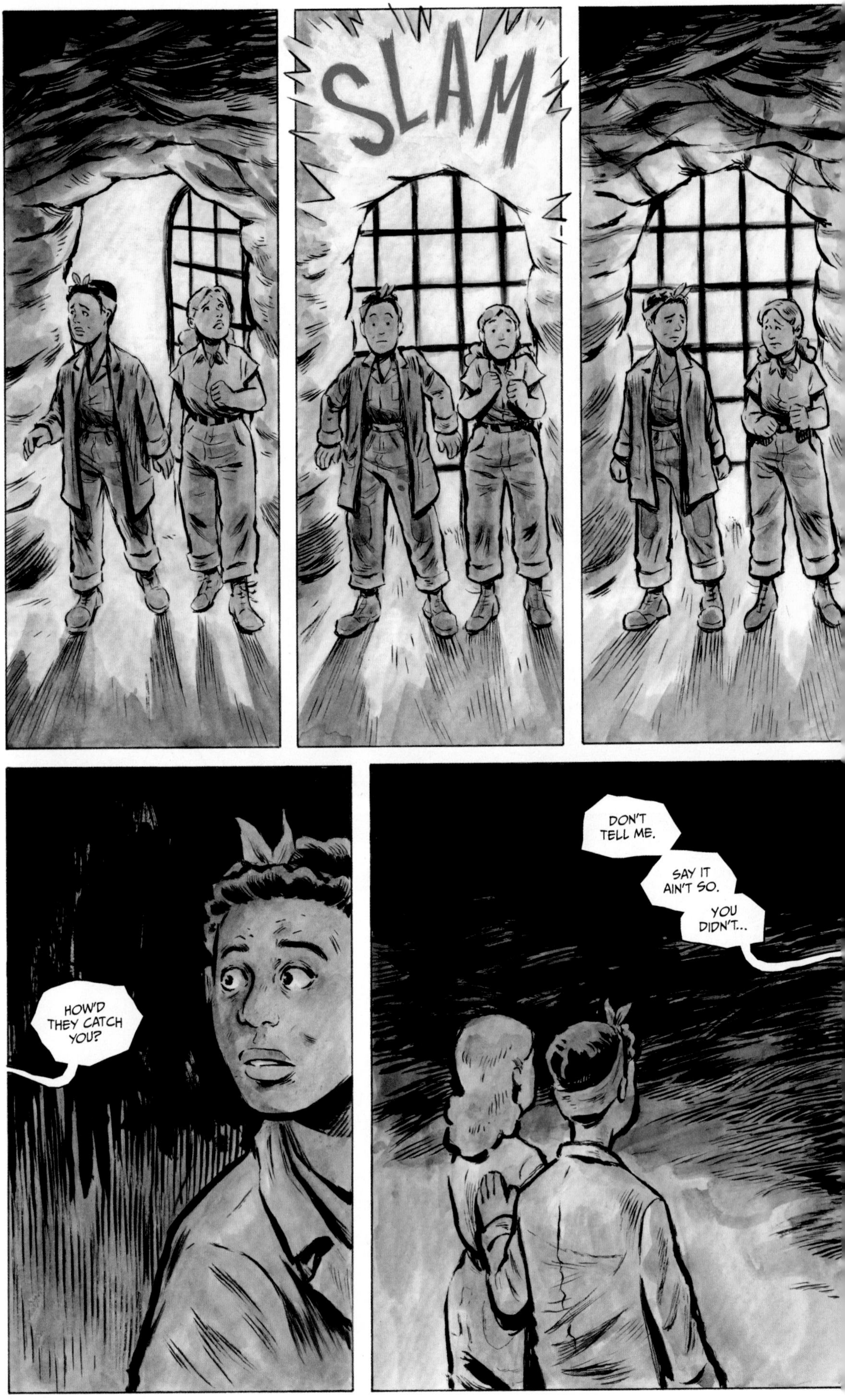
SLAM
HOW'D THEY CATCH YOU?
DON'T TELL ME.
SAY IT AIN'T SO.
YOU DIDN'T...

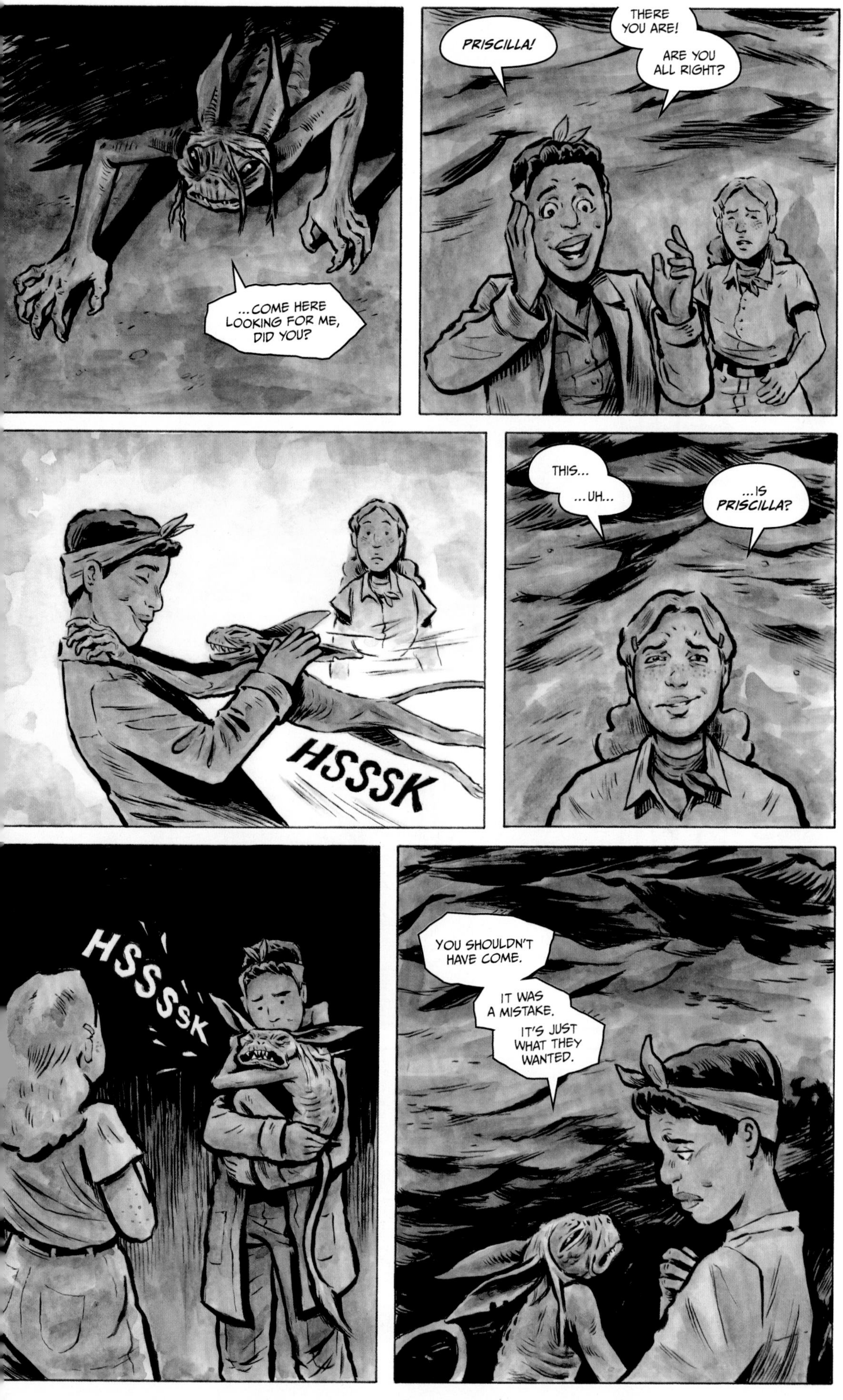
...COME HERE LOOKING FOR ME, DID YOU?
PRISCILLA!
THERE YOU ARE!
ARE YOU ALL RIGHT?
HSSSK
THIS...
...UH...
...IS PRISCILLA?
HSSSsSK
YOU SHOULDN'T HAVE COME.
IT WAS A MISTAKE.
IT'S JUST WHAT THEY WANTED.

FROM TIME TO TIME, BERNICE HAD FELT *TRAPPED*.

TRAPPED BY *FAMILY OBLIGATIONS*.

TRAPPED BY A SENSE OF *RESPONSIBILITY*.

SHE MIGHT NOT EVER ADMIT IT, BUT SHE SOMETIMES FELT A LITTLE *JEALOUS*.

JEALOUS OF EMMY.

BECAUSE SHE JUST PICKED UP AND LEFT ALL THIS BEHIND.

SHE WAS SOMEWHERE OUT THERE, EXPLORING A WORLD BERNICE HAD NEVER KNOWN.

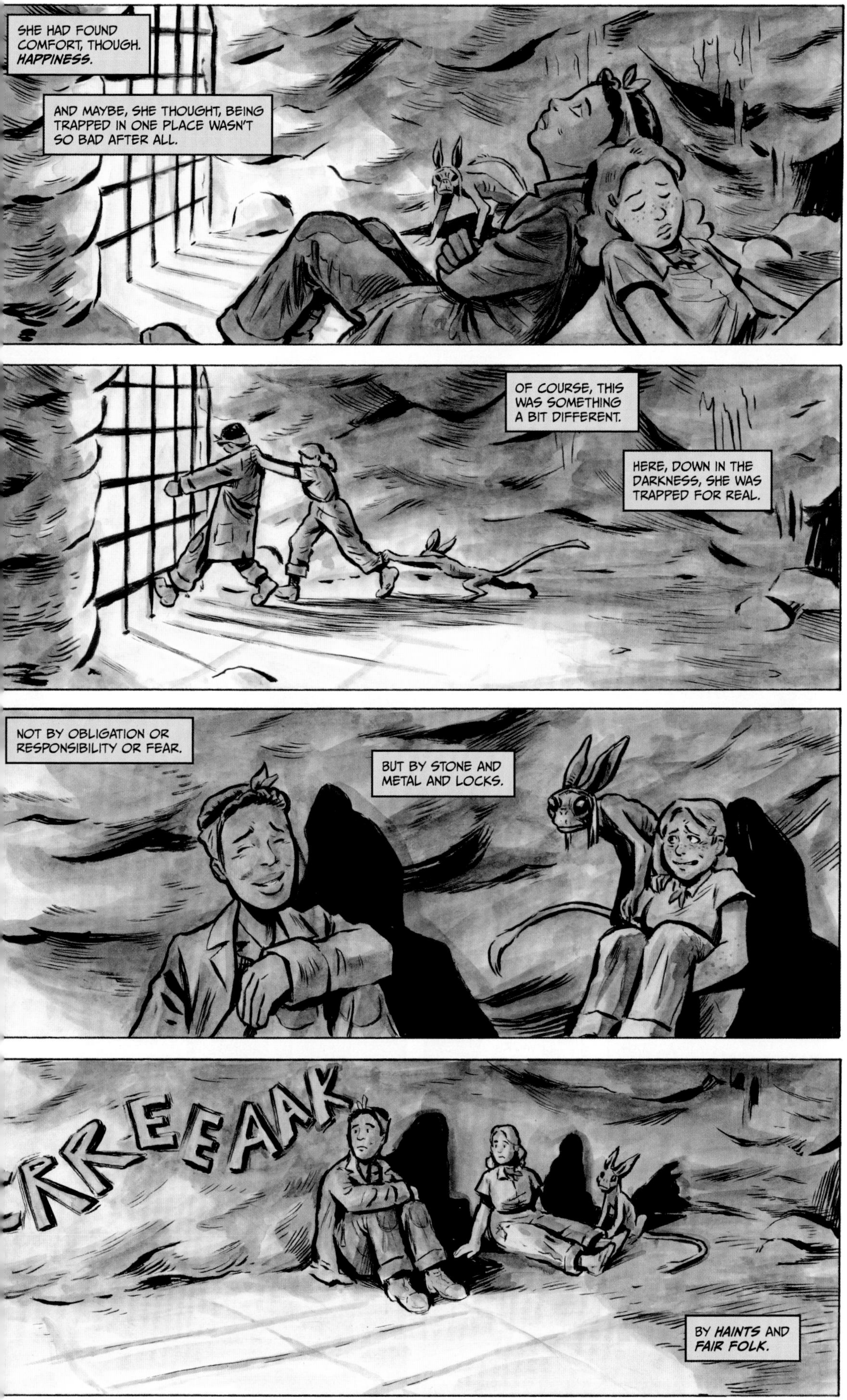
SHE HAD FOUND COMFORT, THOUGH. *HAPPINESS.*
AND MAYBE, SHE THOUGHT, BEING TRAPPED IN ONE PLACE WASN'T SO BAD AFTER ALL.
OF COURSE, THIS WAS SOMETHING A BIT DIFFERENT.
HERE, DOWN IN THE DARKNESS, SHE WAS TRAPPED FOR REAL.
NOT BY OBLIGATION OR RESPONSIBILITY OR FEAR.
BUT BY STONE AND METAL AND LOCKS.
CRREEAAK
BY *HAINTS* AND *FAIR FOLK.*

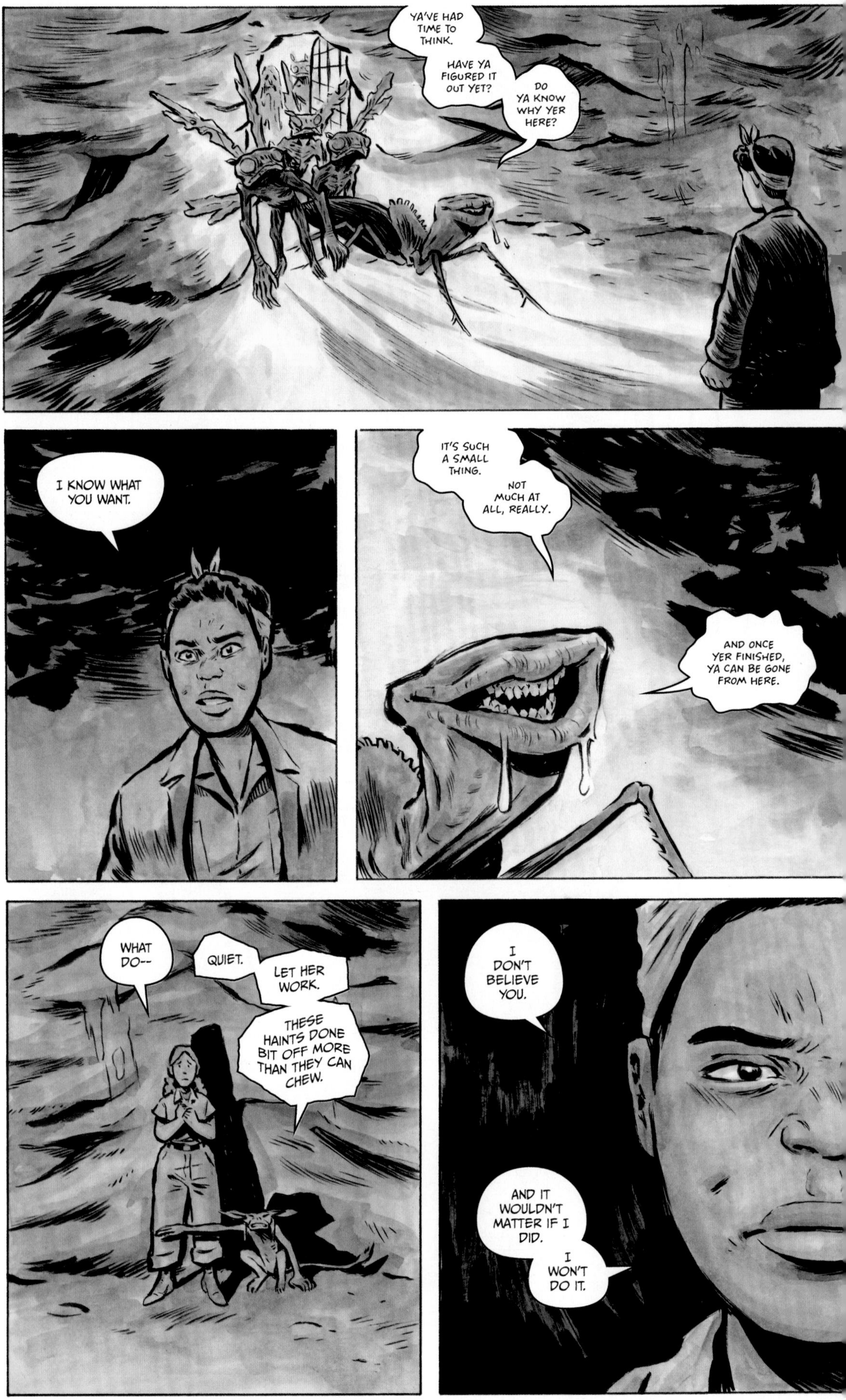
YA'VE HAD TIME TO THINK.
HAVE YA FIGURED IT OUT YET?
DO YA KNOW WHY YER HERE?
I KNOW WHAT YOU WANT.
IT'S SUCH A SMALL THING.
NOT MUCH AT ALL, REALLY.
AND ONCE YER FINISHED, YA CAN BE GONE FROM HERE.
WHAT DO--
QUIET.
LET HER WORK.
THESE HAINTS DONE BIT OFF MORE THAN THEY CAN CHEW.
I DON'T BELIEVE YOU.
AND IT WOULDN'T MATTER IF I DID.
I WON'T DO IT.

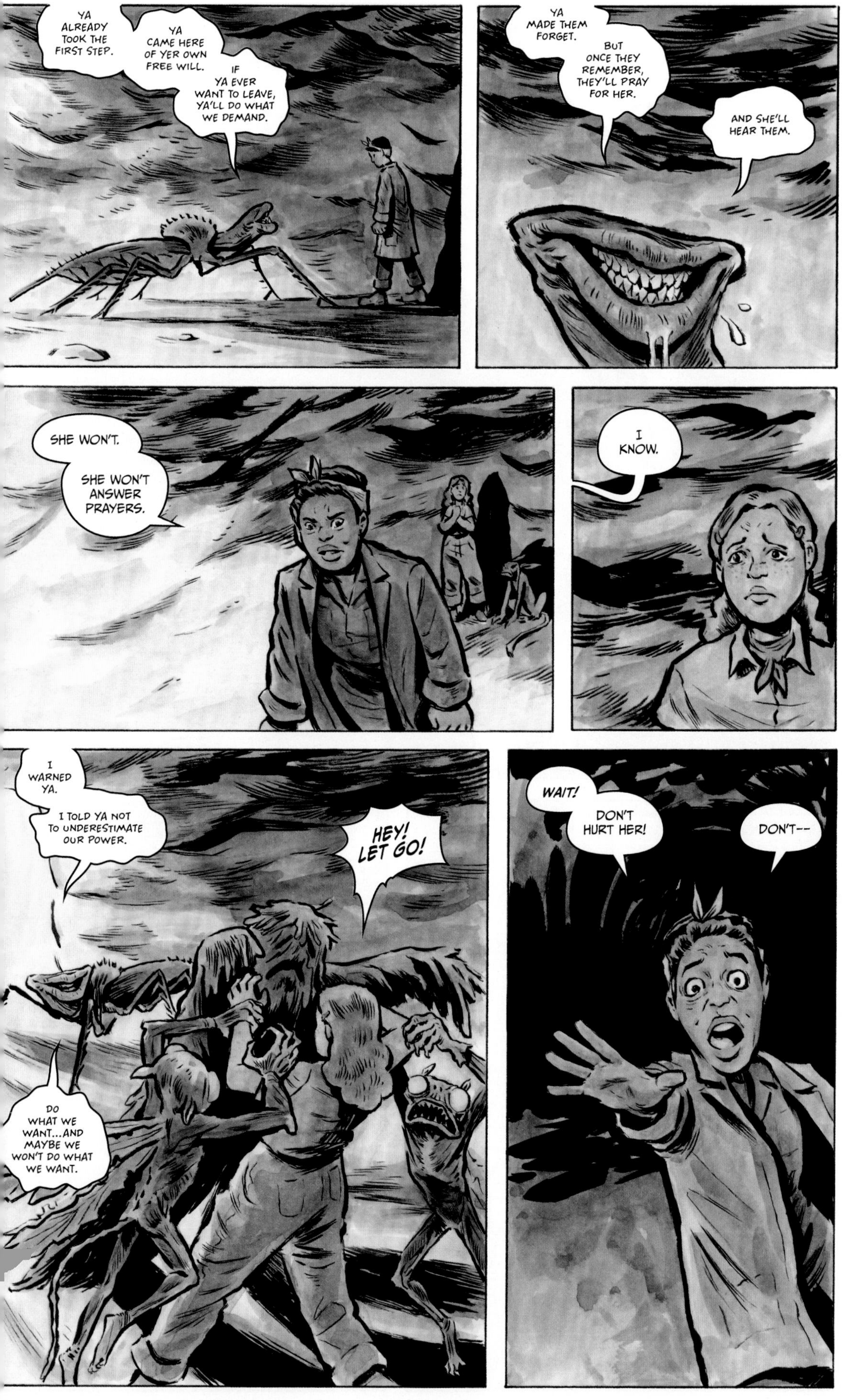

YA ALREADY TOOK THE FIRST STEP.
YA CAME HERE OF YER OWN FREE WILL.
IF YA EVER WANT TO LEAVE, YA'LL DO WHAT WE DEMAND.
YA MADE THEM FORGET.
BUT ONCE THEY REMEMBER, THEY'LL PRAY FOR HER.
AND SHE'LL HEAR THEM.
SHE WON'T.
SHE WON'T ANSWER PRAYERS.
I KNOW.
I WARNED YA.
I TOLD YA NOT TO UNDERESTIMATE OUR POWER.
HEY! LET GO!
DO WHAT WE WANT...AND MAYBE WE WON'T DO WHAT WE WANT.
WAIT!
DON'T HURT HER!
DON'T--

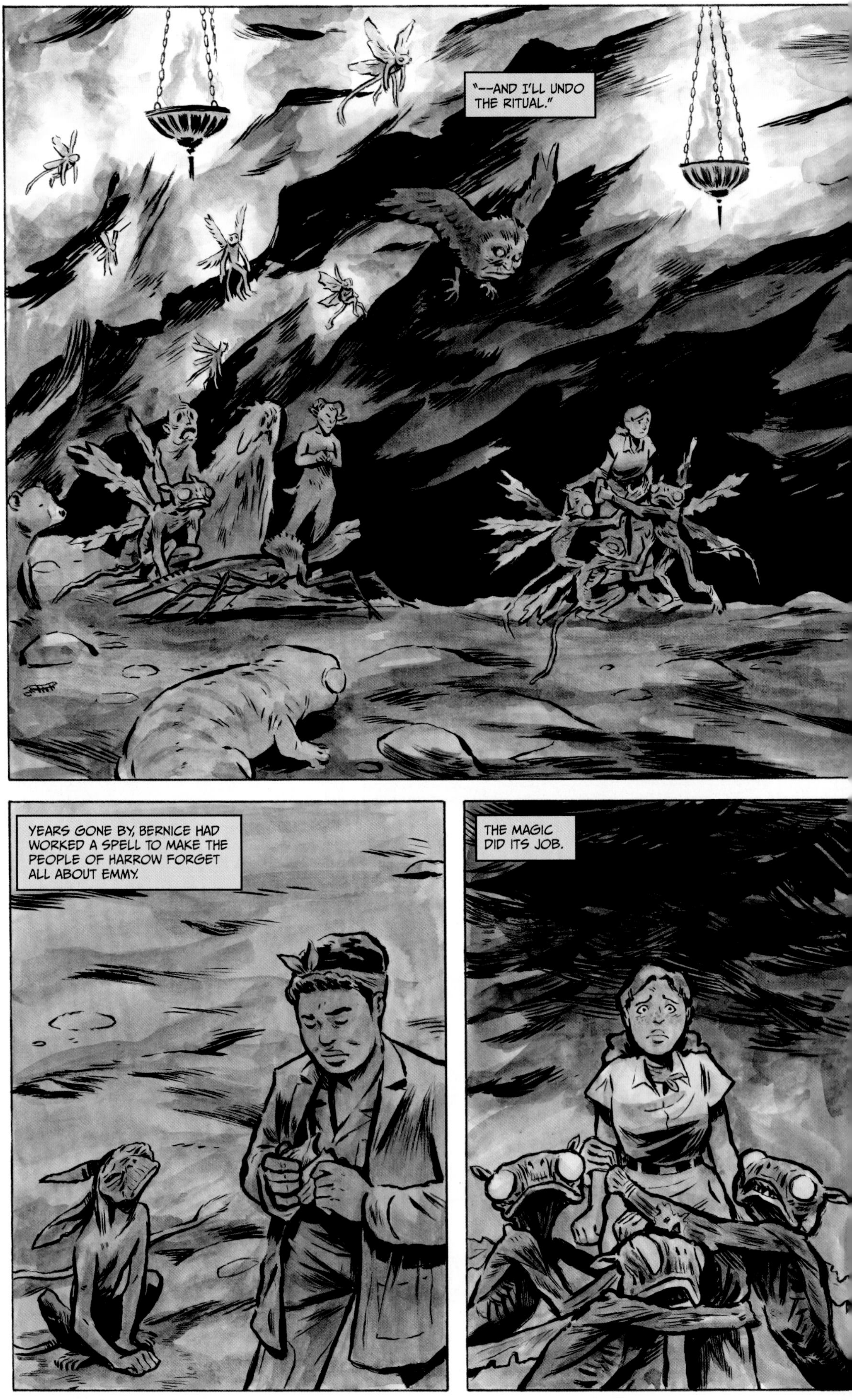
"--AND I'LL UNDO THE RITUAL."
YEARS GONE BY, BERNICE HAD WORKED A SPELL TO MAKE THE PEOPLE OF HARROW FORGET ALL ABOUT EMMY.
THE MAGIC DID ITS JOB.

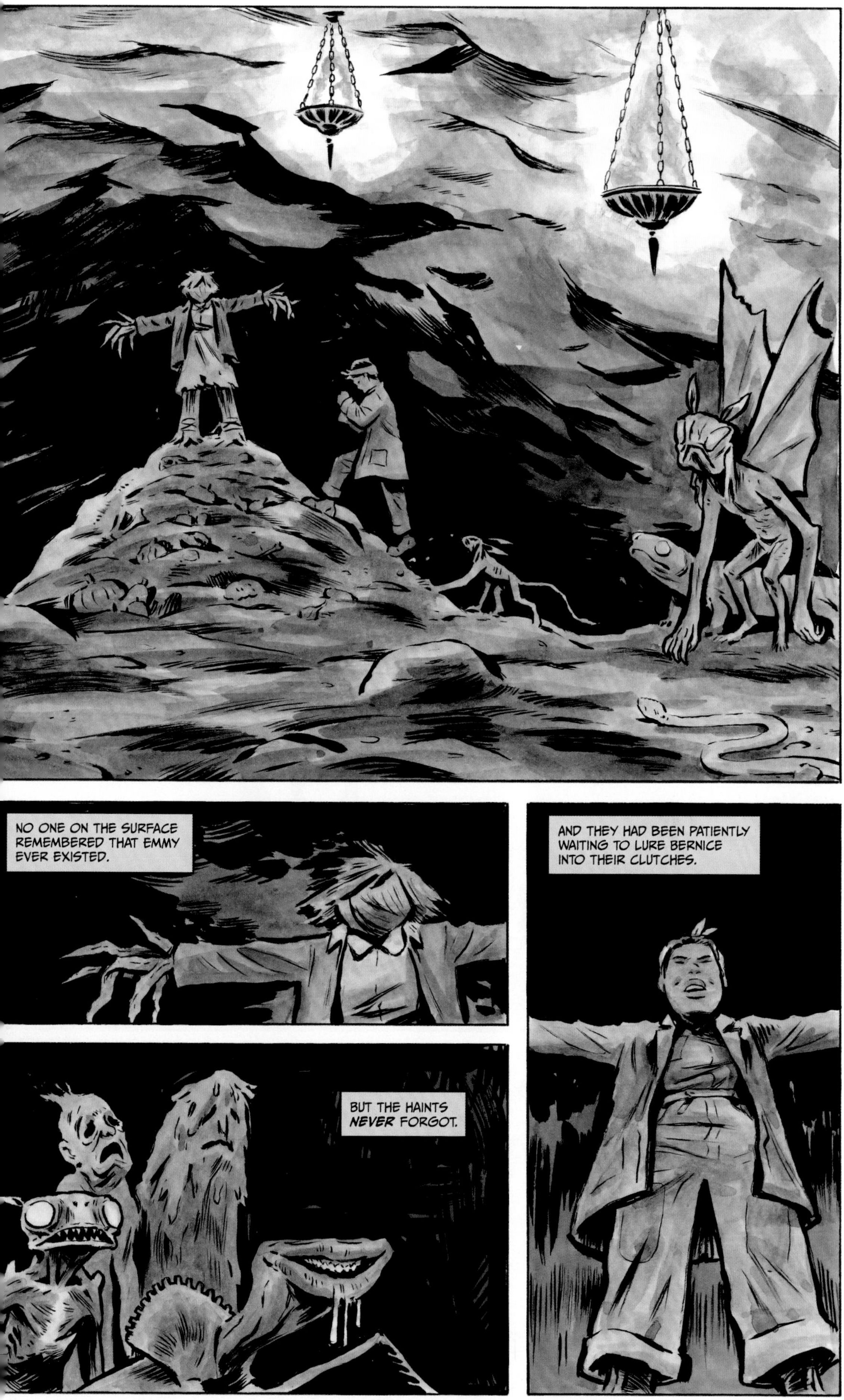
NO ONE ON THE SURFACE REMEMBERED THAT EMMY EVER EXISTED.
BUT THE HAINTS *NEVER* FORGOT.
AND THEY HAD BEEN PATIENTLY WAITING TO LURE BERNICE INTO THEIR CLUTCHES.

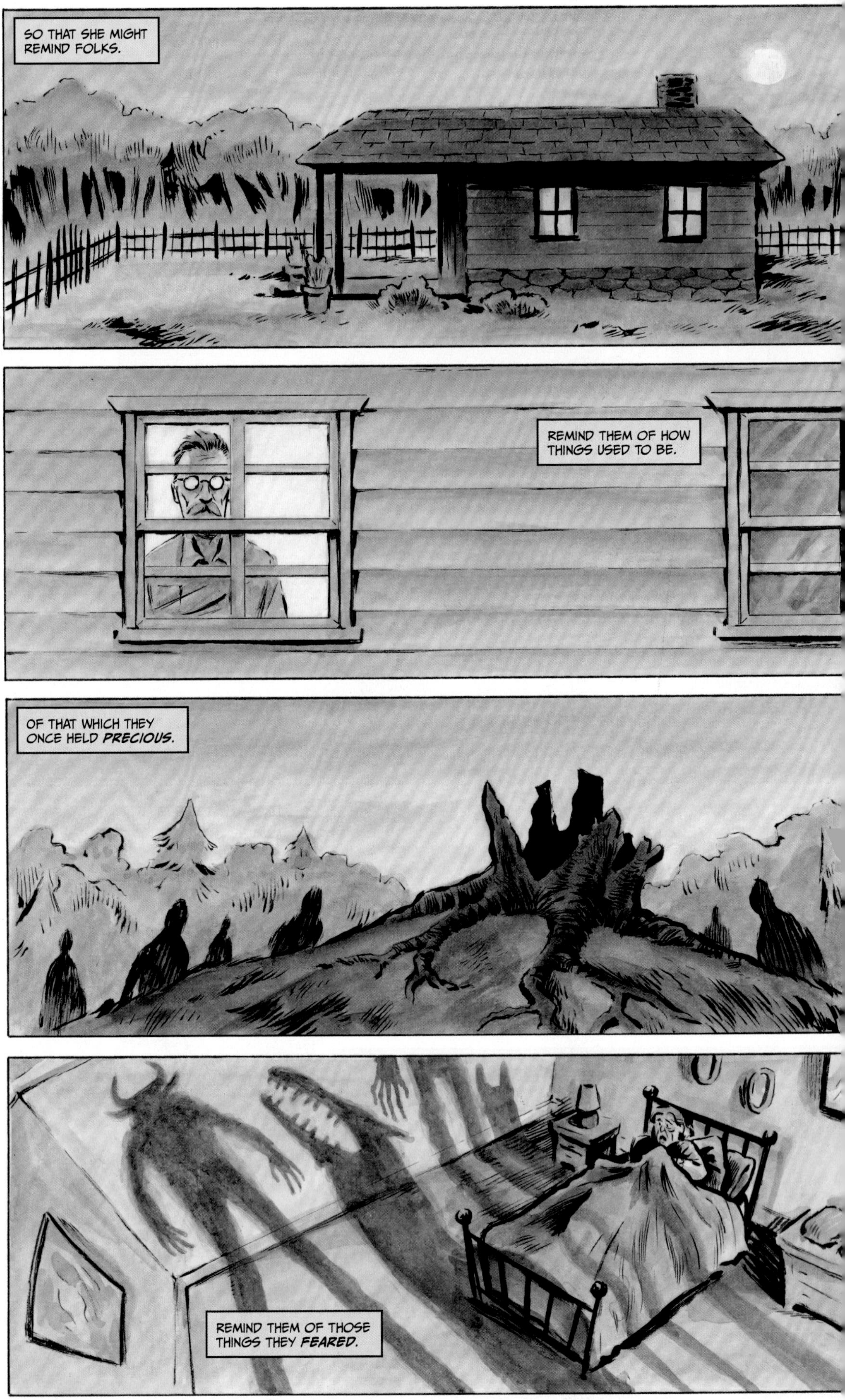
SO THAT SHE MIGHT REMIND FOLKS.
REMIND THEM OF HOW THINGS USED TO BE.
OF THAT WHICH THEY ONCE HELD *PRECIOUS*.
REMIND THEM OF THOSE THINGS THEY *FEARED*.

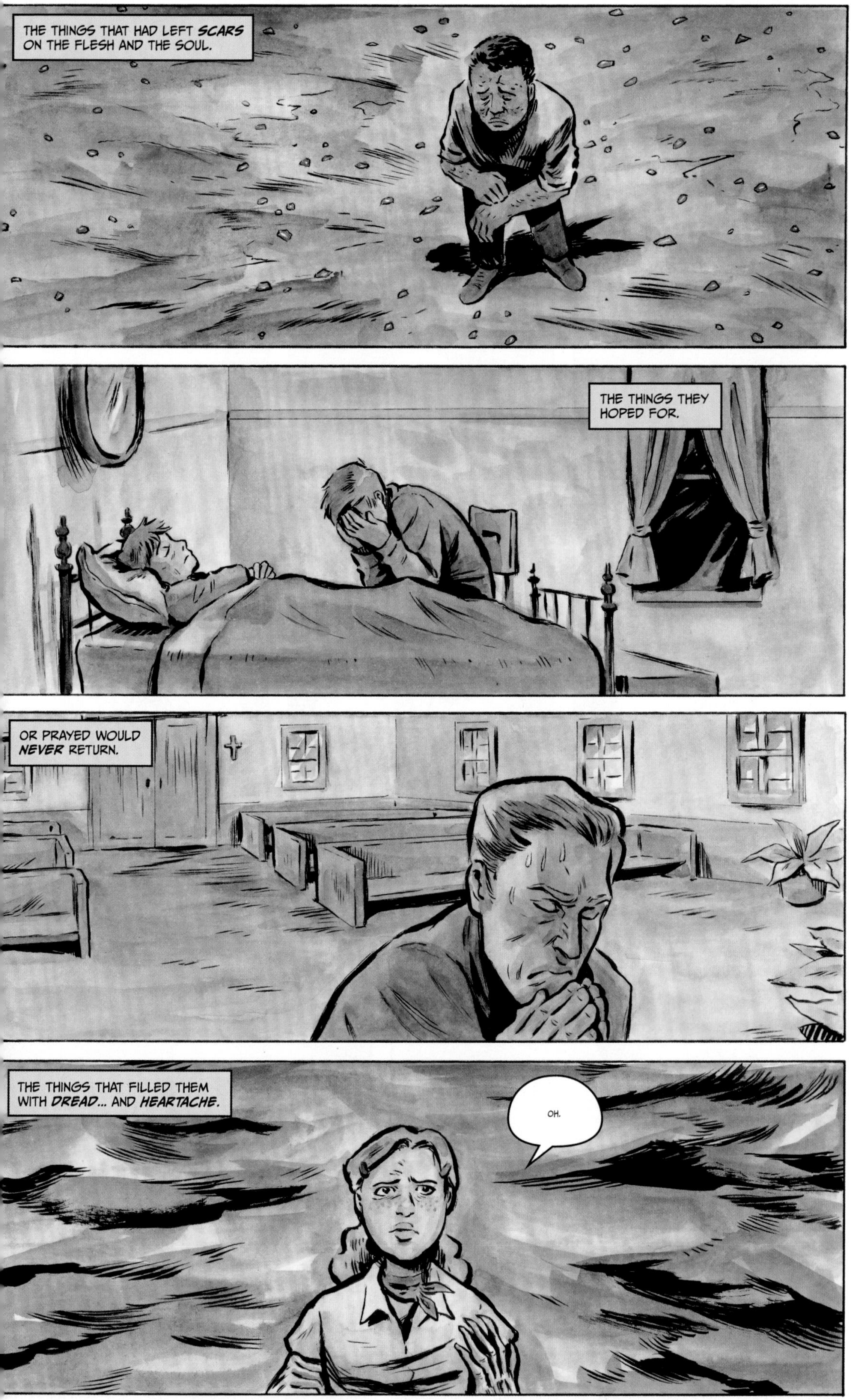
THE THINGS THAT HAD LEFT SCARS ON THE FLESH AND THE SOUL.
THE THINGS THEY HOPED FOR.
OR PRAYED WOULD NEVER RETURN.
THE THINGS THAT FILLED THEM WITH DREAD... AND HEARTACHE.
OH.

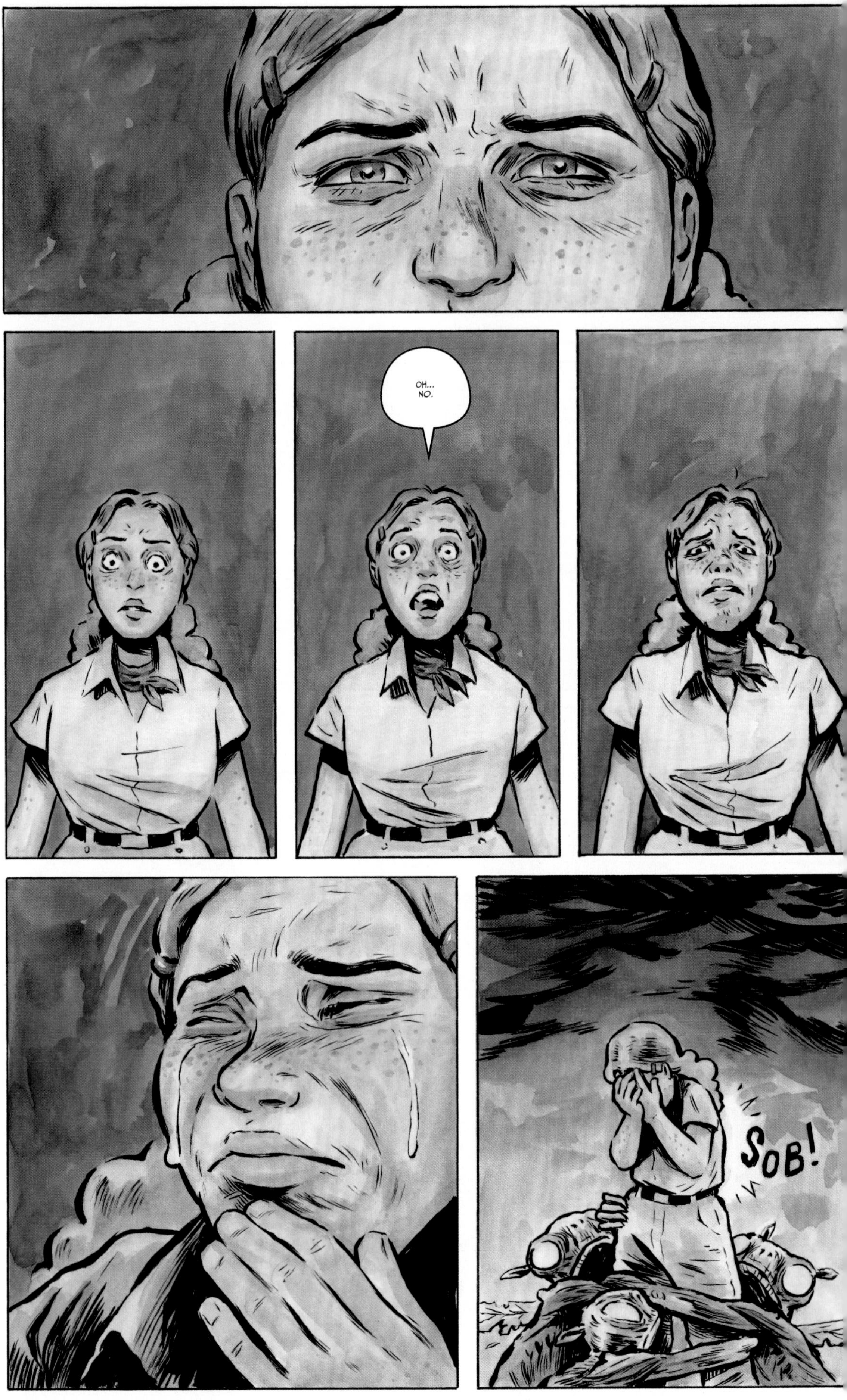
OH... NO.
SOB!

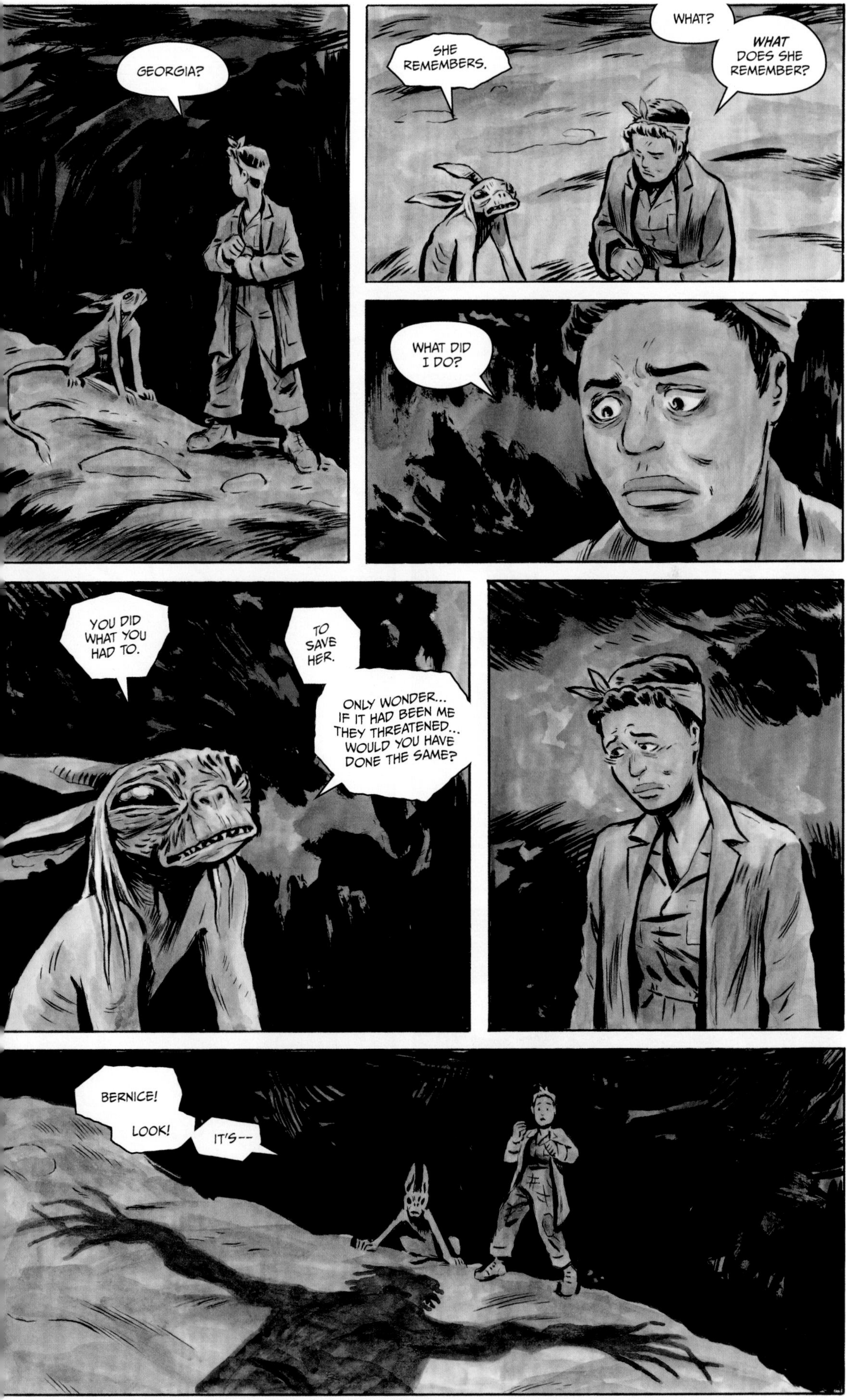
GEORGIA?
SHE REMEMBERS.
WHAT?
WHAT DOES SHE REMEMBER?
WHAT DID I DO?
YOU DID WHAT YOU HAD TO.
TO SAVE HER.
ONLY WONDER... IF IT HAD BEEN ME THEY THREATENED... WOULD YOU HAVE DONE THE SAME?
BERNICE!
LOOK!
IT'S--

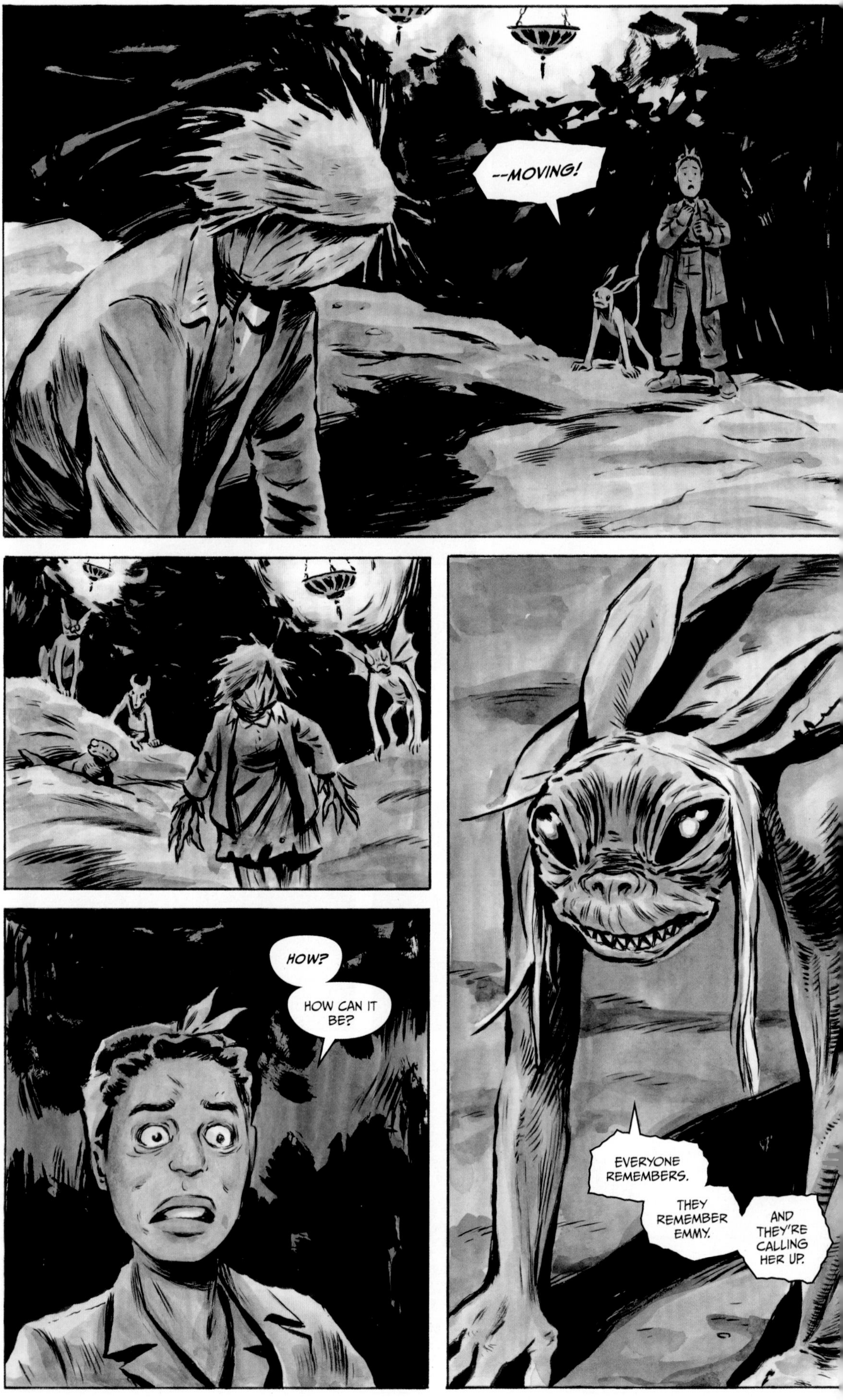
--MOVING!
HOW?
HOW CAN IT BE?
EVERYONE REMEMBERS.
THEY REMEMBER EMMY.
AND THEY'RE CALLING HER UP.

SHE'S GOING ABOVE!

THEY'RE SUMMONING HER!

CALLING TO HER!

CALLING TO US ALL!

IT'S OUR TIME OF RETURNING!

WE MUST FOLLOW!

HHHHHHHHHHH

NO!

YA MUST STAY BEHIND!

FOR NOW, LEASTWAYS!

YA FIGURED ME RIGHT ON THAT COUNT.

I LIED.

I CAN'T JUST LET YA GO.

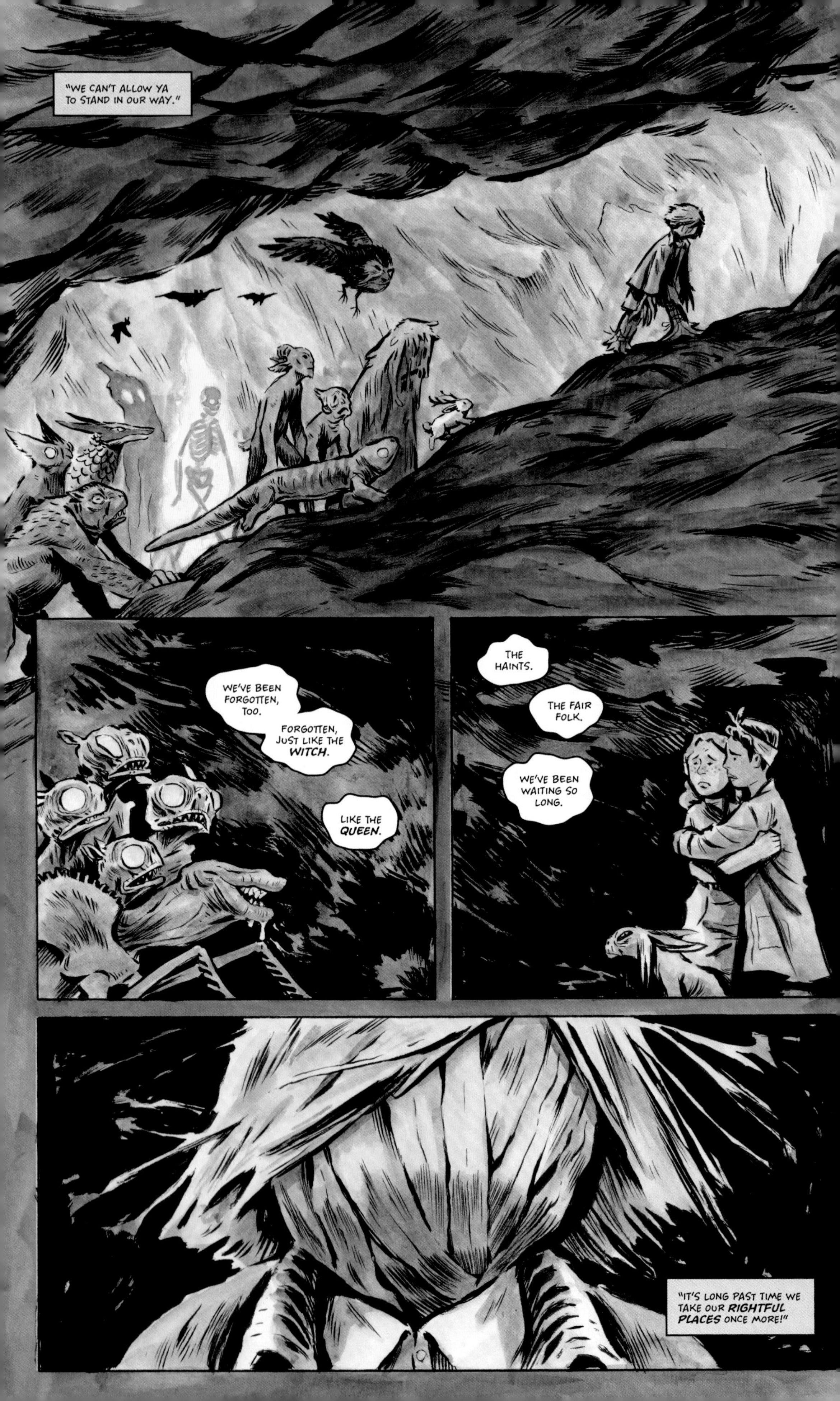
"WE CAN'T ALLOW YA TO STAND IN OUR WAY."
WE'VE BEEN FORGOTTEN, TOO.
FORGOTTEN, JUST LIKE THE WITCH.
LIKE THE QUEEN.
THE HAINTS.
THE FAIR FOLK.
WE'VE BEEN WAITING SO LONG.
"IT'S LONG PAST TIME WE TAKE OUR RIGHTFUL PLACES ONCE MORE!"

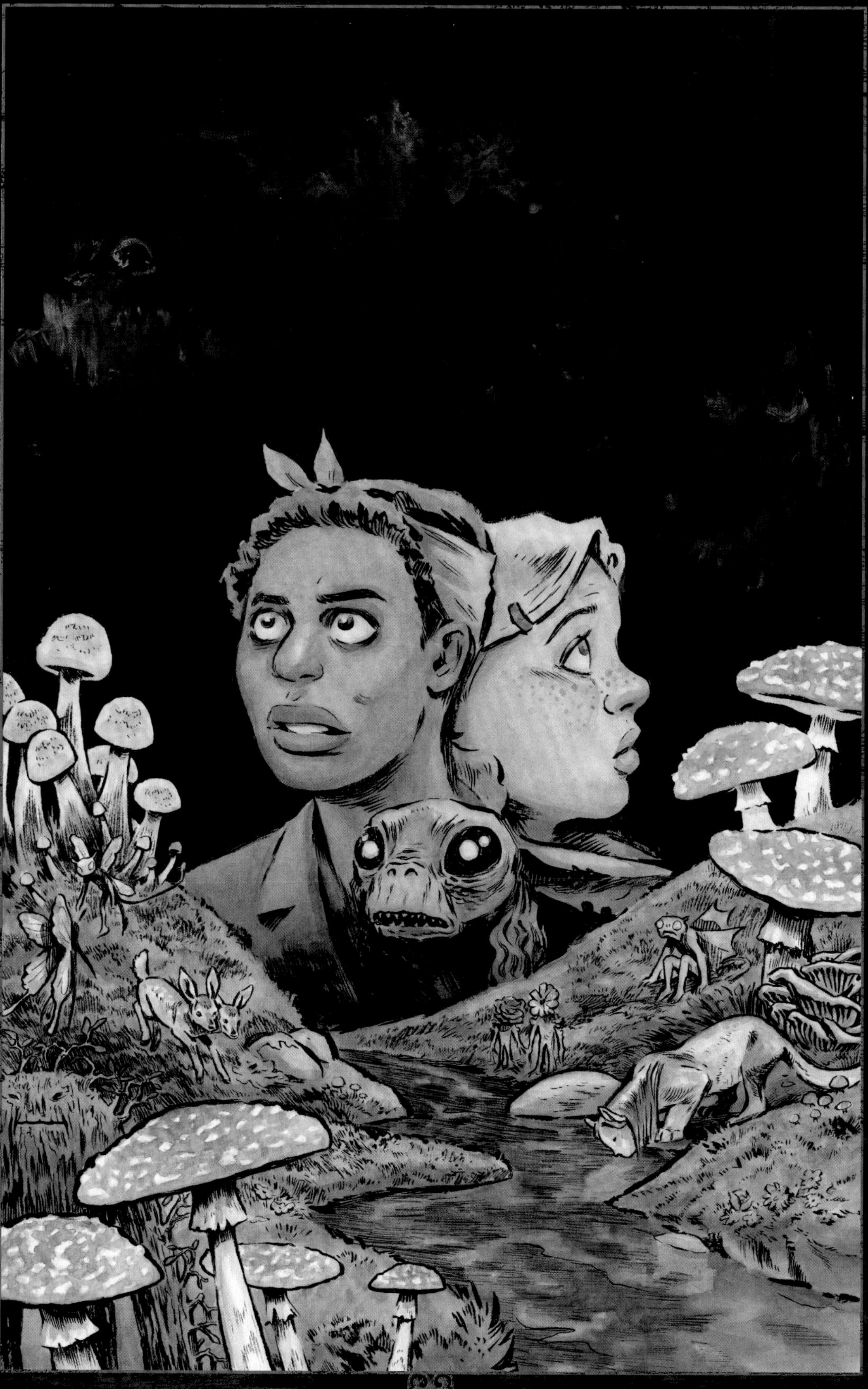

THREE

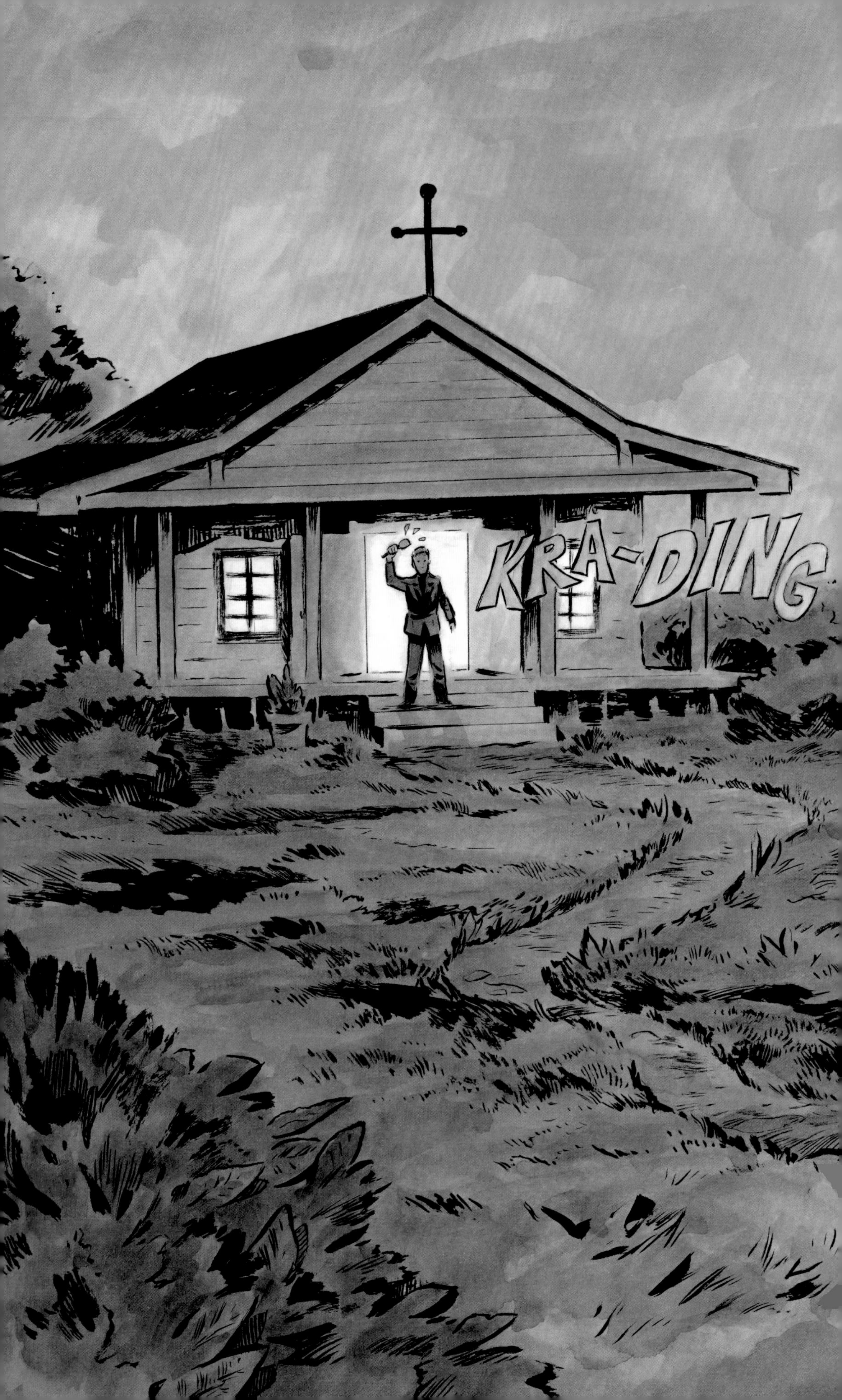
KRA-DING

RECOLLECTION FLOODED BACK TO THE HEARTS AND MINDS OF THE GOOD PEOPLE OF HARROW.
AND, WITH RECOLLECTION, *FEAR*.
KRA-DING
KRA-DING
FOR, IF MEMORIES COULD RETURN, COULDN'T THE *WITCH* COME BACK, TOO?
HARROW COUNTY
CULLEN BUNN

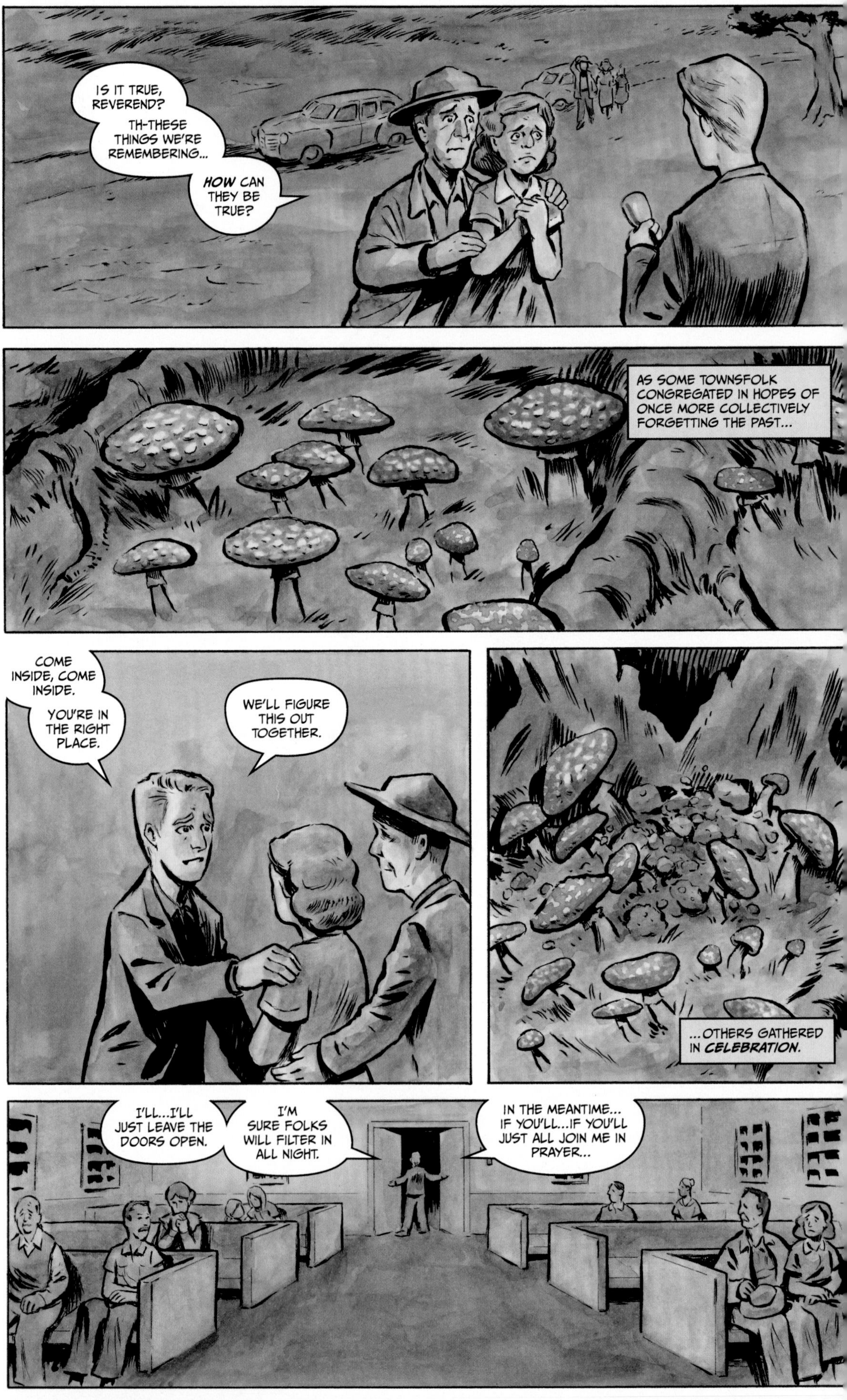
IS IT TRUE, REVEREND?
TH-THESE THINGS WE'RE REMEMBERING...
HOW CAN THEY BE TRUE?
AS SOME TOWNSFOLK CONGREGATED IN HOPES OF ONCE MORE COLLECTIVELY FORGETTING THE PAST...
COME INSIDE, COME INSIDE.
YOU'RE IN THE RIGHT PLACE.
WE'LL FIGURE THIS OUT TOGETHER.
...OTHERS GATHERED IN *CELEBRATION.*
I'LL...I'LL JUST LEAVE THE DOORS OPEN.
I'M SURE FOLKS WILL FILTER IN ALL NIGHT.
IN THE MEANTIME... IF YOU'LL...IF YOU'LL JUST ALL JOIN ME IN PRAYER...

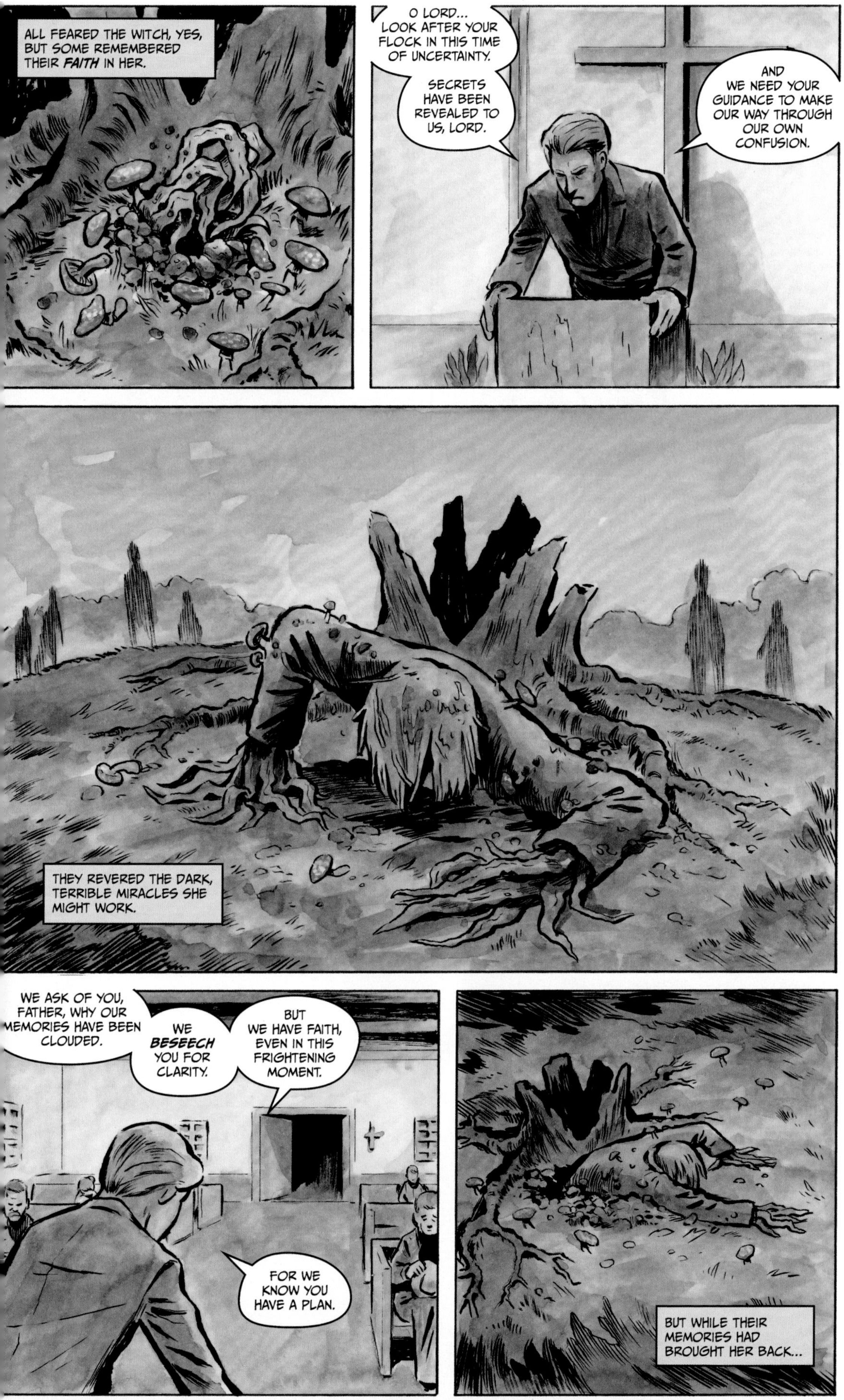
ALL FEARED THE WITCH, YES, BUT SOME REMEMBERED THEIR *FAITH* IN HER.
O LORD... LOOK AFTER YOUR FLOCK IN THIS TIME OF UNCERTAINTY.
SECRETS HAVE BEEN REVEALED TO US, LORD.
AND WE NEED YOUR GUIDANCE TO MAKE OUR WAY THROUGH OUR OWN CONFUSION.
THEY REVERED THE DARK, TERRIBLE MIRACLES SHE MIGHT WORK.
WE ASK OF YOU, FATHER, WHY OUR MEMORIES HAVE BEEN CLOUDED.
WE *BESEECH* YOU FOR CLARITY.
BUT WE HAVE FAITH, EVEN IN THIS FRIGHTENING MOMENT.
FOR WE KNOW YOU HAVE A PLAN.
BUT WHILE THEIR MEMORIES HAD BROUGHT HER BACK...

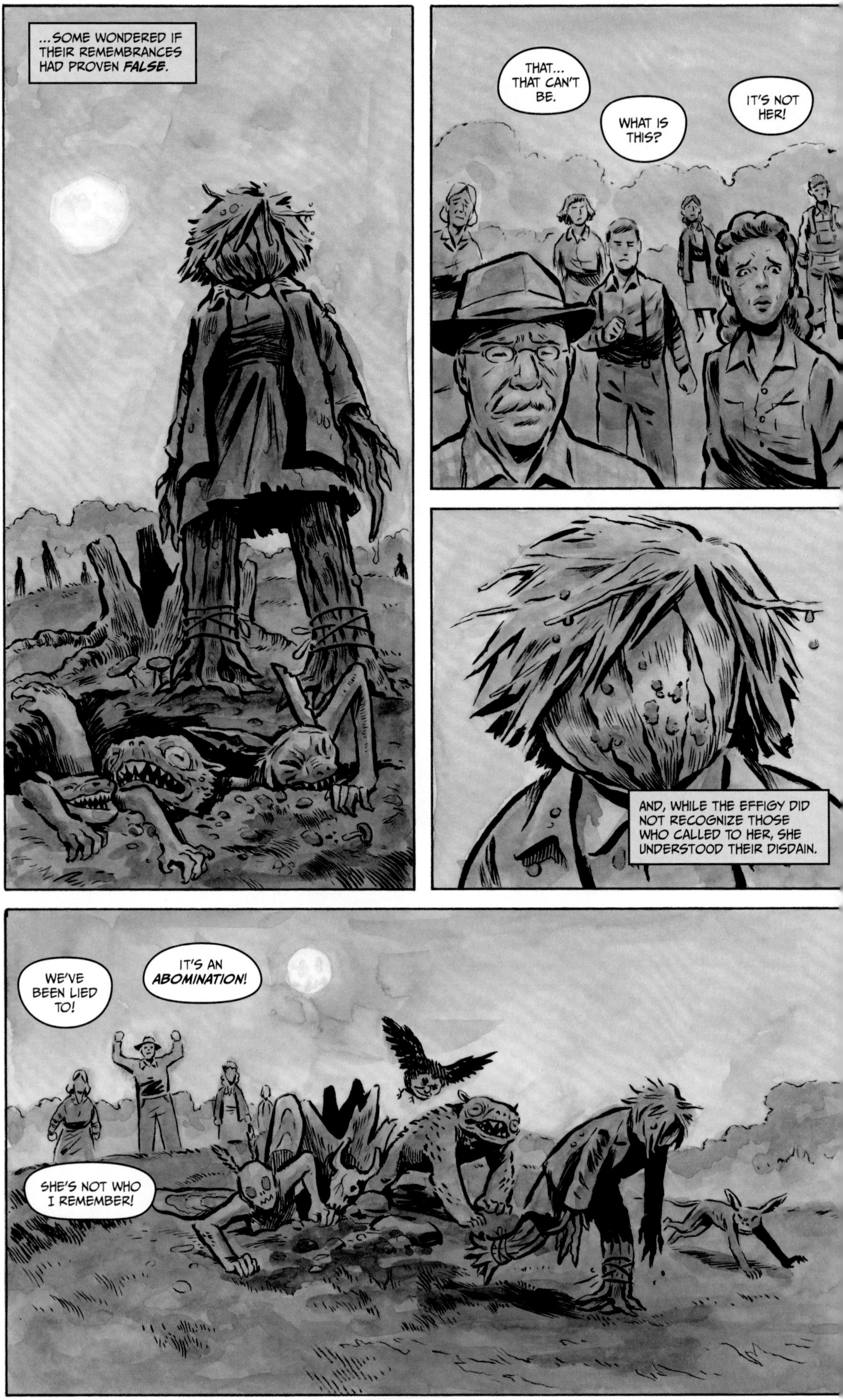
...SOME WONDERED IF THEIR REMEMBRANCES HAD PROVEN *FALSE*.
THAT... THAT CAN'T BE.
WHAT IS THIS?
IT'S NOT HER!
AND, WHILE THE EFFIGY DID NOT RECOGNIZE THOSE WHO CALLED TO HER, SHE UNDERSTOOD THEIR DISDAIN.
WE'VE BEEN LIED TO!
IT'S AN *ABOMINATION*!
SHE'S NOT WHO I REMEMBER!

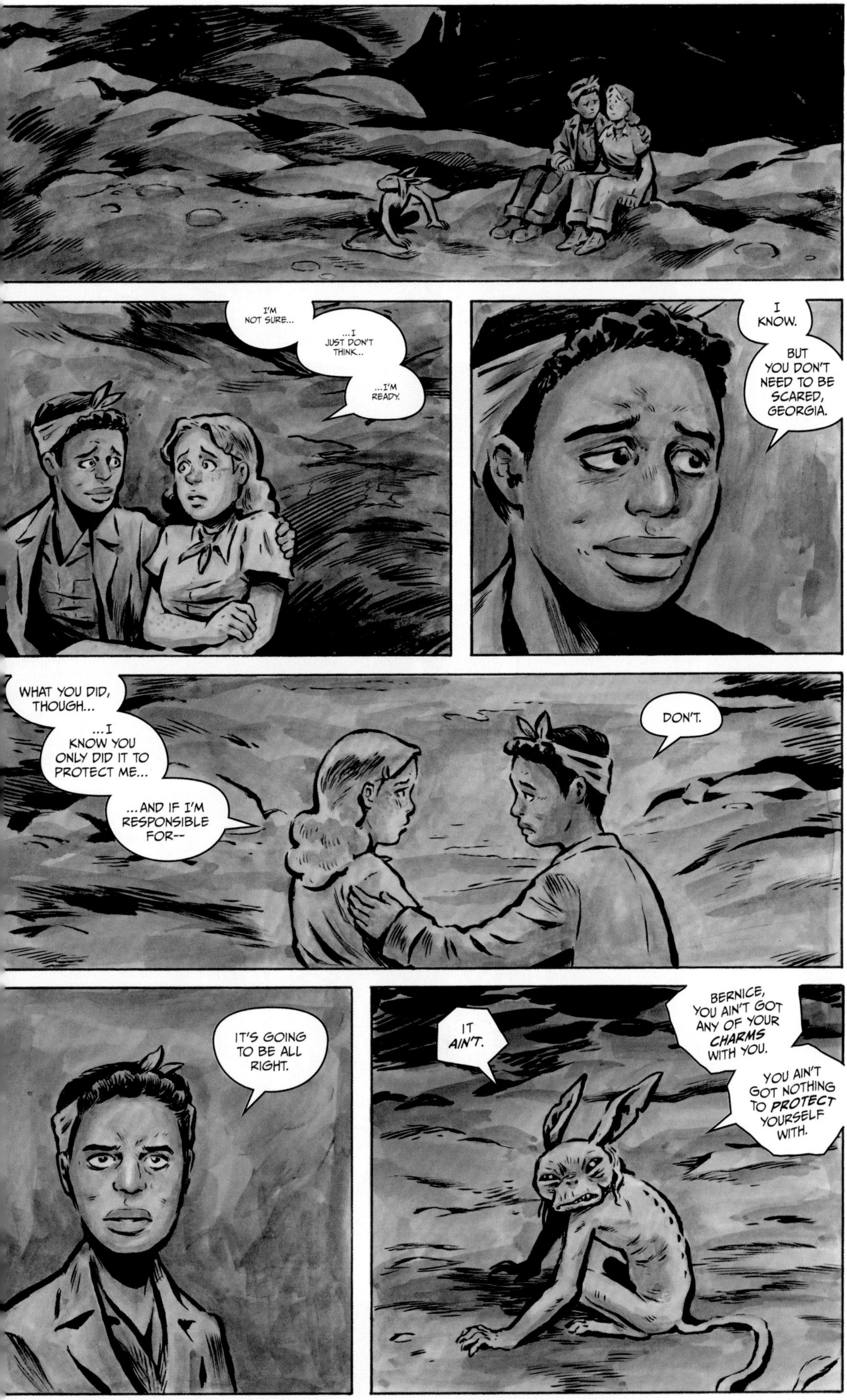
I'M NOT SURE...
...I JUST DON'T THINK..
...I'M READY.
I KNOW.
BUT YOU DON'T NEED TO BE SCARED, GEORGIA.
WHAT YOU DID, THOUGH...
...I KNOW YOU ONLY DID IT TO PROTECT ME...
...AND IF I'M RESPONSIBLE FOR--
DON'T.
IT'S GOING TO BE ALL RIGHT.
IT AIN'T.
BERNICE, YOU AIN'T GOT ANY OF YOUR CHARMS WITH YOU.
YOU AIN'T GOT NOTHING TO PROTECT YOURSELF WITH.

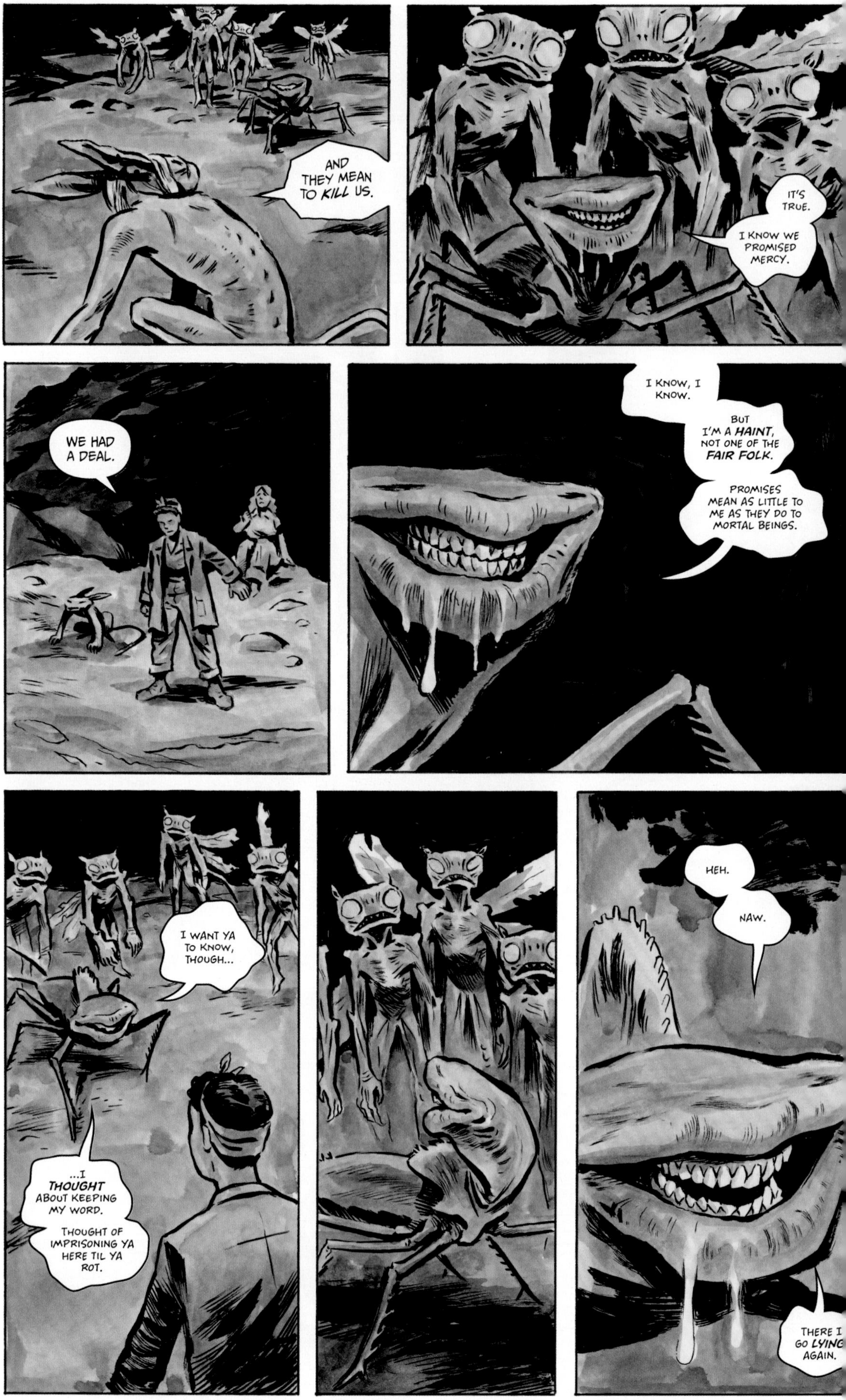
AND THEY MEAN TO KILL US.
IT'S TRUE.
I KNOW WE PROMISED MERCY.
WE HAD A DEAL.
I KNOW, I KNOW.
BUT I'M A HAINT, NOT ONE OF THE FAIR FOLK.
PROMISES MEAN AS LITTLE TO ME AS THEY DO TO MORTAL BEINGS.
I WANT YA TO KNOW, THOUGH...
...I THOUGHT ABOUT KEEPING MY WORD.
THOUGHT OF IMPRISONING YA HERE TIL YA ROT.
HEH.
NAW.
THERE I GO LYING AGAIN.

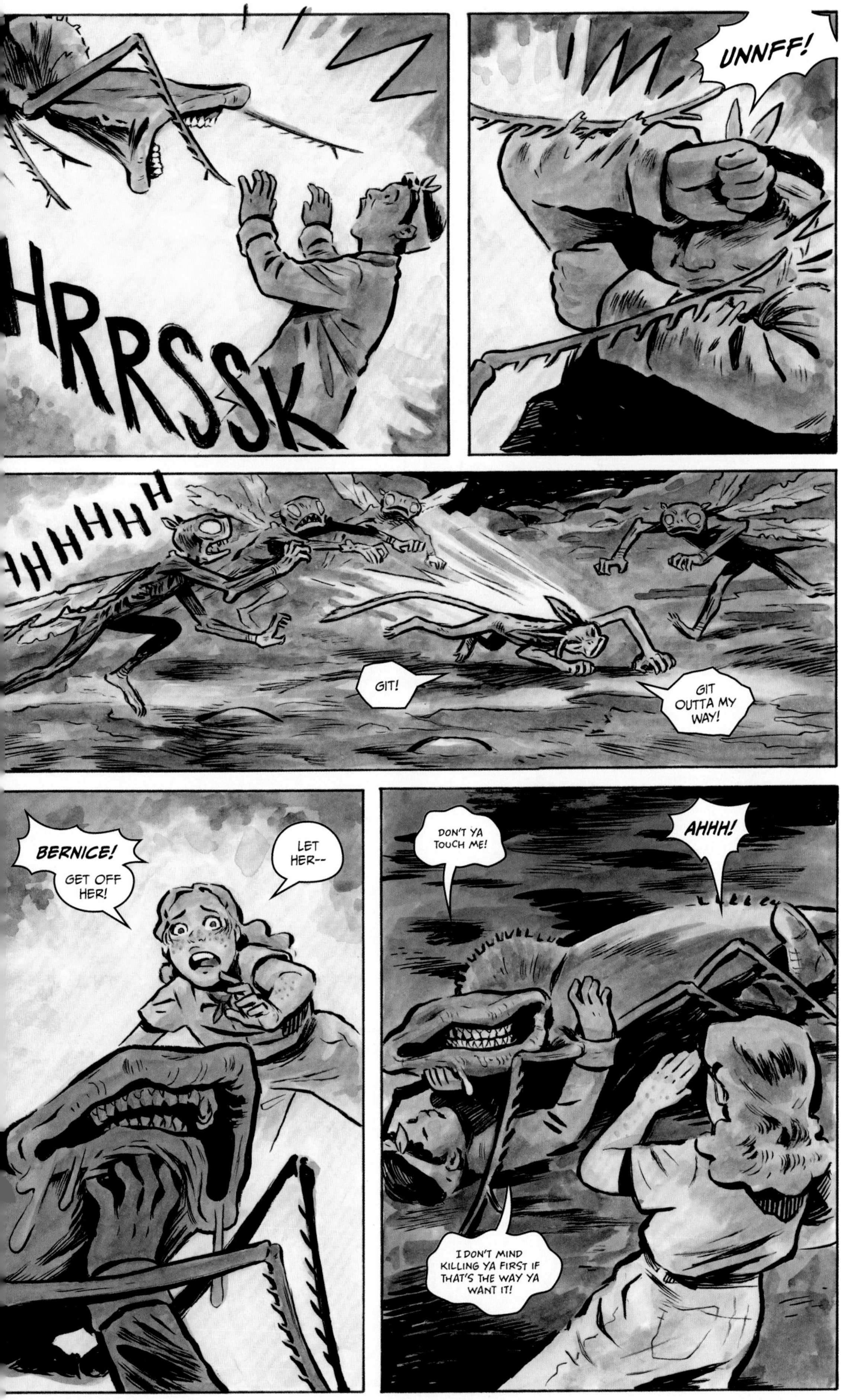
HRRSSK
UNNFF!
HHHHHHHH
GIT!
GIT OUTTA MY WAY!
BERNICE! GET OFF HER!
LET HER--
DON'T YA TOUCH ME!
AHHH!
I DON'T MIND KILLING YA FIRST IF THAT'S THE WAY YA WANT IT!

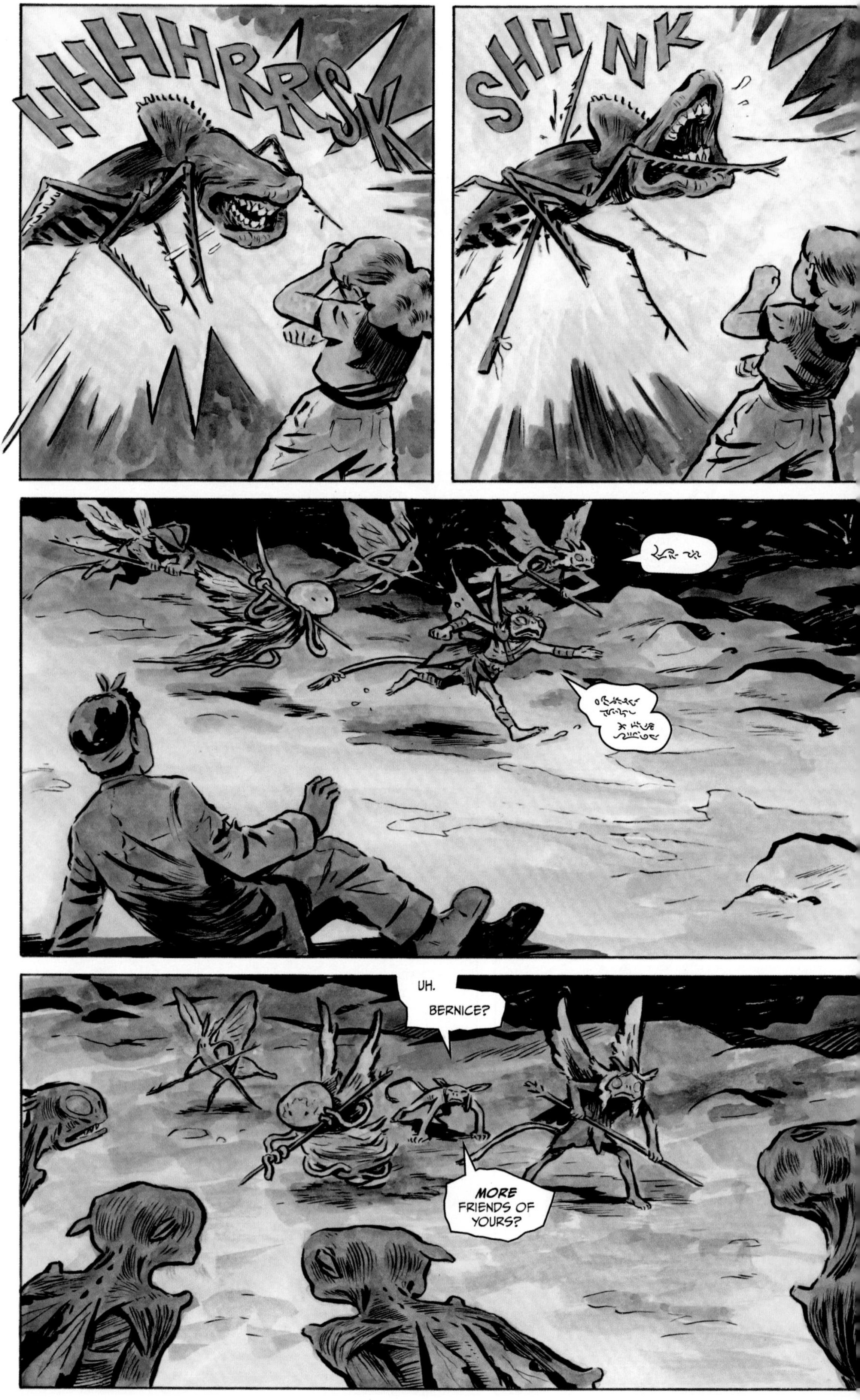
HHHHRRRSK
SHHNK
UH.
BERNICE?
MORE FRIENDS OF YOURS?

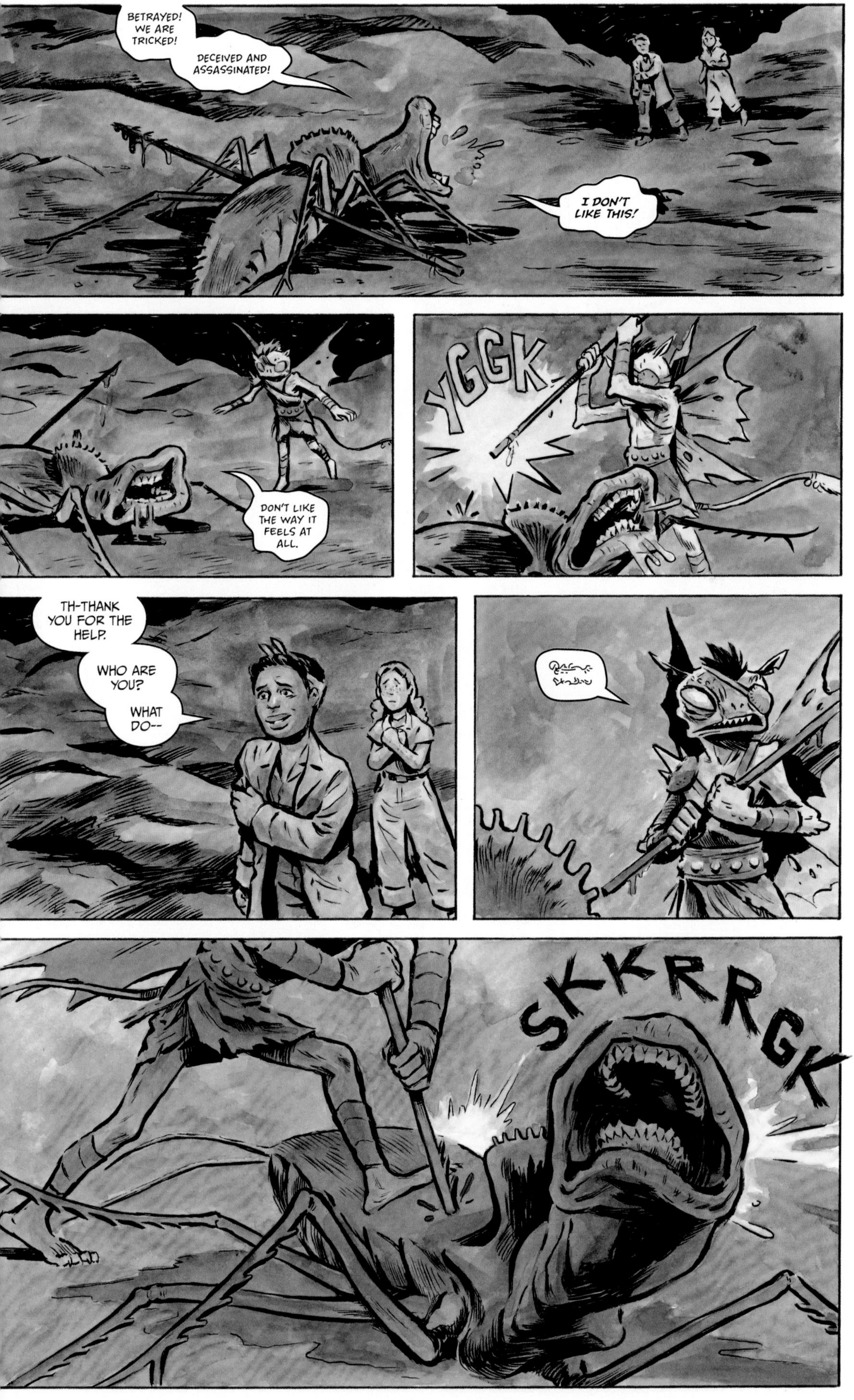
BETRAYED! WE ARE TRICKED!
DECEIVED AND ASSASSINATED!
I DON'T LIKE THIS!
DON'T LIKE THE WAY IT FEELS AT ALL.
YGGK
TH-THANK YOU FOR THE HELP.
WHO ARE YOU?
WHAT DO--
SKRRRGK

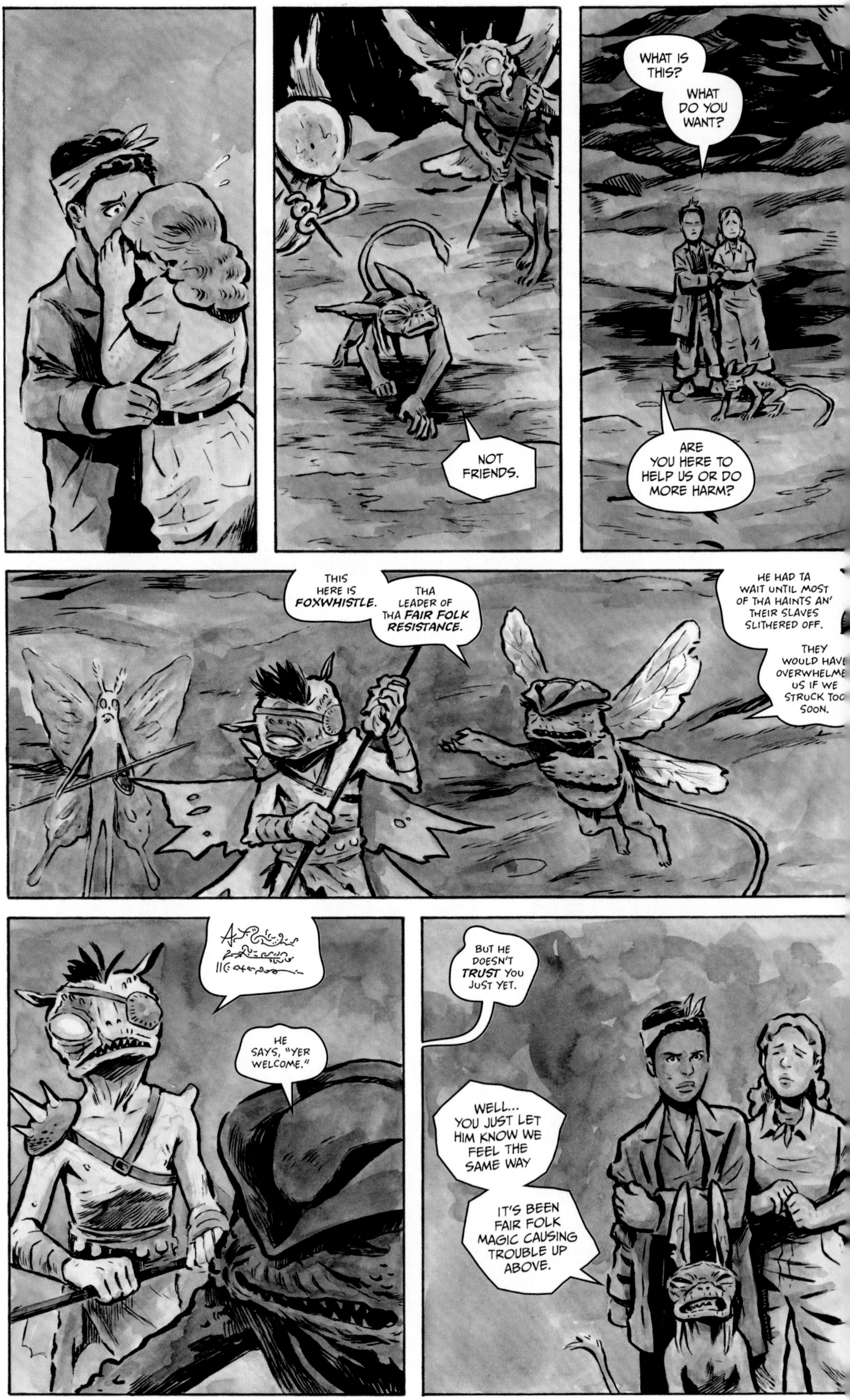

NOT FRIENDS.
WHAT IS THIS?
WHAT DO YOU WANT?
ARE YOU HERE TO HELP US OR DO MORE HARM?
THIS HERE IS FOXWHISTLE.
THA LEADER OF THA FAIR FOLK RESISTANCE.
HE HAD TA WAIT UNTIL MOST OF THA HAINTS AN' THEIR SLAVES SLITHERED OFF.
THEY WOULD HAVE OVERWHELME US IF WE STRUCK TOO SOON.
HE SAYS, "YER WELCOME."
BUT HE DOESN'T TRUST YOU JUST YET.
WELL... YOU JUST LET HIM KNOW WE FEEL THE SAME WAY
IT'S BEEN FAIR FOLK MAGIC CAUSING TROUBLE UP ABOVE.

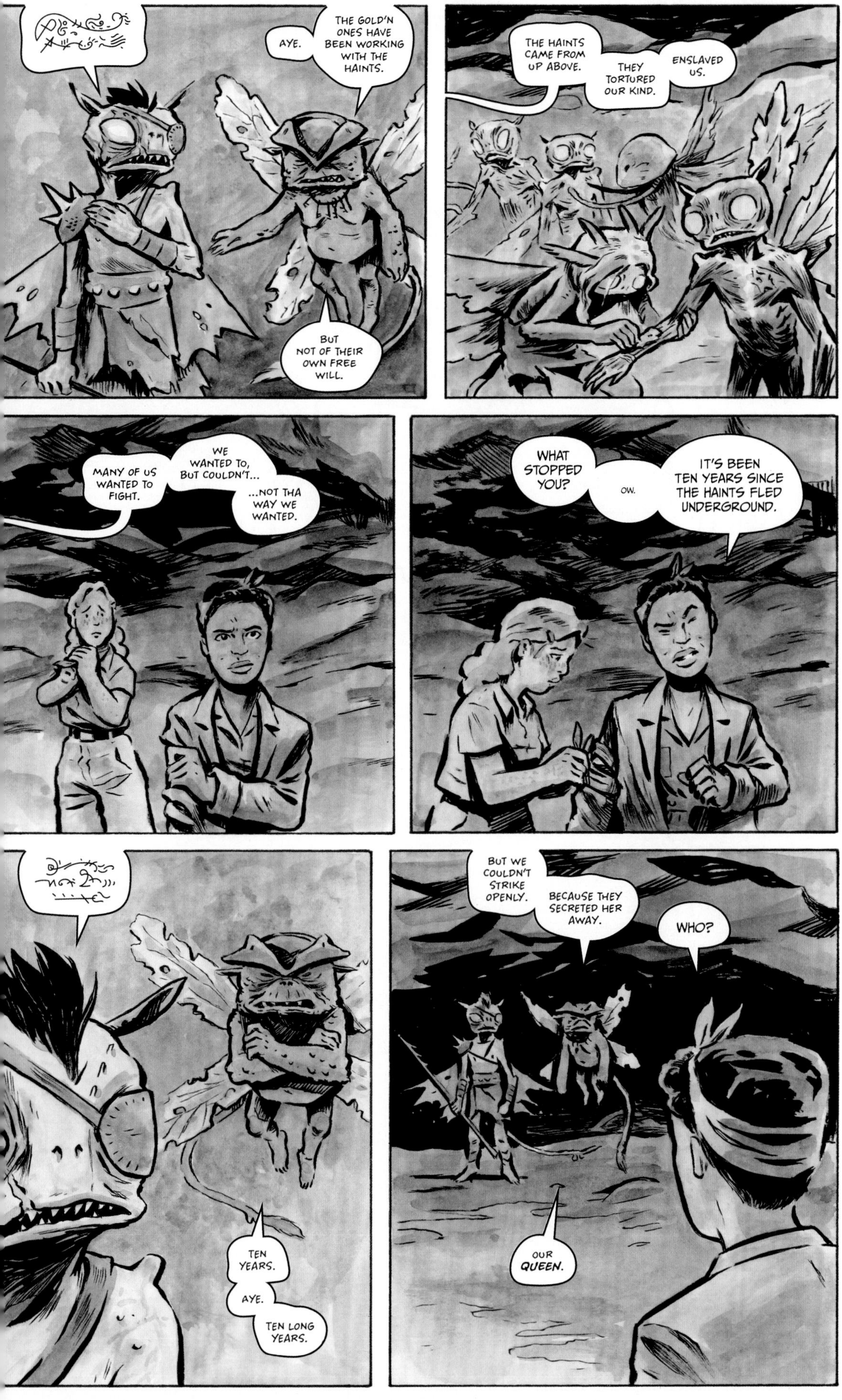

AYE.
THE GOLD'N ONES HAVE BEEN WORKING WITH THE HAINTS.
BUT NOT OF THEIR OWN FREE WILL.
THE HAINTS CAME FROM UP ABOVE.
THEY TORTURED OUR KIND.
ENSLAVED US.
MANY OF US WANTED TO FIGHT.
WE WANTED TO, BUT COULDN'T...
...NOT THA WAY WE WANTED.
WHAT STOPPED YOU?
OW.
IT'S BEEN TEN YEARS SINCE THE HAINTS FLED UNDERGROUND.
TEN YEARS.
AYE.
TEN LONG YEARS.
BUT WE COULDN'T STRIKE OPENLY.
BECAUSE THEY SECRETED HER AWAY.
WHO?
OUR QUEEN.

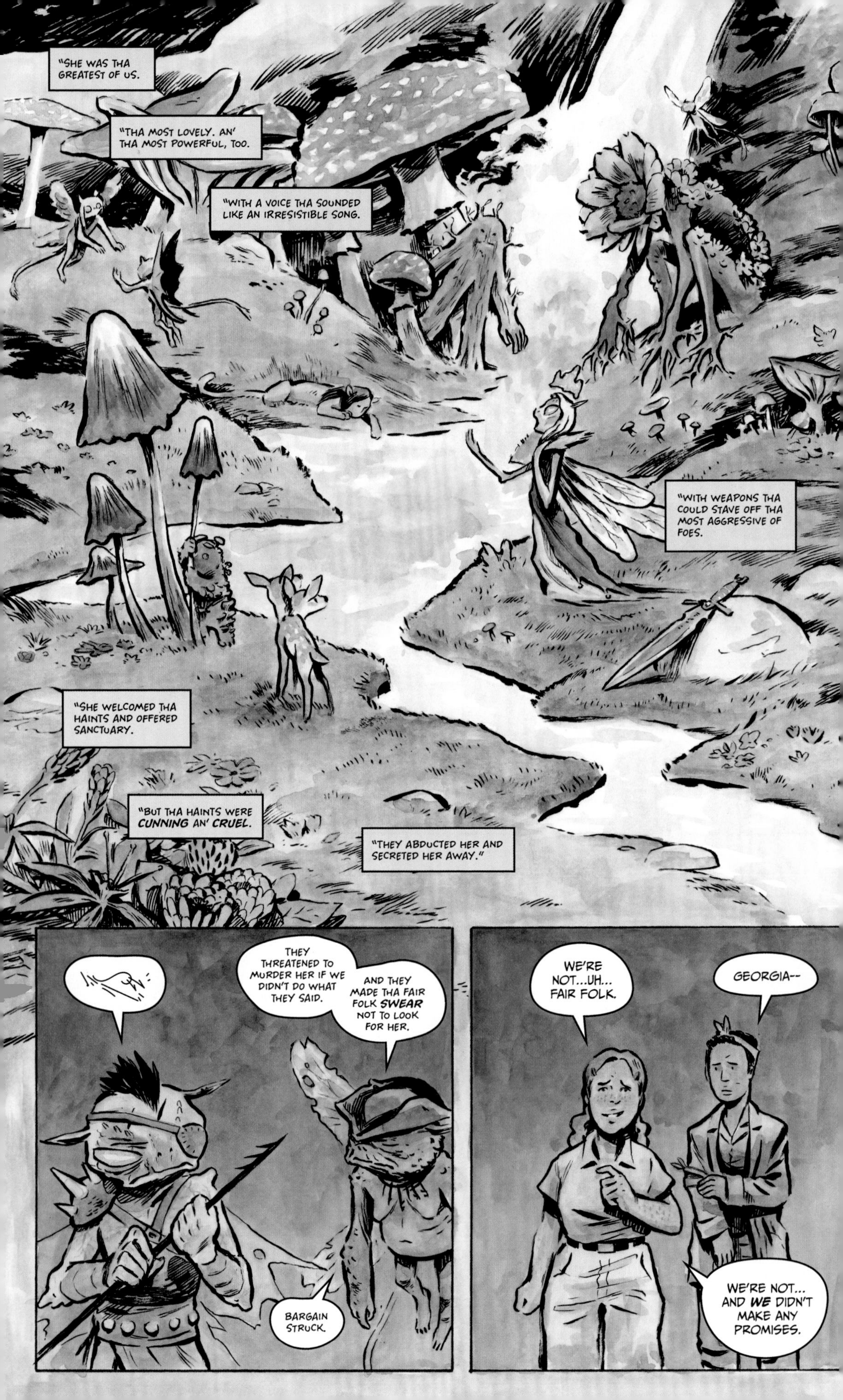
"SHE WAS THA GREATEST OF US.
"THA MOST LOVELY. AN' THA MOST POWERFUL, TOO.
"WITH A VOICE THA SOUNDED LIKE AN IRRESISTIBLE SONG.
"WITH WEAPONS THA COULD STAVE OFF THA MOST AGGRESSIVE OF FOES.
"SHE WELCOMED THA HAINTS AND OFFERED SANCTUARY.
"BUT THA HAINTS WERE CUNNING AN' CRUEL.
"THEY ABDUCTED HER AND SECRETED HER AWAY."
THEY THREATENED TO MURDER HER IF WE DIDN'T DO WHAT THEY SAID.
AND THEY MADE THA FAIR FOLK SWEAR NOT TO LOOK FOR HER.
BARGAIN STRUCK.
WE'RE NOT...UH... FAIR FOLK.
GEORGIA--
WE'RE NOT... AND WE DIDN'T MAKE ANY PROMISES.

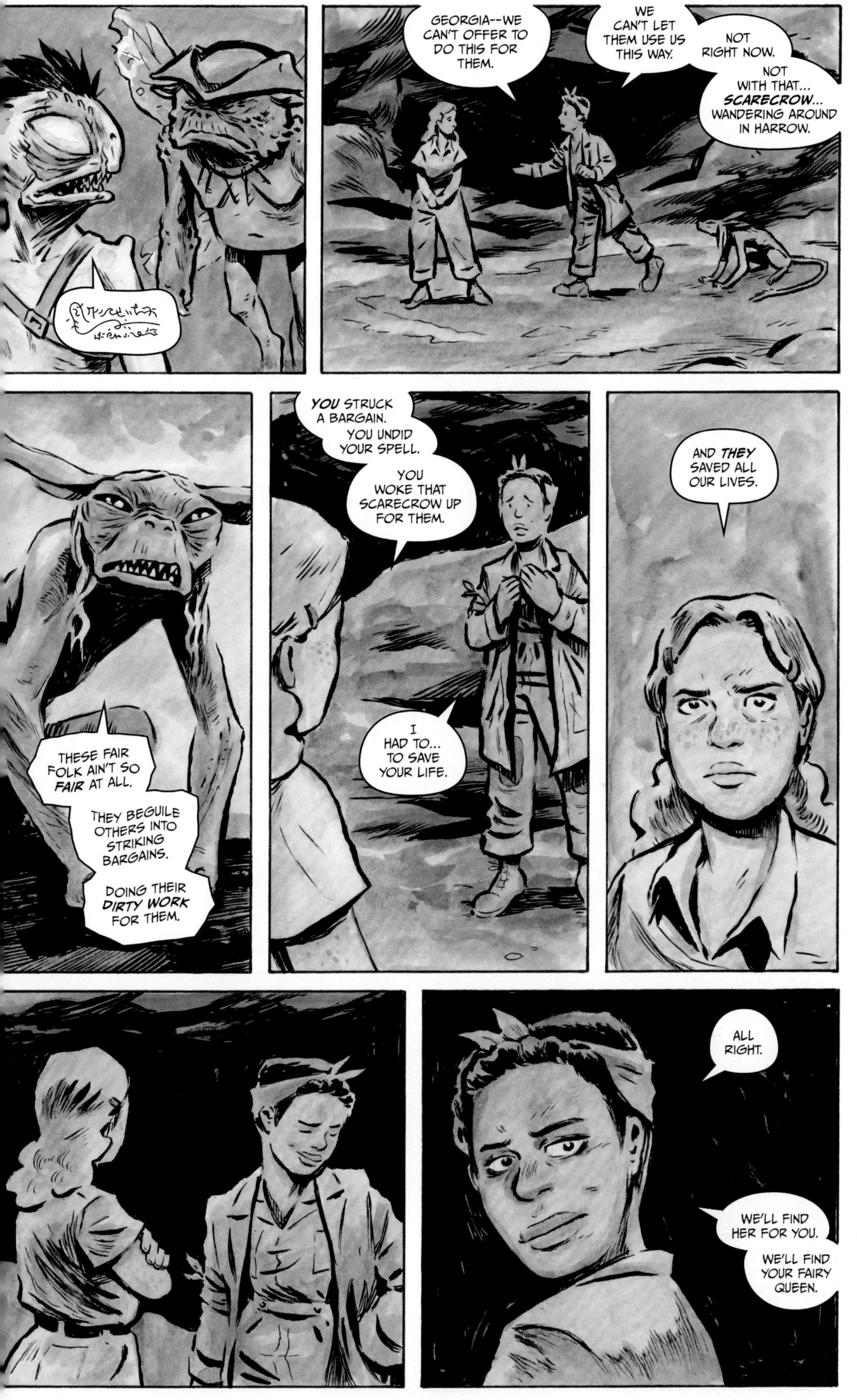
GEORGIA--WE CAN'T OFFER TO DO THIS FOR THEM.
WE CAN'T LET THEM USE US THIS WAY.
NOT RIGHT NOW.
NOT WITH THAT... SCARECROW... WANDERING AROUND IN HARROW.
THESE FAIR FOLK AIN'T SO FAIR AT ALL.
THEY BEGUILE OTHERS INTO STRIKING BARGAINS.
DOING THEIR DIRTY WORK FOR THEM.
YOU STRUCK A BARGAIN.
YOU UNDID YOUR SPELL.
YOU WOKE THAT SCARECROW UP FOR THEM.
I HAD TO... TO SAVE YOUR LIFE.
AND THEY SAVED ALL OUR LIVES.
ALL RIGHT.
WE'LL FIND HER FOR YOU.
WE'LL FIND YOUR FAIRY QUEEN.

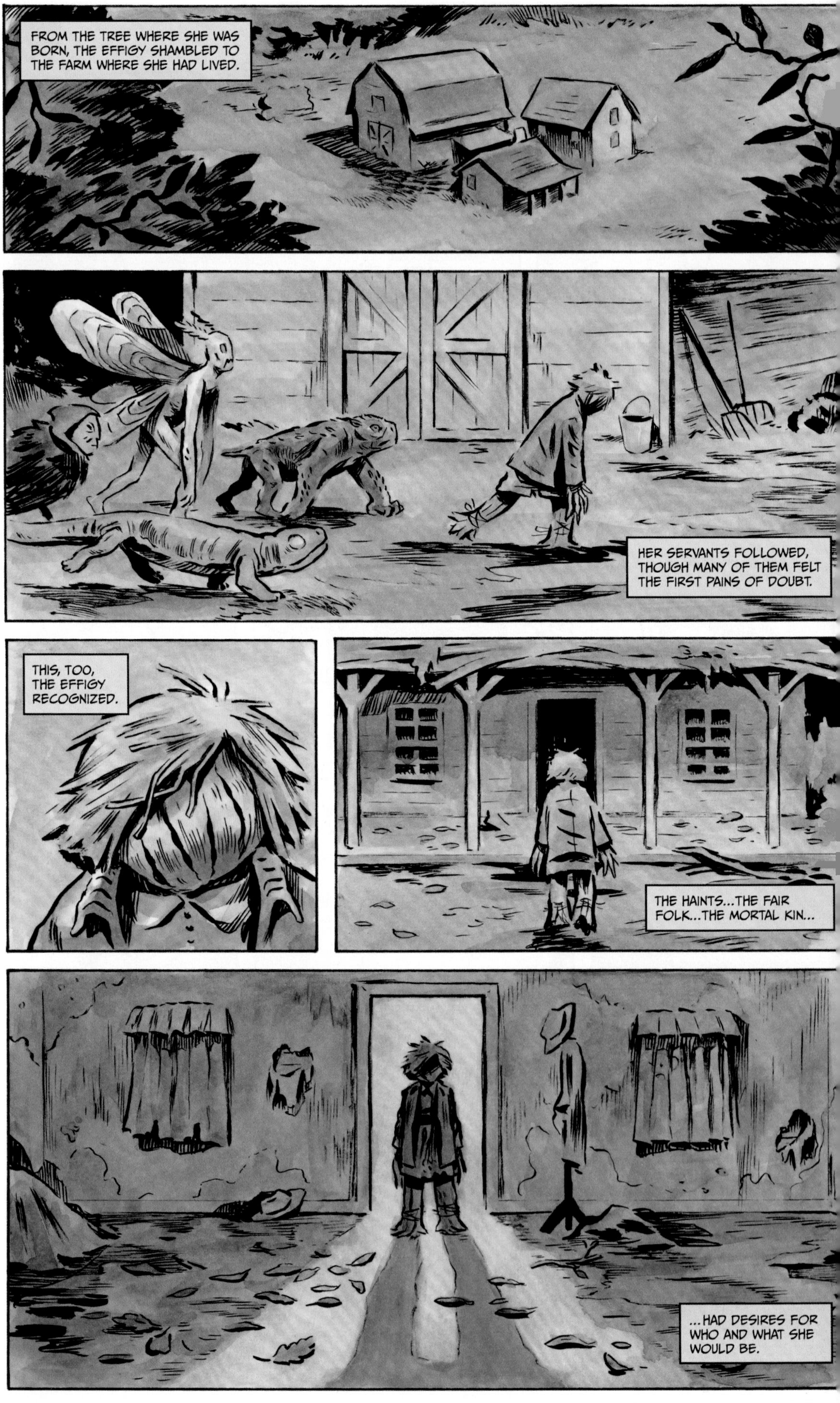
FROM THE TREE WHERE SHE WAS BORN, THE EFFIGY SHAMBLED TO THE FARM WHERE SHE HAD LIVED.
HER SERVANTS FOLLOWED, THOUGH MANY OF THEM FELT THE FIRST PAINS OF DOUBT.
THIS, TOO, THE EFFIGY RECOGNIZED.
THE HAINTS...THE FAIR FOLK...THE MORTAL KIN...
...HAD DESIRES FOR WHO AND WHAT SHE WOULD BE.

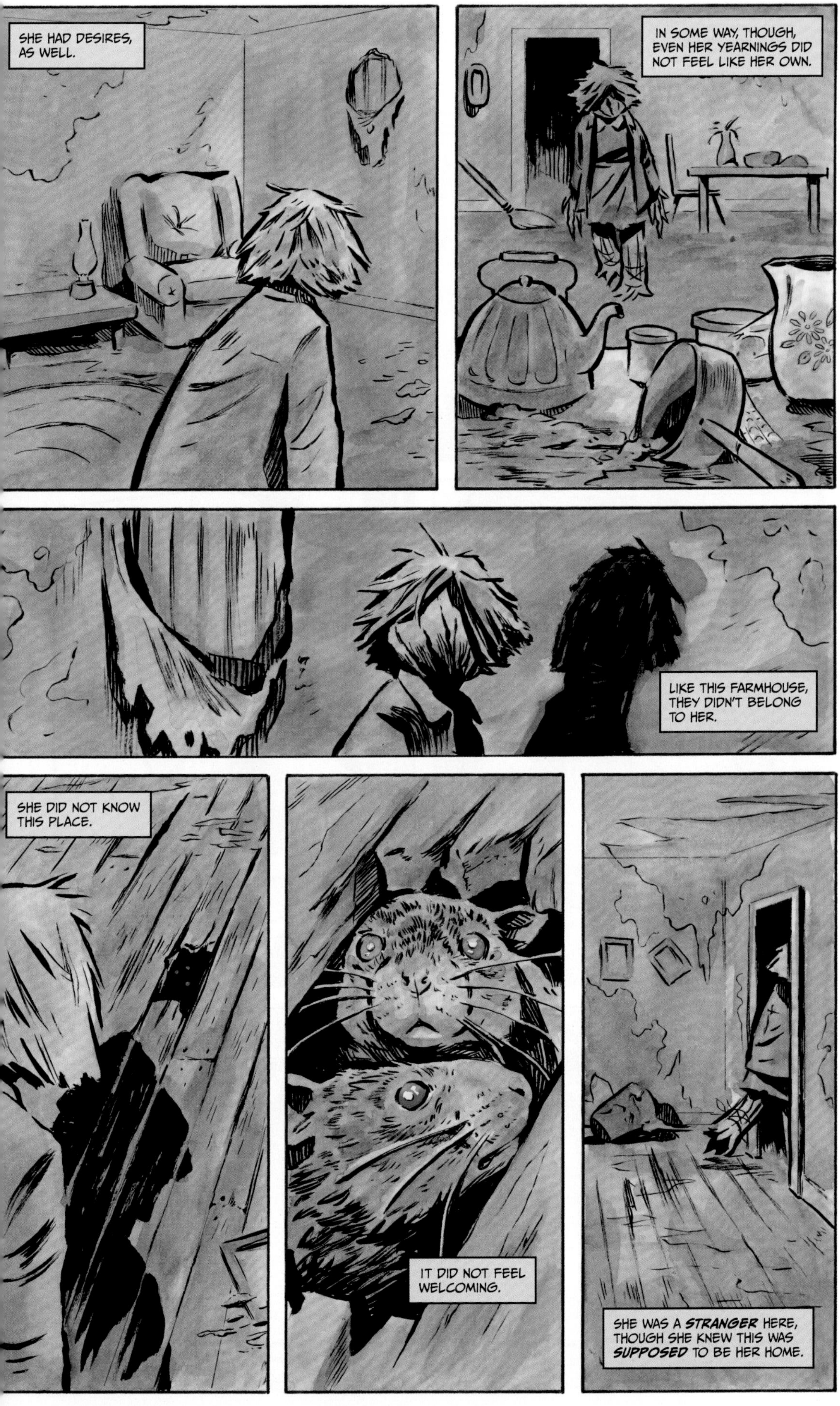
SHE HAD DESIRES, AS WELL.
IN SOME WAY, THOUGH, EVEN HER YEARNINGS DID NOT FEEL LIKE HER OWN.
LIKE THIS FARMHOUSE, THEY DIDN'T BELONG TO HER.
SHE DID NOT KNOW THIS PLACE.
IT DID NOT FEEL WELCOMING.
SHE WAS A **STRANGER** HERE, THOUGH SHE KNEW THIS WAS **SUPPOSED** TO BE HER HOME.

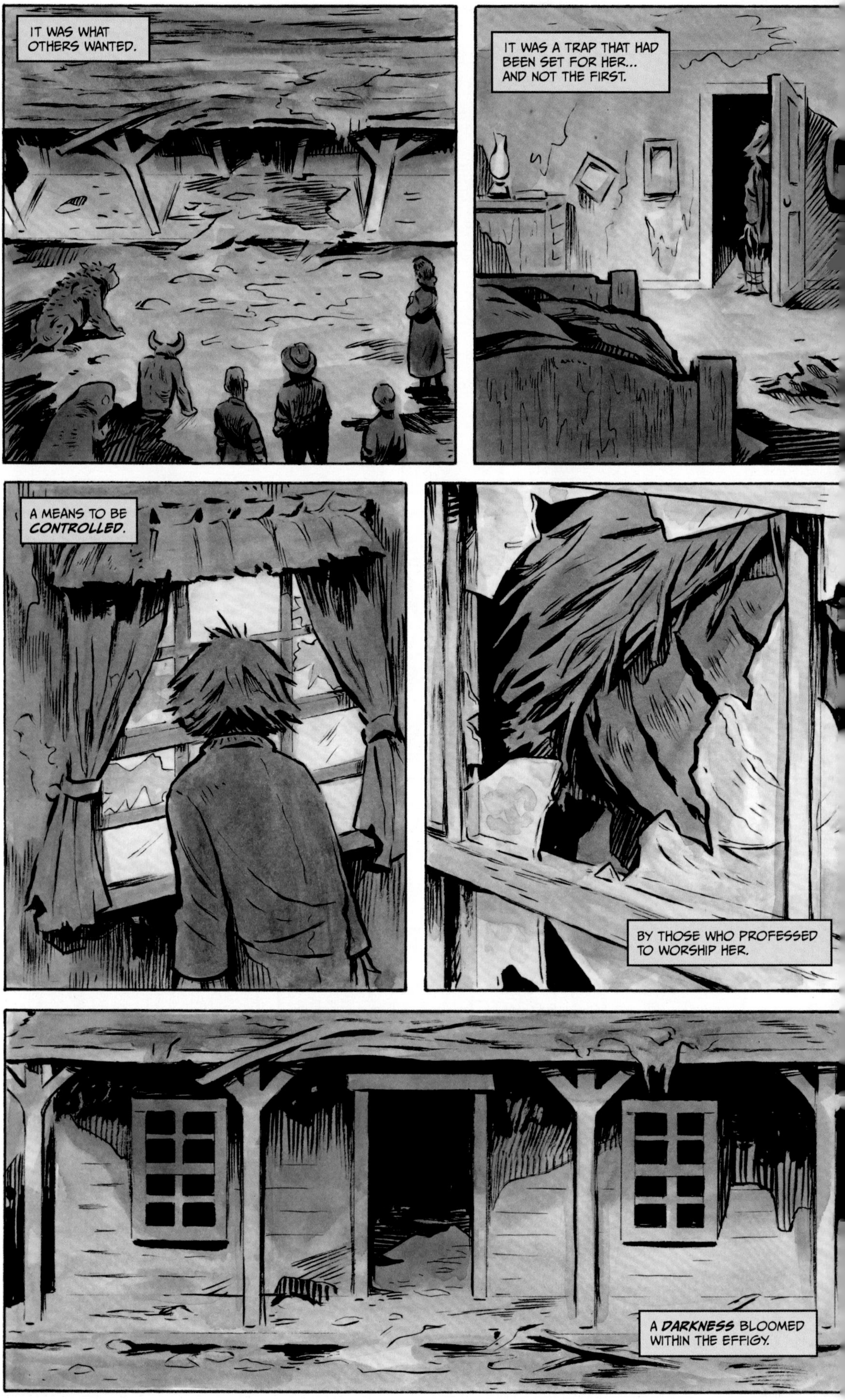
IT WAS WHAT OTHERS WANTED.
IT WAS A TRAP THAT HAD BEEN SET FOR HER... AND NOT THE FIRST.
A MEANS TO BE *CONTROLLED*.
BY THOSE WHO PROFESSED TO WORSHIP HER.
A *DARKNESS* BLOOMED WITHIN THE EFFIGY.

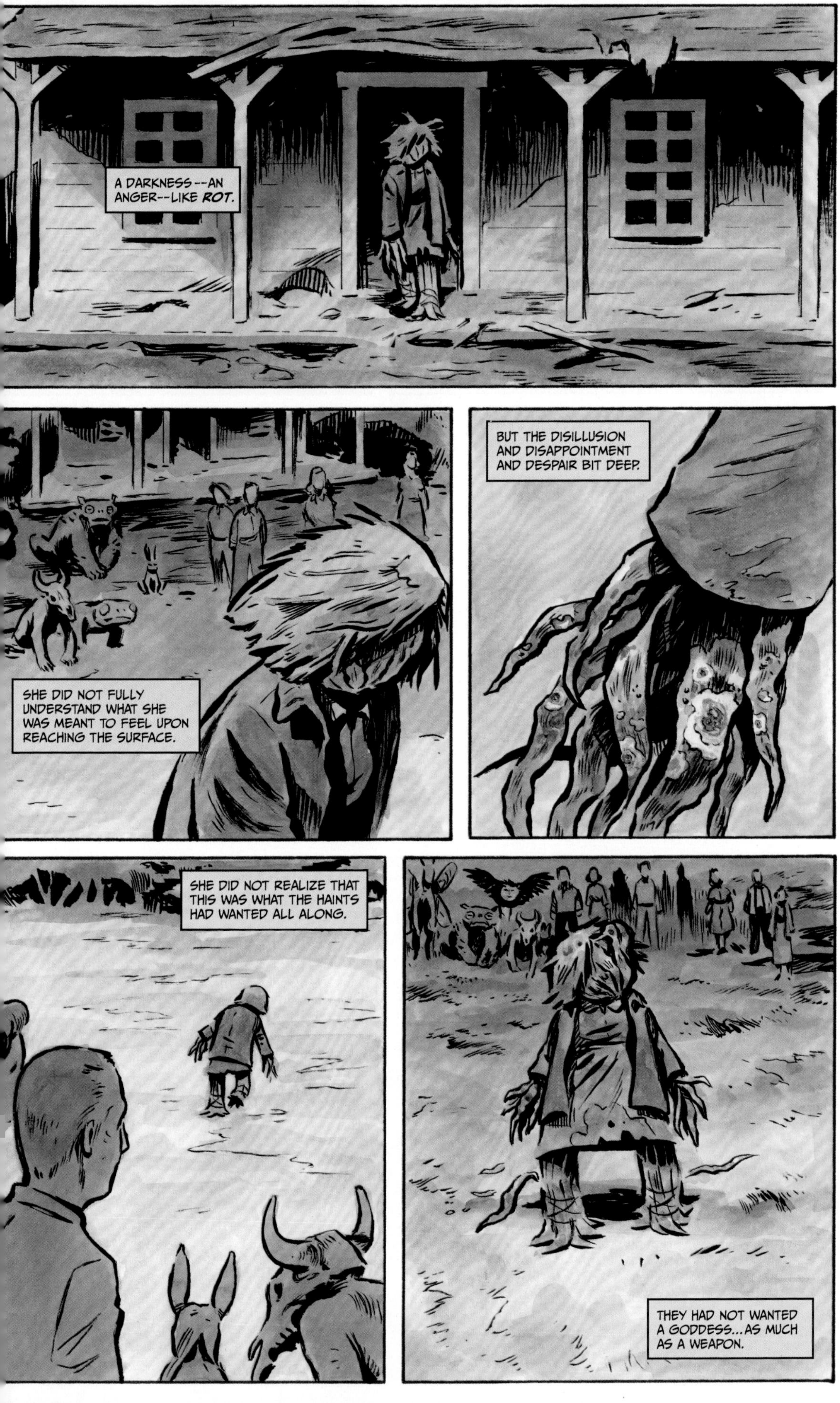
A DARKNESS--AN ANGER--LIKE *ROT*.
SHE DID NOT FULLY UNDERSTAND WHAT SHE WAS MEANT TO FEEL UPON REACHING THE SURFACE.
BUT THE DISILLUSION AND DISAPPOINTMENT AND DESPAIR BIT DEEP.
SHE DID NOT REALIZE THAT THIS WAS WHAT THE HAINTS HAD WANTED ALL ALONG.
THEY HAD NOT WANTED A GODDESS...AS MUCH AS A WEAPON.

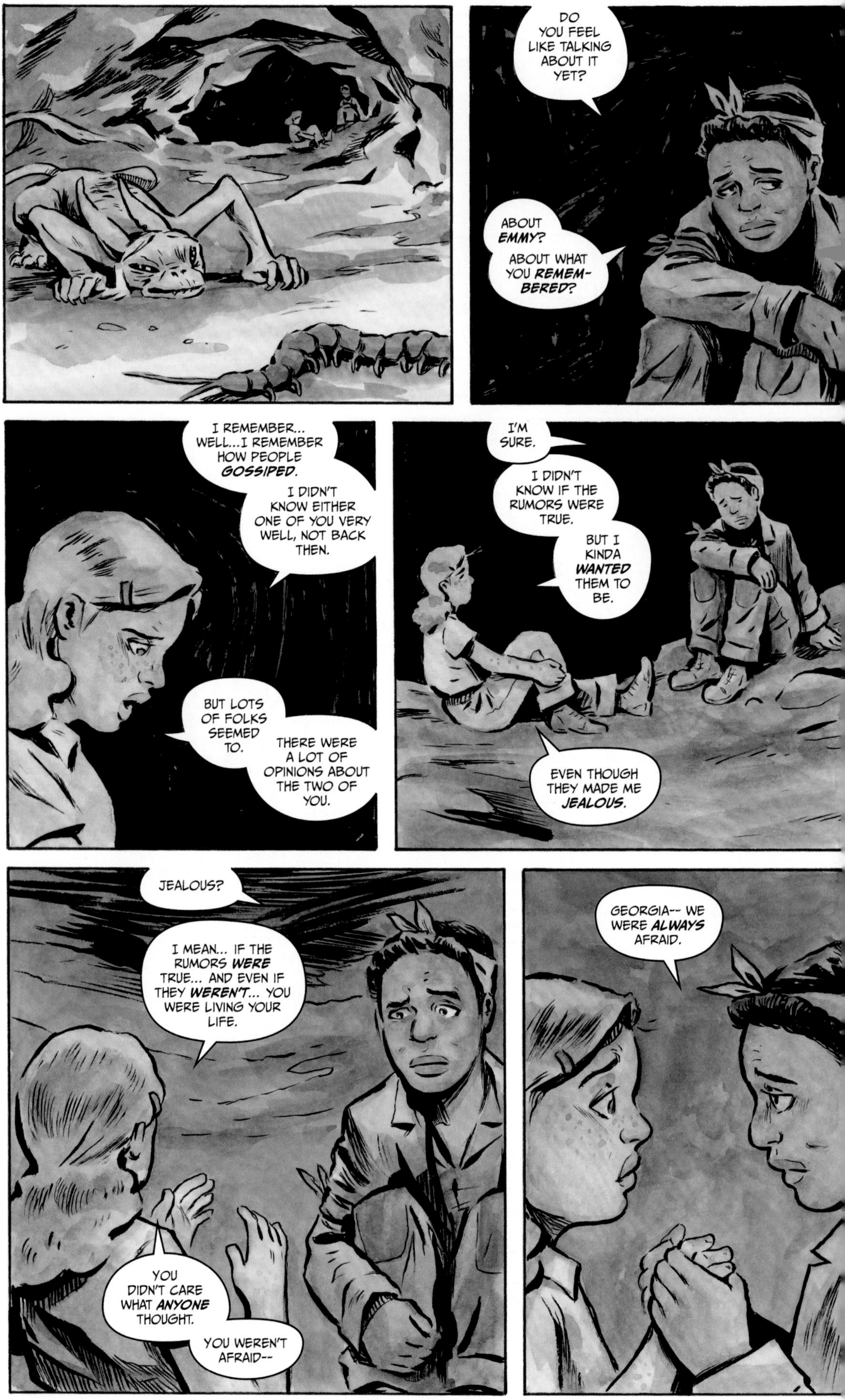
DO YOU FEEL LIKE TALKING ABOUT IT YET?
ABOUT EMMY?
ABOUT WHAT YOU REMEMBERED?
I REMEMBER... WELL...I REMEMBER HOW PEOPLE GOSSIPED.
I DIDN'T KNOW EITHER ONE OF YOU VERY WELL, NOT BACK THEN.
BUT LOTS OF FOLKS SEEMED TO.
THERE WERE A LOT OF OPINIONS ABOUT THE TWO OF YOU.
I'M SURE.
I DIDN'T KNOW IF THE RUMORS WERE TRUE.
BUT I KINDA WANTED THEM TO BE.
EVEN THOUGH THEY MADE ME JEALOUS.
JEALOUS?
I MEAN... IF THE RUMORS WERE TRUE... AND EVEN IF THEY WEREN'T... YOU WERE LIVING YOUR LIFE.
YOU DIDN'T CARE WHAT ANYONE THOUGHT.
YOU WEREN'T AFRAID--
GEORGIA-- WE WERE ALWAYS AFRAID.

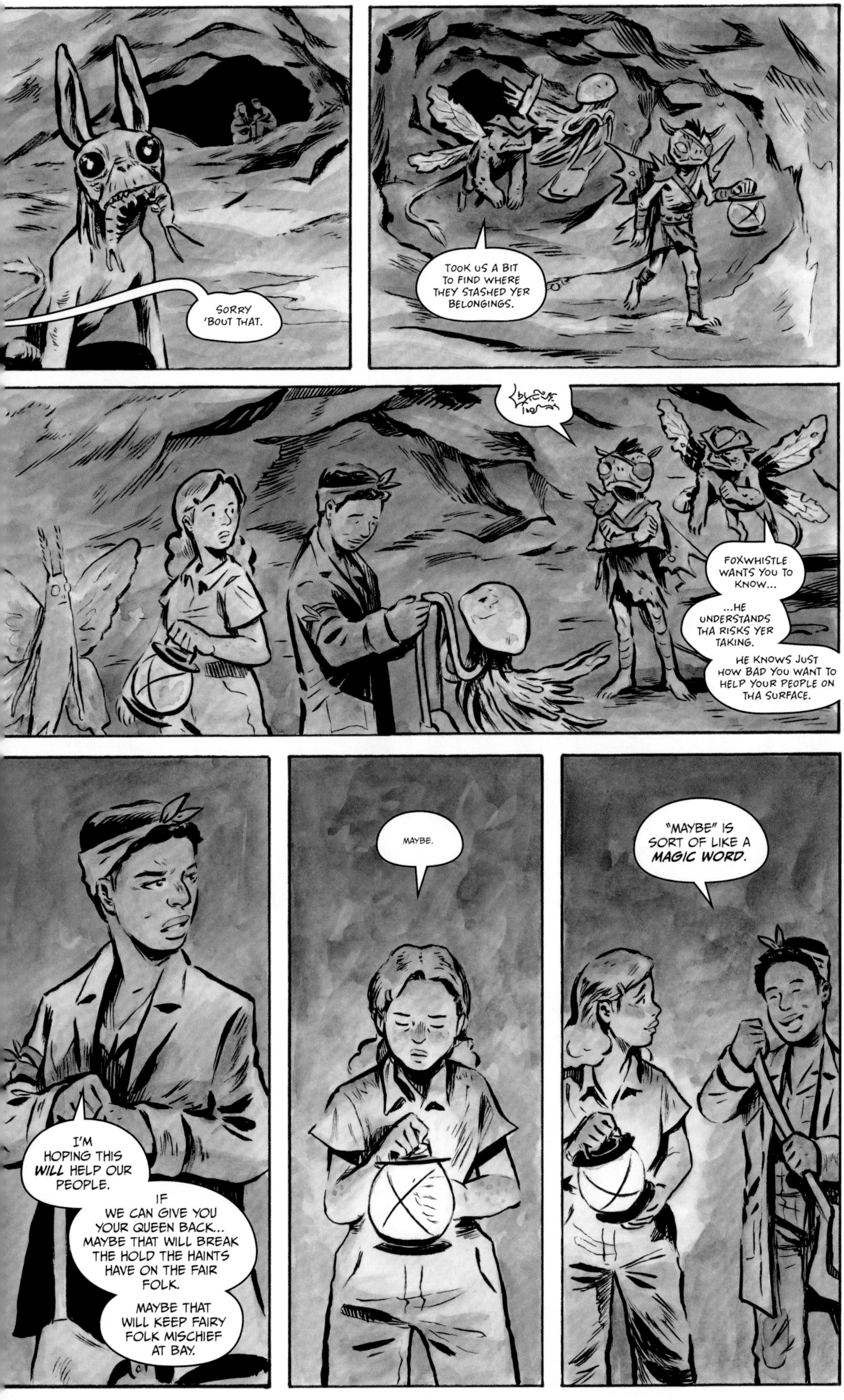
SORRY 'BOUT THAT.
TOOK US A BIT TO FIND WHERE THEY STASHED YER BELONGINGS.
FOXWHISTLE WANTS YOU TO KNOW...
...HE UNDERSTANDS THA RISKS YER TAKING.
HE KNOWS JUST HOW BAD YOU WANT TO HELP YOUR PEOPLE ON THA SURFACE.
I'M HOPING THIS WILL HELP OUR PEOPLE.
IF WE CAN GIVE YOU YOUR QUEEN BACK... MAYBE THAT WILL BREAK THE HOLD THE HAINTS HAVE ON THE FAIR FOLK.
MAYBE THAT WILL KEEP FAIRY FOLK MISCHIEF AT BAY.
MAYBE.
"MAYBE" IS SORT OF LIKE A MAGIC WORD.

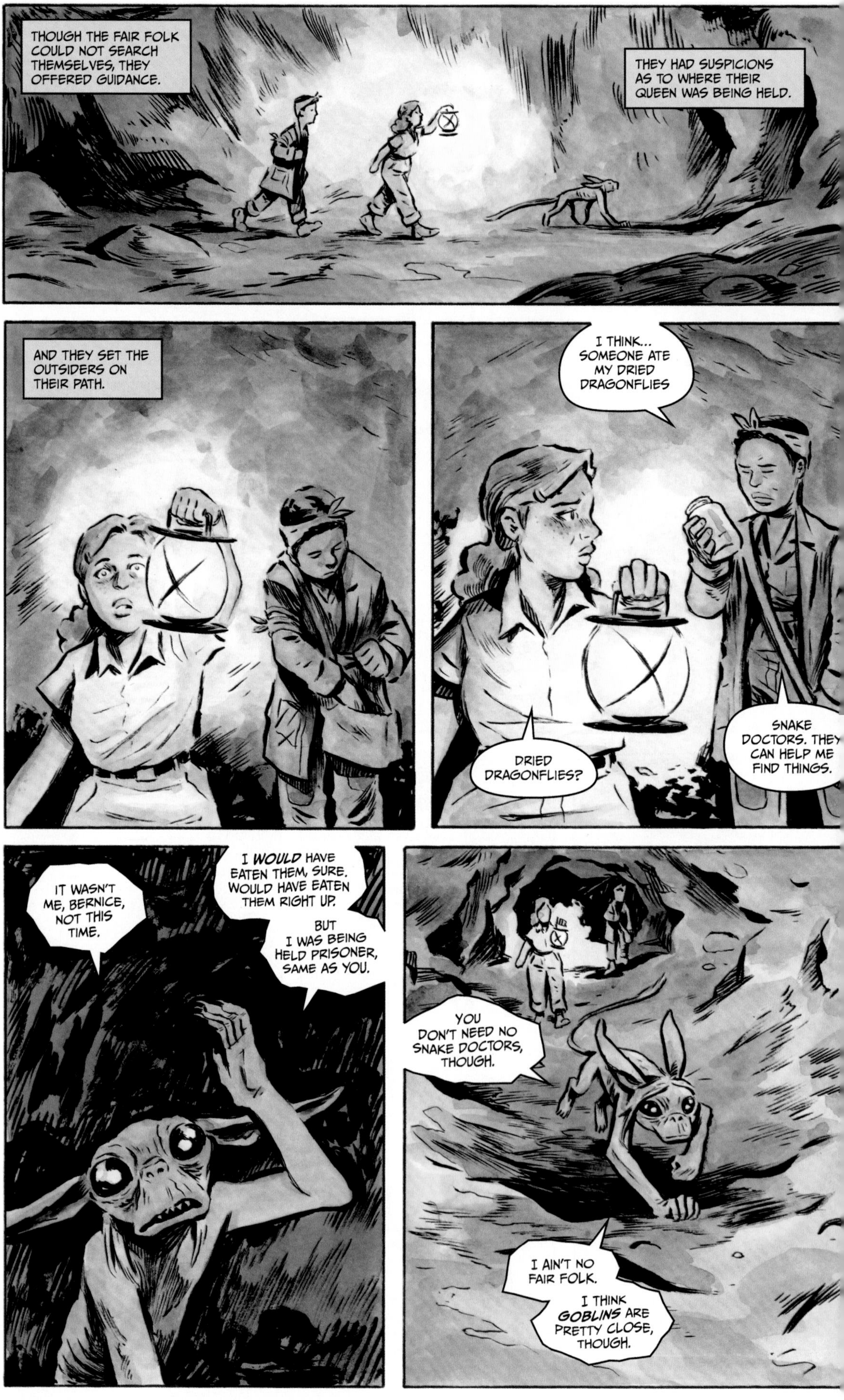
THOUGH THE FAIR FOLK COULD NOT SEARCH THEMSELVES, THEY OFFERED GUIDANCE.
THEY HAD SUSPICIONS AS TO WHERE THEIR QUEEN WAS BEING HELD.
AND THEY SET THE OUTSIDERS ON THEIR PATH.
I THINK... SOMEONE ATE MY DRIED DRAGONFLIES
DRIED DRAGONFLIES?
SNAKE DOCTORS. THEY CAN HELP ME FIND THINGS.
IT WASN'T ME, BERNICE, NOT THIS TIME.
I WOULD HAVE EATEN THEM, SURE. WOULD HAVE EATEN THEM RIGHT UP.
BUT I WAS BEING HELD PRISONER, SAME AS YOU.
YOU DON'T NEED NO SNAKE DOCTORS, THOUGH.
I AIN'T NO FAIR FOLK.
I THINK GOBLINS ARE PRETTY CLOSE, THOUGH.

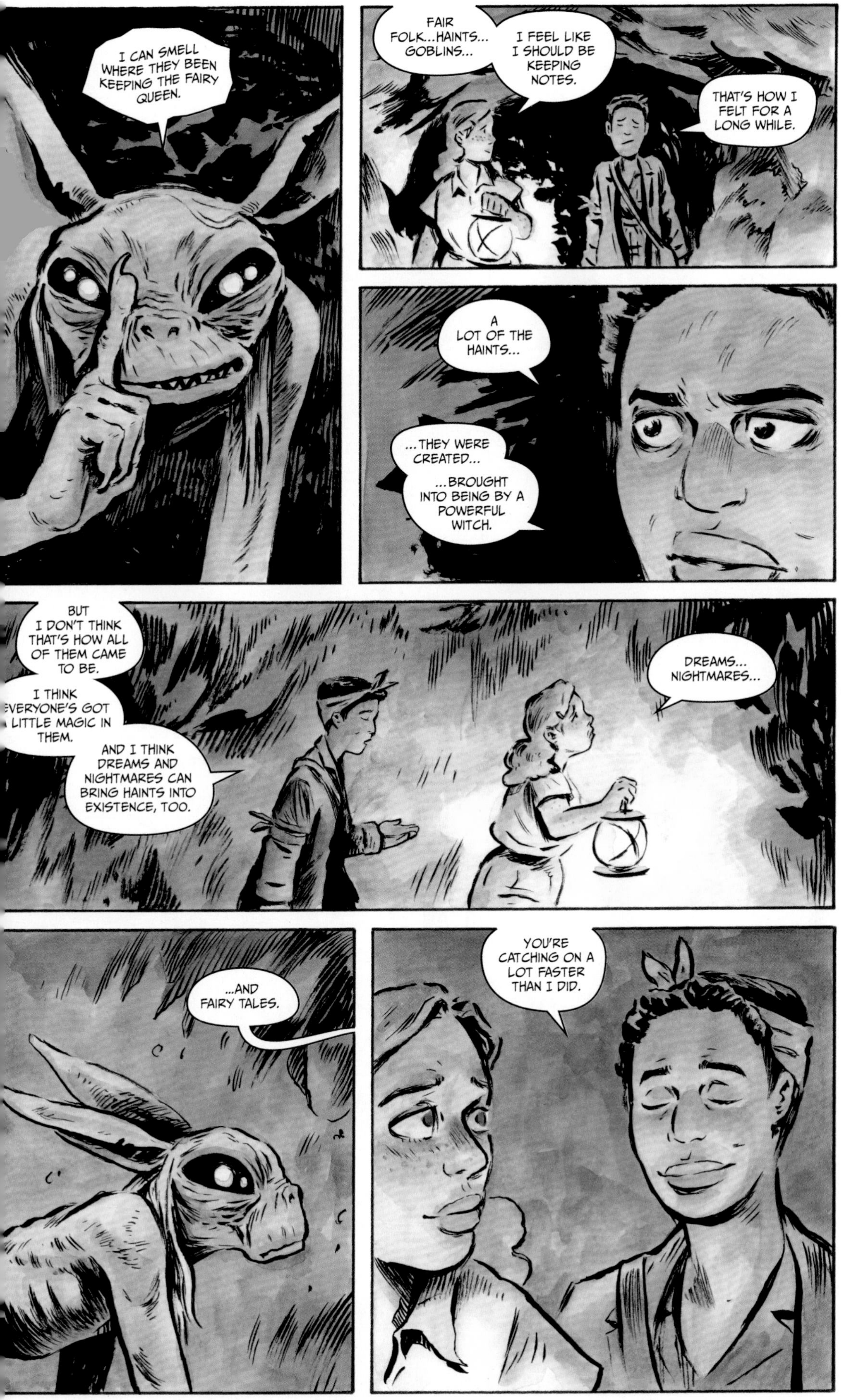
I CAN SMELL WHERE THEY BEEN KEEPING THE FAIRY QUEEN.
FAIR FOLK...HAINTS... GOBLINS...
I FEEL LIKE I SHOULD BE KEEPING NOTES.
THAT'S HOW I FELT FOR A LONG WHILE.
A LOT OF THE HAINTS...
...THEY WERE CREATED...
...BROUGHT INTO BEING BY A POWERFUL WITCH.
BUT I DON'T THINK THAT'S HOW ALL OF THEM CAME TO BE.
I THINK EVERYONE'S GOT A LITTLE MAGIC IN THEM.
AND I THINK DREAMS AND NIGHTMARES CAN BRING HAINTS INTO EXISTENCE, TOO.
DREAMS... NIGHTMARES...
...AND FAIRY TALES.
YOU'RE CATCHING ON A LOT FASTER THAN I DID.

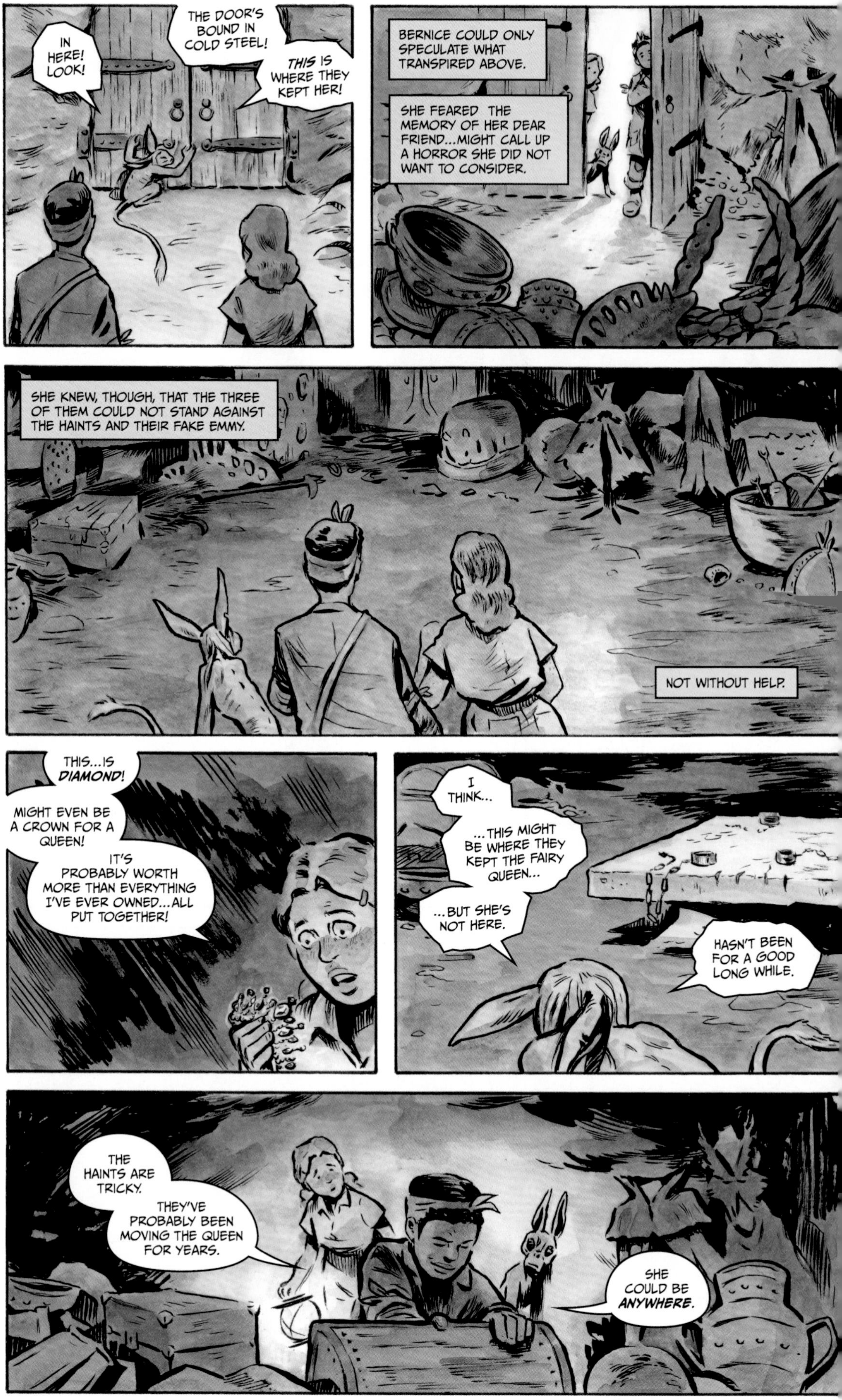

IN HERE! LOOK!
THE DOOR'S BOUND IN COLD STEEL!
THIS IS WHERE THEY KEPT HER!
BERNICE COULD ONLY SPECULATE WHAT TRANSPIRED ABOVE.
SHE FEARED THE MEMORY OF HER DEAR FRIEND...MIGHT CALL UP A HORROR SHE DID NOT WANT TO CONSIDER.
SHE KNEW, THOUGH, THAT THE THREE OF THEM COULD NOT STAND AGAINST THE HAINTS AND THEIR FAKE EMMY.
NOT WITHOUT HELP.
THIS...IS *DIAMOND*!
MIGHT EVEN BE A CROWN FOR A QUEEN!
IT'S PROBABLY WORTH MORE THAN EVERYTHING I'VE EVER OWNED...ALL PUT TOGETHER!
I THINK...
...THIS MIGHT BE WHERE THEY KEPT THE FAIRY QUEEN...
...BUT SHE'S NOT HERE.
HASN'T BEEN FOR A GOOD LONG WHILE.
THE HAINTS ARE TRICKY.
THEY'VE PROBABLY BEEN MOVING THE QUEEN FOR YEARS.
SHE COULD BE *ANYWHERE*.

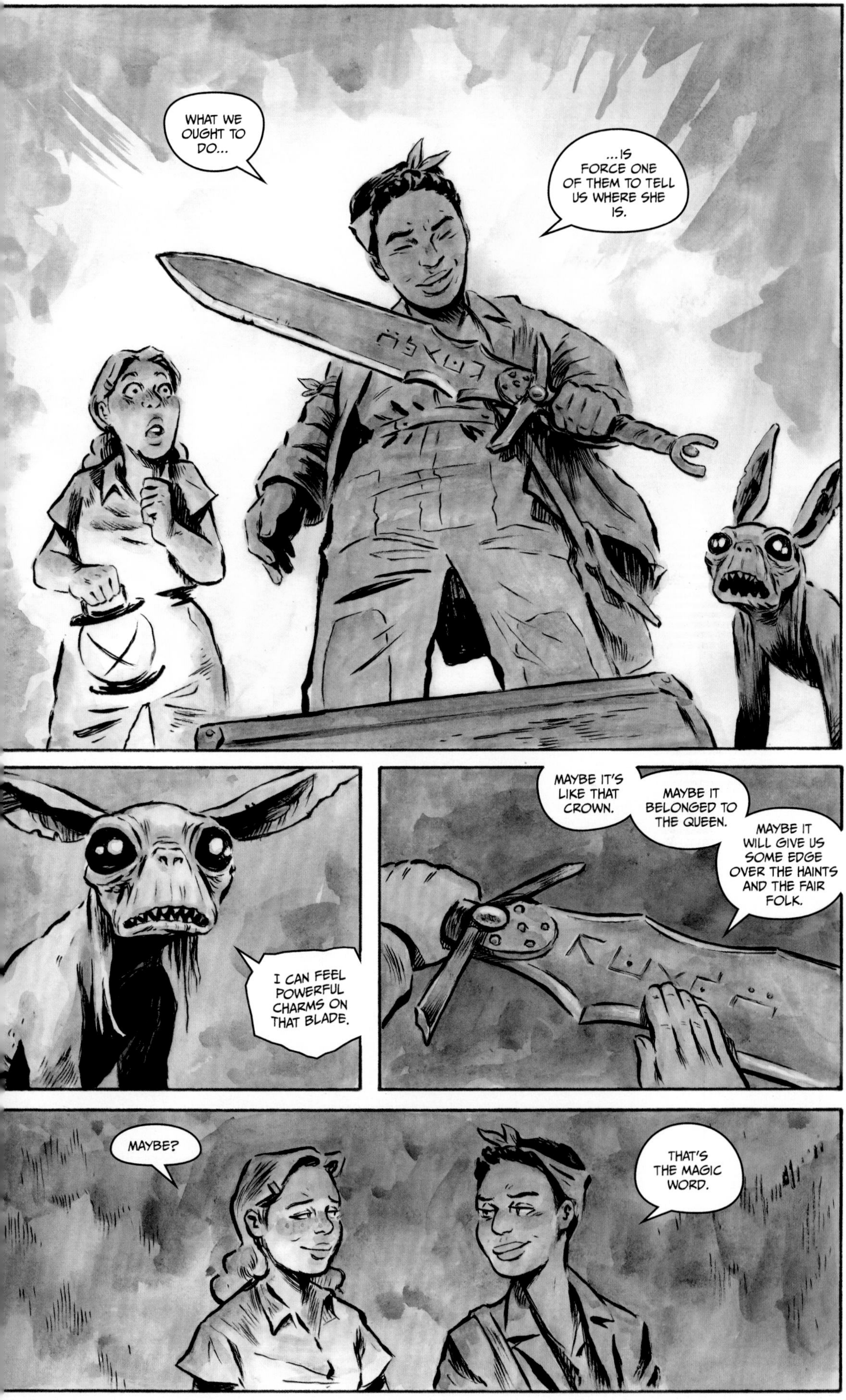
WHAT WE OUGHT TO DO...
...IS FORCE ONE OF THEM TO TELL US WHERE SHE IS.
I CAN FEEL POWERFUL CHARMS ON THAT BLADE.
MAYBE IT'S LIKE THAT CROWN.
MAYBE IT BELONGED TO THE QUEEN.
MAYBE IT WILL GIVE US SOME EDGE OVER THE HAINTS AND THE FAIR FOLK.
MAYBE?
THAT'S THE MAGIC WORD.

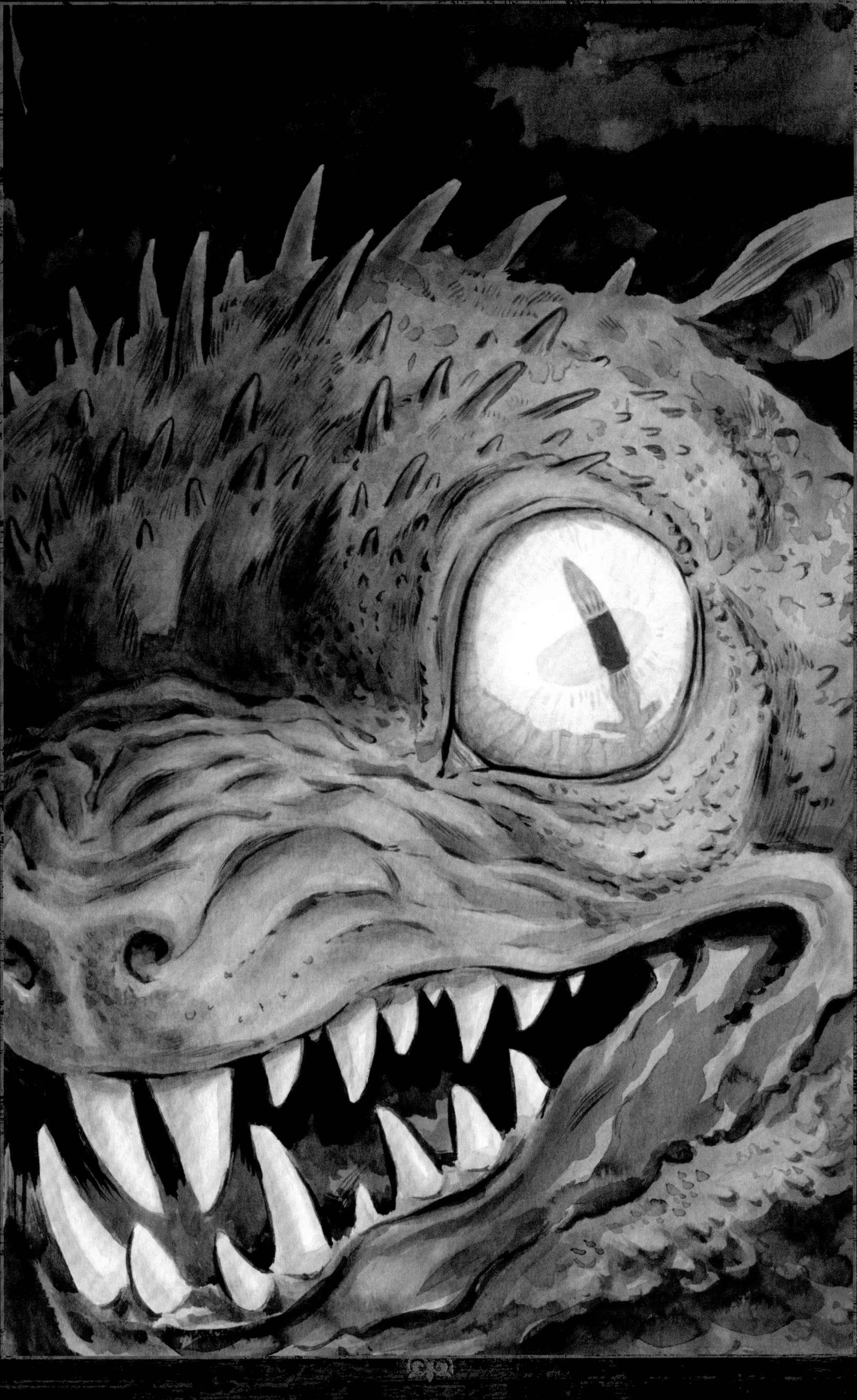

FOUR

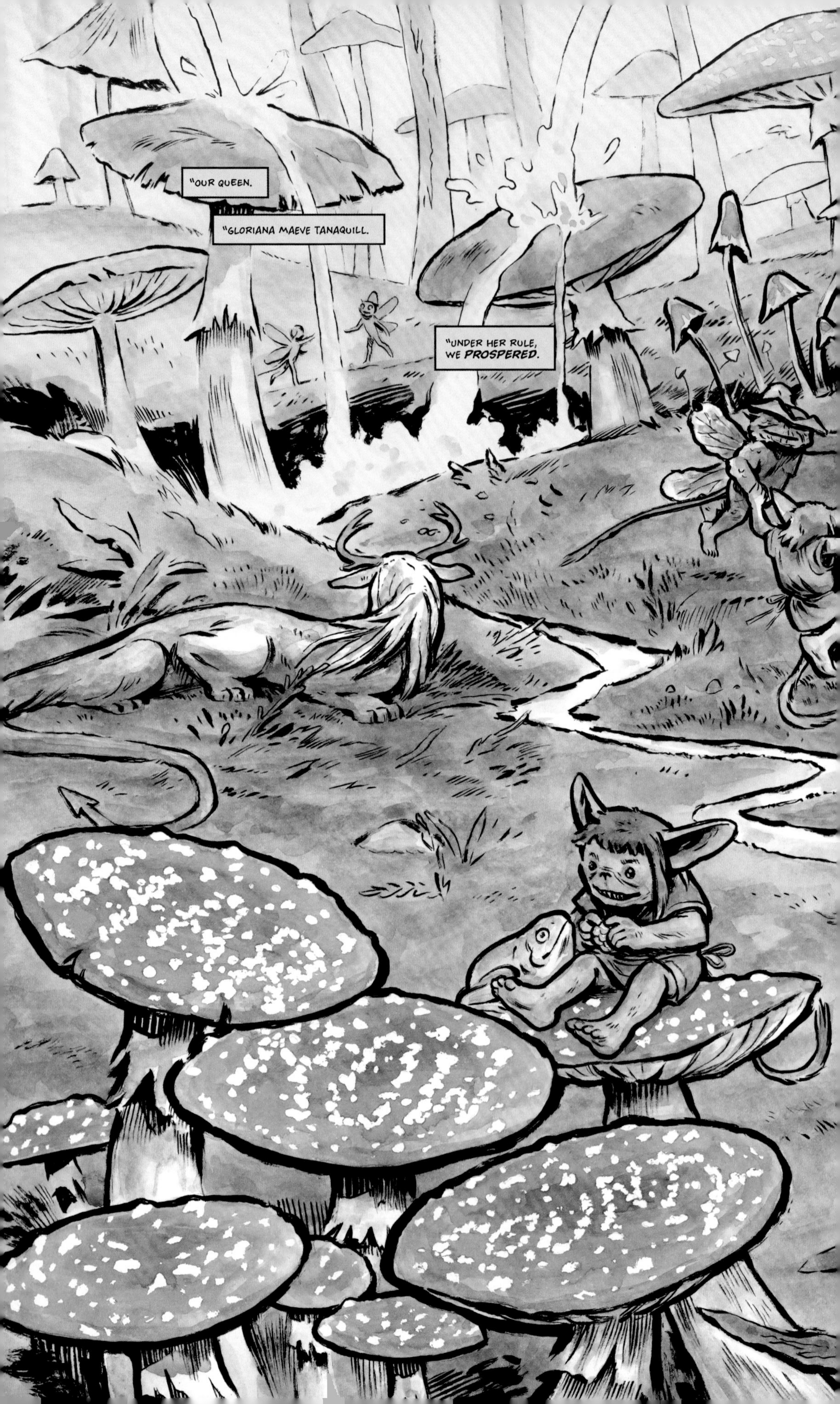
"OUR QUEEN.
"GLORIANA MAEVE TANAQUILL.
"UNDER HER RULE, WE PROSPERED.

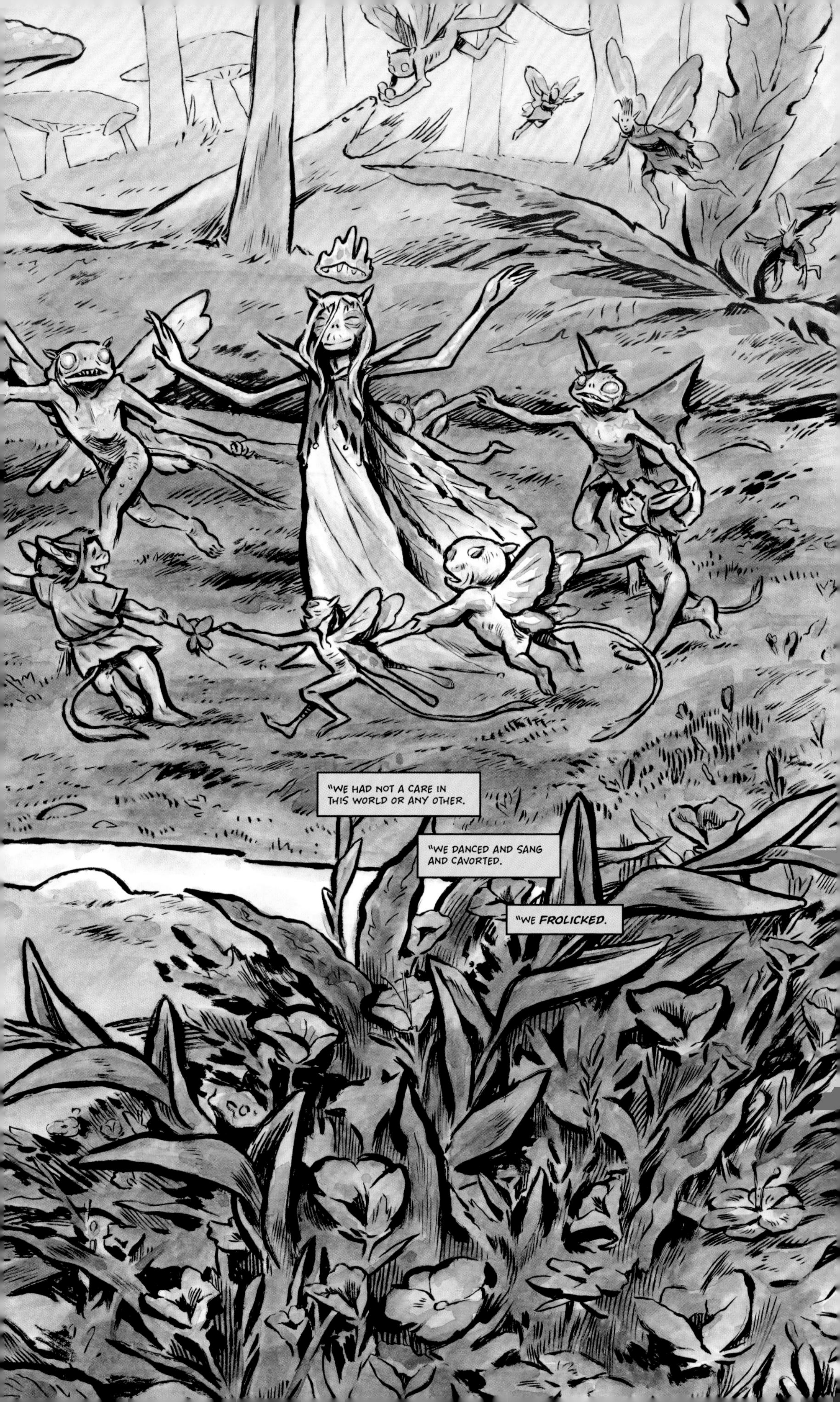
"WE HAD NOT A CARE IN THIS WORLD OR ANY OTHER.
"WE DANCED AND SANG AND CAVORTED.
"WE *FROLICKED*.

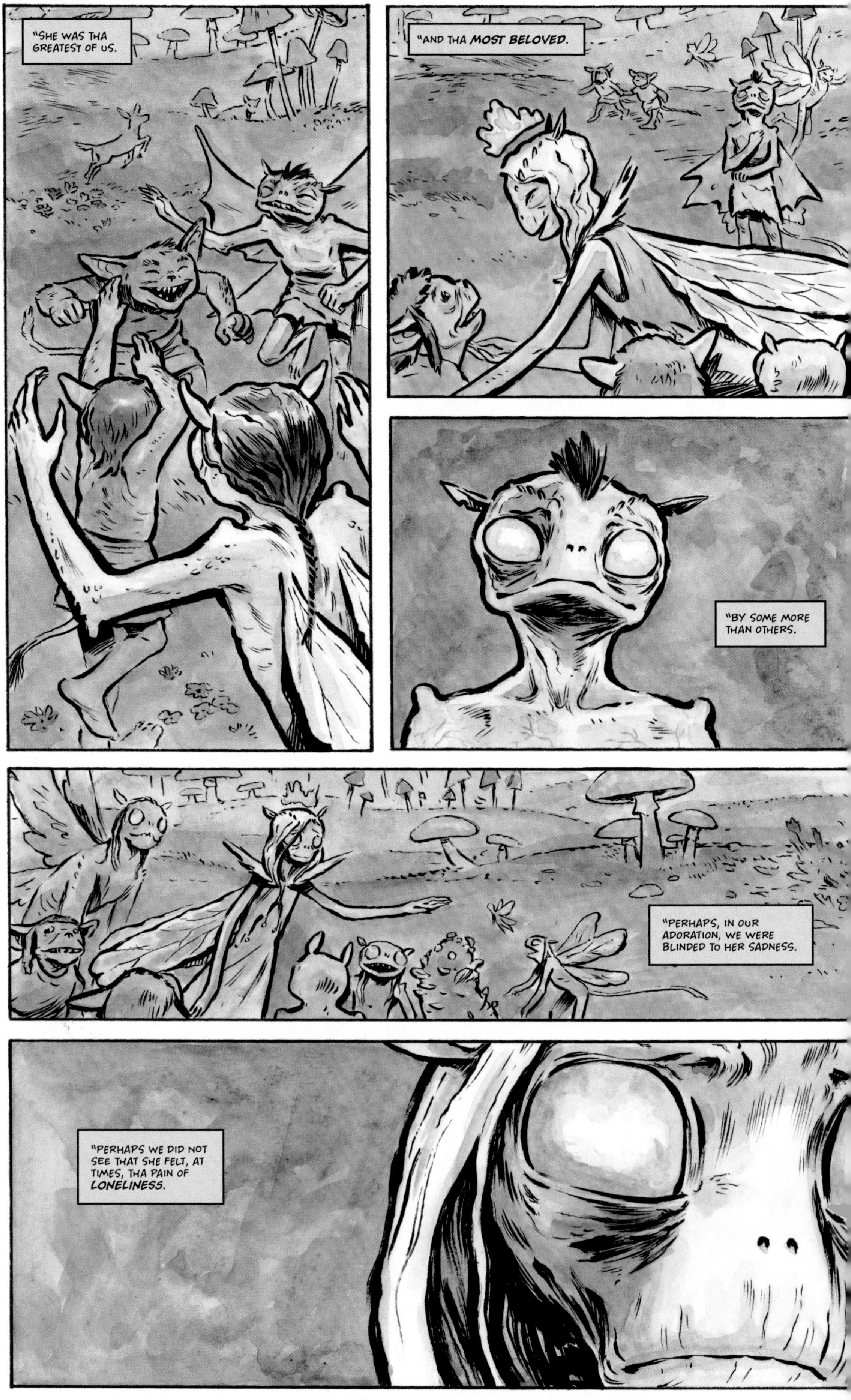
"SHE WAS THA GREATEST OF US.
"AND THA MOST BELOVED.
"BY SOME MORE THAN OTHERS.
"PERHAPS, IN OUR ADORATION, WE WERE BLINDED TO HER SADNESS.
"PERHAPS WE DID NOT SEE THAT SHE FELT, AT TIMES, THA PAIN OF LONELINESS.

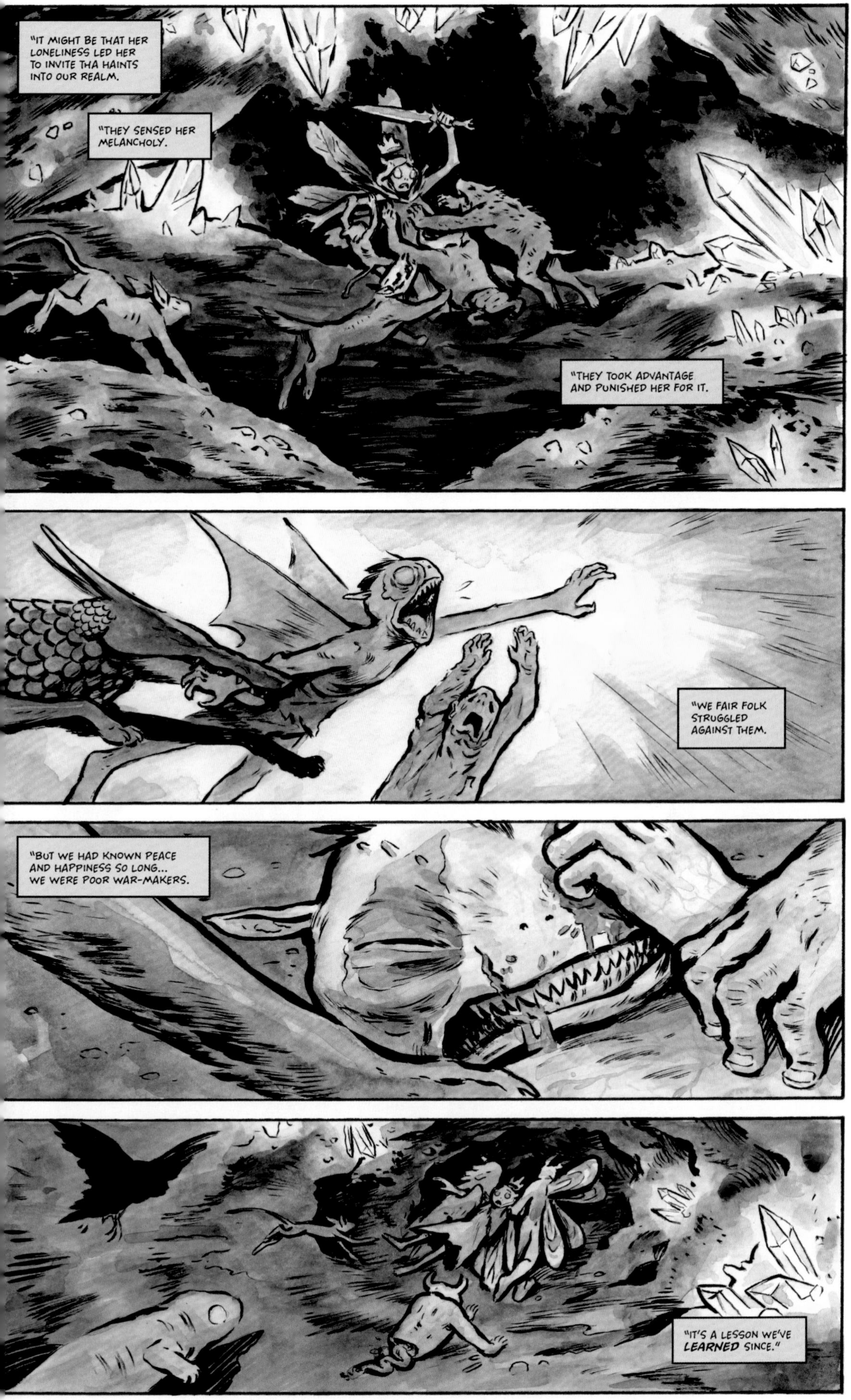
"IT MIGHT BE THAT HER LONELINESS LED HER TO INVITE THA HAINTS INTO OUR REALM.
"THEY SENSED HER MELANCHOLY.
"THEY TOOK ADVANTAGE AND PUNISHED HER FOR IT.
"WE FAIR FOLK STRUGGLED AGAINST THEM.
"BUT WE HAD KNOWN PEACE AND HAPPINESS SO LONG... WE WERE POOR WAR-MAKERS.
"IT'S A LESSON WE'VE *LEARNED* SINCE."

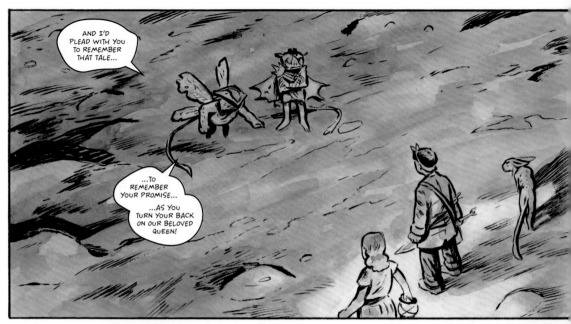

AND I'D PLEAD WITH YOU TO REMEMBER THAT TALE...

...TO REMEMBER YOUR PROMISE... ...AS YOU TURN YOUR BACK ON OUR BELOVED QUEEN!

I'VE FORGOTTEN NOTHING.

I LOOKED FOR YOUR QUEEN.

COULDN'T FIND HER.

BUT IF I CAN BREAK THE POWER THE HAINTS HOLD OVER YOU...

...I CAN FORCE THEM TO TELL US WHERE THEY'VE IMPRISONED YOUR QUEEN.

YOU WERE NO MATCH FOR THA HAINTS AND FAIR FOLK BEFORE!

YOU FOLDED TO THEIR WISHES!

WHAT MAKES YOU THINK YOU CAN STAND 'GAINST THEM NOW?

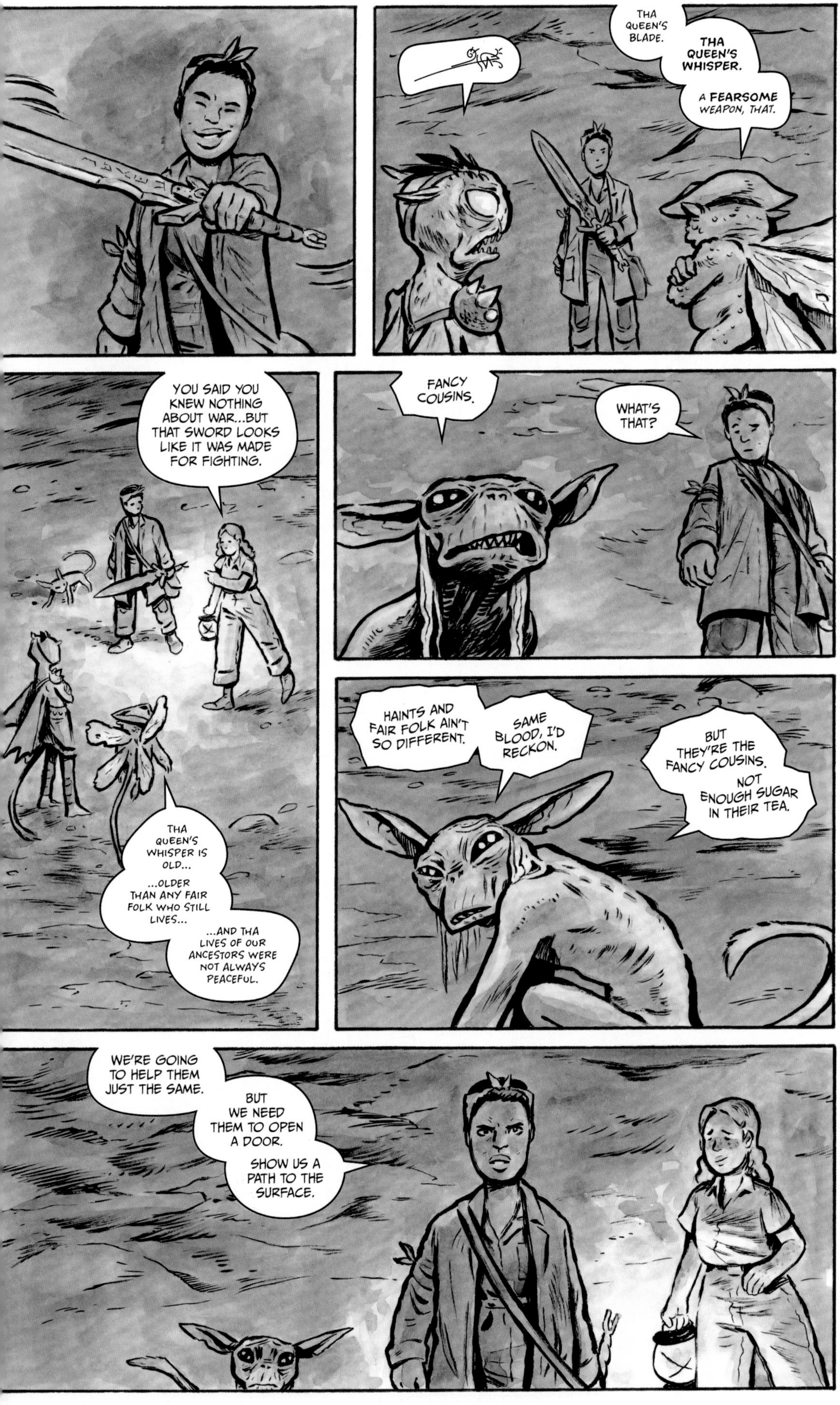

THA QUEEN'S BLADE.
THA QUEEN'S WHISPER.
A FEARSOME WEAPON, THAT.
YOU SAID YOU KNEW NOTHING ABOUT WAR...BUT THAT SWORD LOOKS LIKE IT WAS MADE FOR FIGHTING.
THA QUEEN'S WHISPER IS OLD...
...OLDER THAN ANY FAIR FOLK WHO STILL LIVES...
...AND THA LIVES OF OUR ANCESTORS WERE NOT ALWAYS PEACEFUL.
FANCY COUSINS.
WHAT'S THAT?
HAINTS AND FAIR FOLK AIN'T SO DIFFERENT.
SAME BLOOD, I'D RECKON.
BUT THEY'RE THE FANCY COUSINS.
NOT ENOUGH SUGAR IN THEIR TEA.
WE'RE GOING TO HELP THEM JUST THE SAME.
BUT WE NEED THEM TO OPEN A DOOR.
SHOW US A PATH TO THE SURFACE.

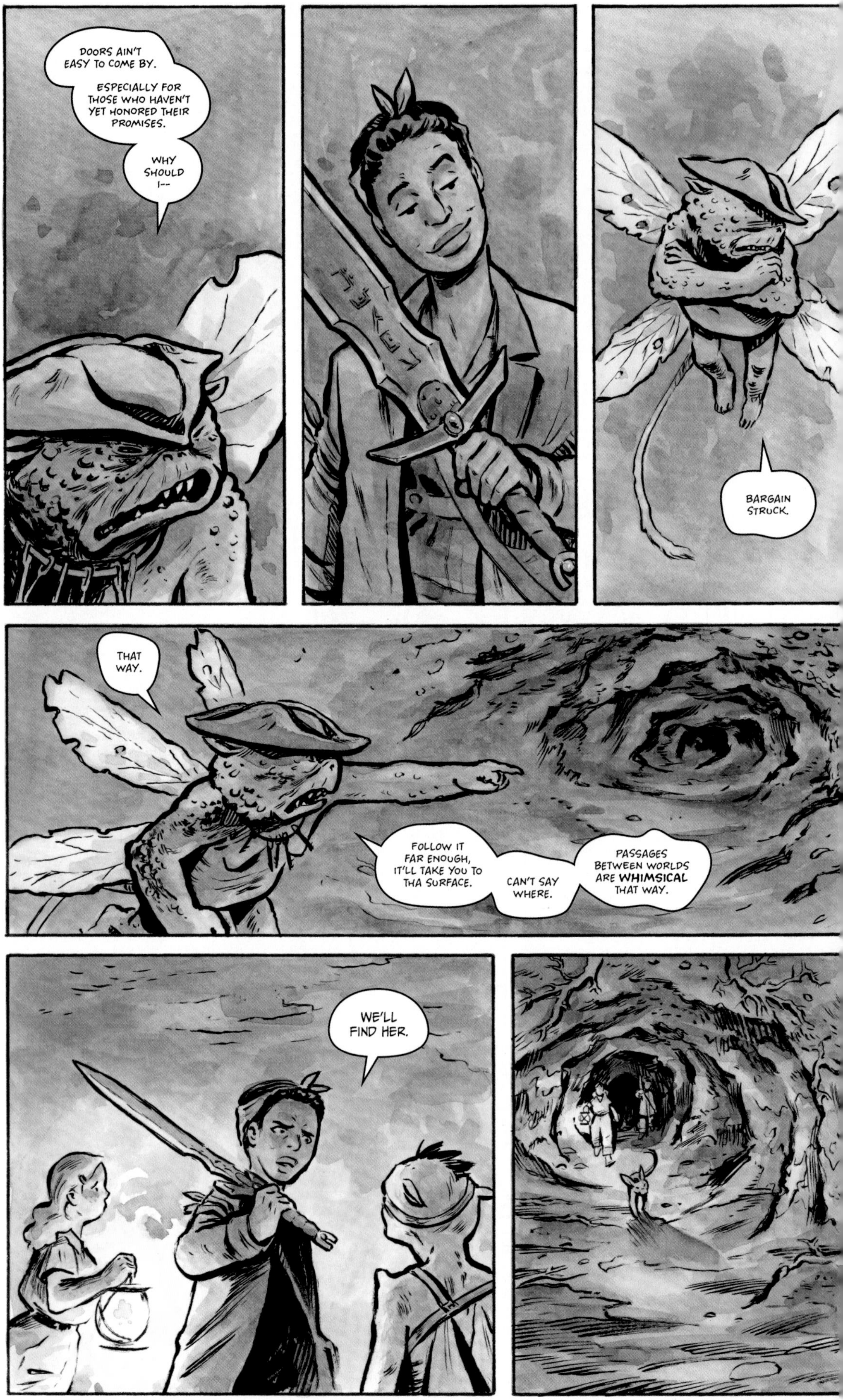
DOORS AIN'T EASY TO COME BY.
ESPECIALLY FOR THOSE WHO HAVEN'T YET HONORED THEIR PROMISES.
WHY SHOULD I--
BARGAIN STRUCK.
THAT WAY.
FOLLOW IT FAR ENOUGH, IT'LL TAKE YOU TO THA SURFACE.
CAN'T SAY WHERE.
PASSAGES BETWEEN WORLDS ARE **WHIMSICAL** THAT WAY.
WE'LL FIND HER.

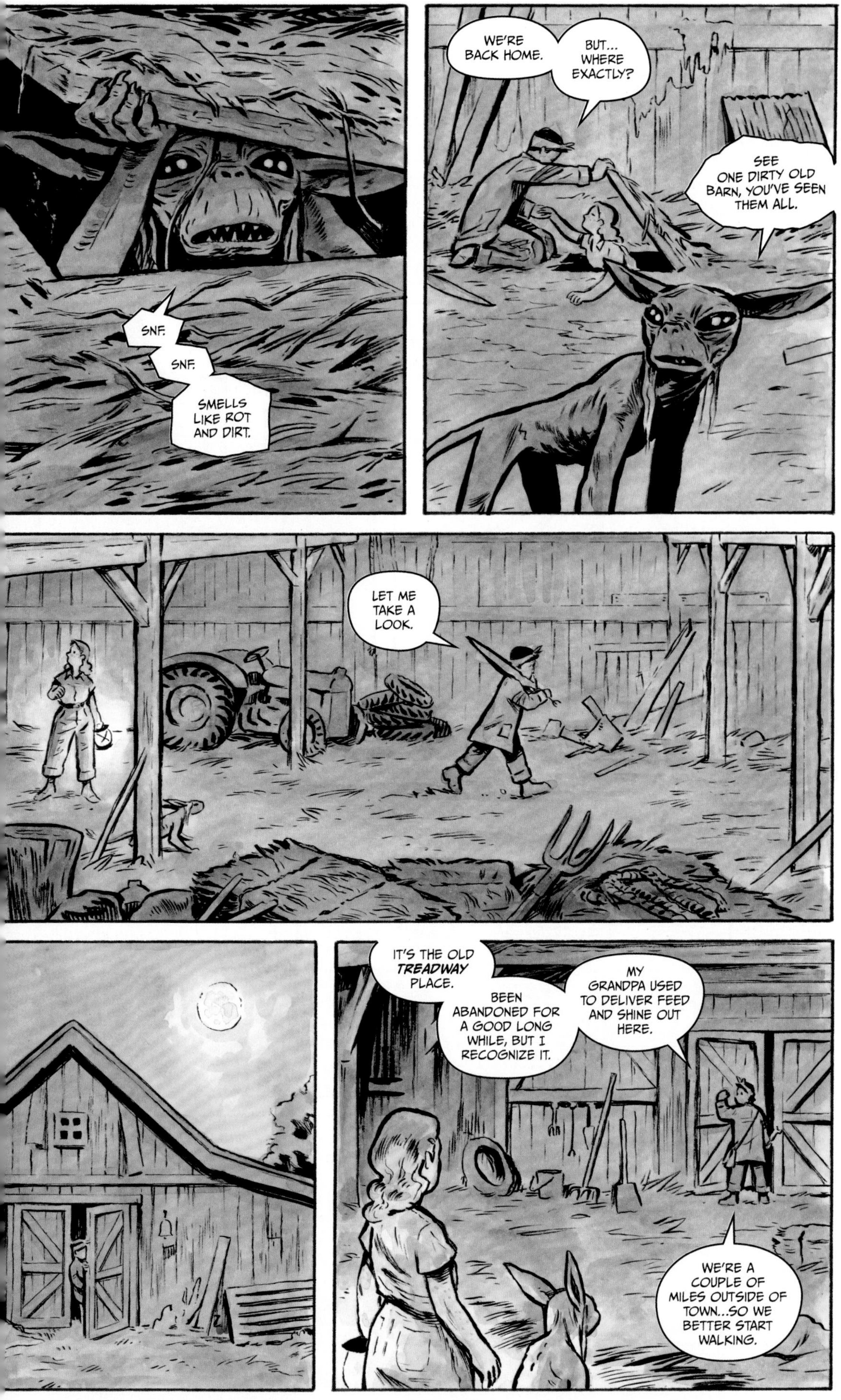

SNF.
SNF.
SMELLS LIKE ROT AND DIRT.
WE'RE BACK HOME.
BUT... WHERE EXACTLY?
SEE ONE DIRTY OLD BARN, YOU'VE SEEN THEM ALL.
LET ME TAKE A LOOK.
IT'S THE OLD *TREADWAY* PLACE.
BEEN ABANDONED FOR A GOOD LONG WHILE, BUT I RECOGNIZE IT.
MY GRANDPA USED TO DELIVER FEED AND SHINE OUT HERE.
WE'RE A COUPLE OF MILES OUTSIDE OF TOWN...SO WE BETTER START WALKING.

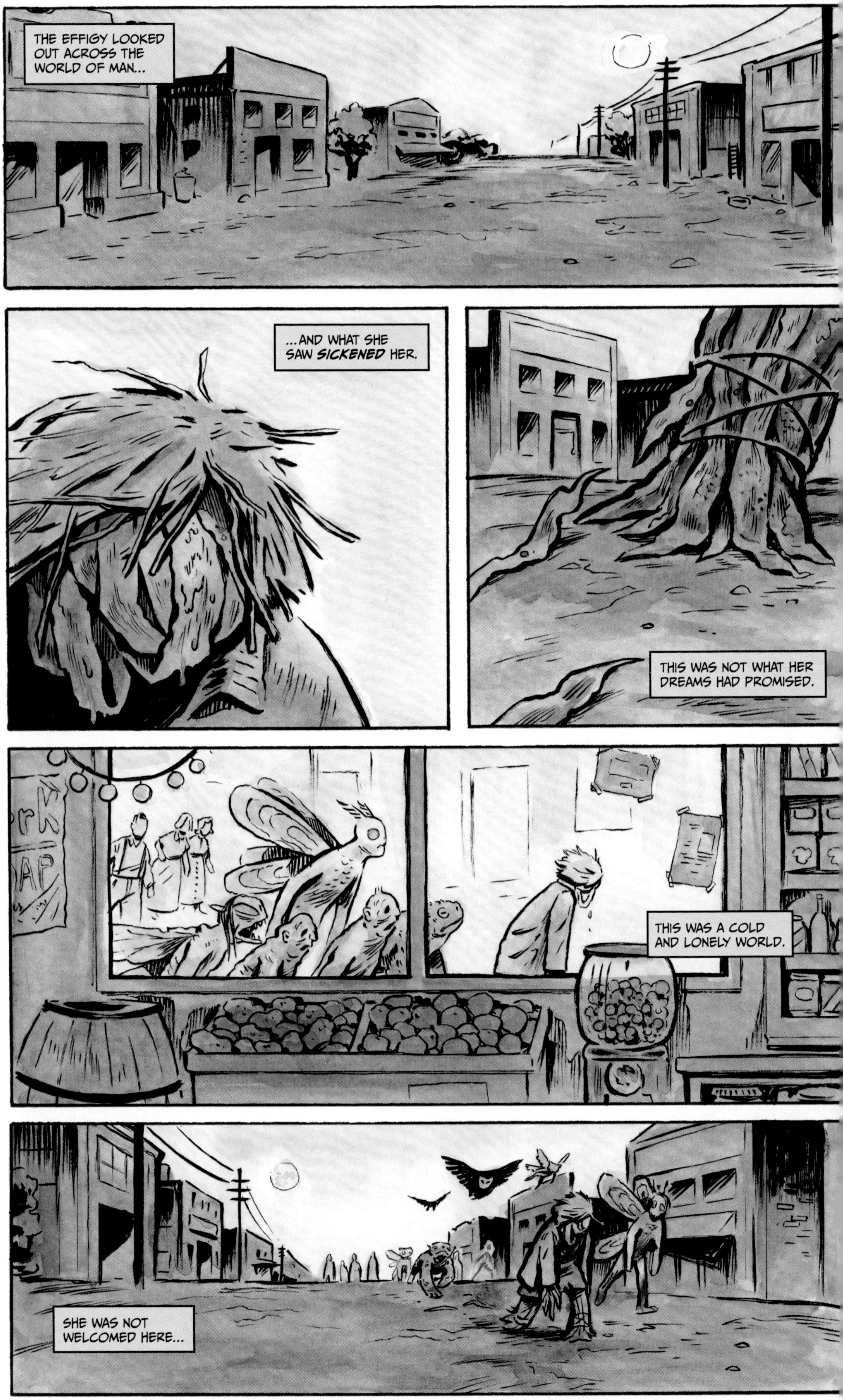
THE EFFIGY LOOKED OUT ACROSS THE WORLD OF MAN...
...AND WHAT SHE SAW *SICKENED* HER.
THIS WAS NOT WHAT HER DREAMS HAD PROMISED.
THIS WAS A COLD AND LONELY WORLD.
SHE WAS NOT WELCOMED HERE...

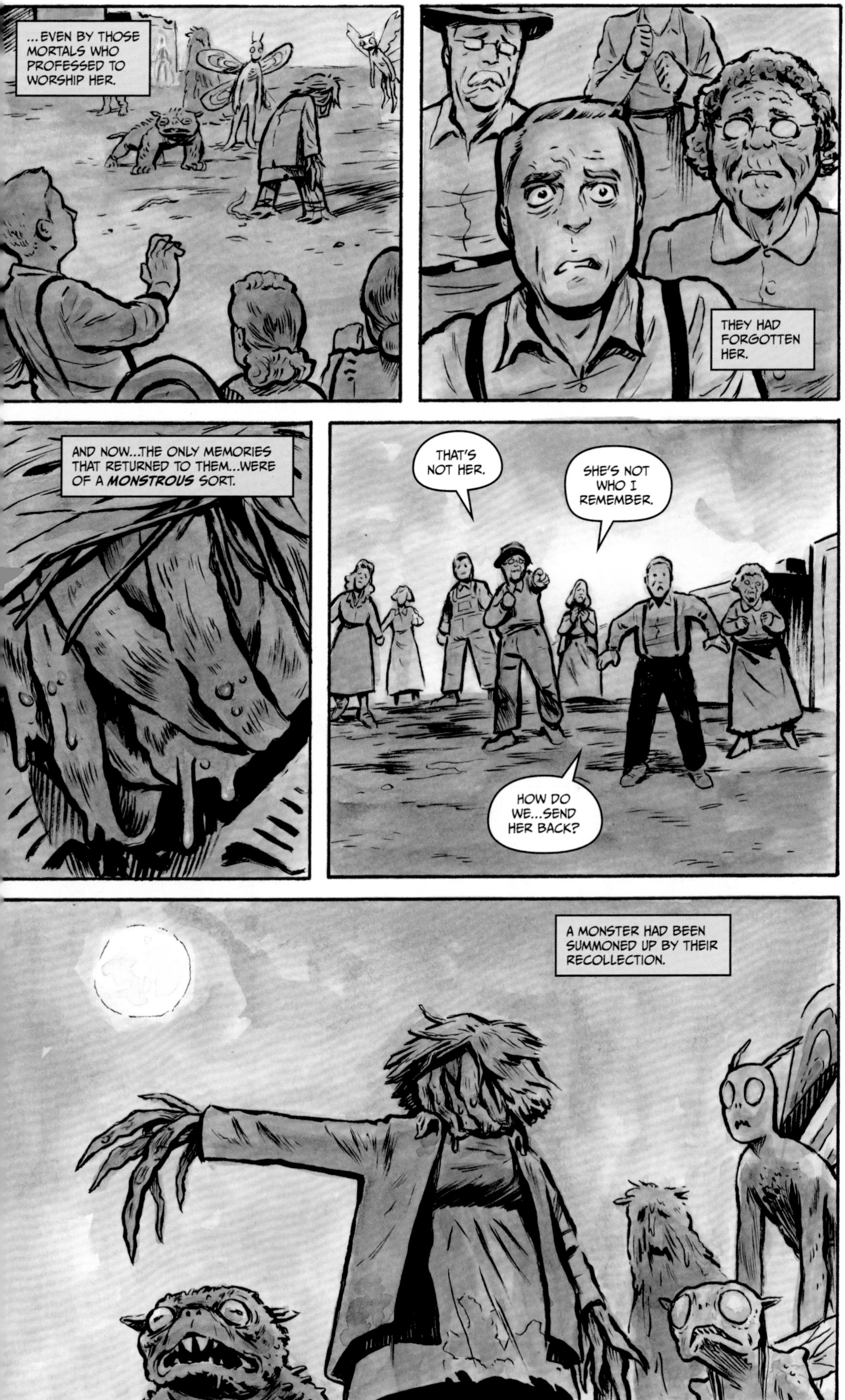
...EVEN BY THOSE MORTALS WHO PROFESSED TO WORSHIP HER.
THEY HAD FORGOTTEN HER.
AND NOW...THE ONLY MEMORIES THAT RETURNED TO THEM...WERE OF A MONSTROUS SORT.
THAT'S NOT HER.
SHE'S NOT WHO I REMEMBER.
HOW DO WE...SEND HER BACK?
A MONSTER HAD BEEN SUMMONED UP BY THEIR RECOLLECTION.

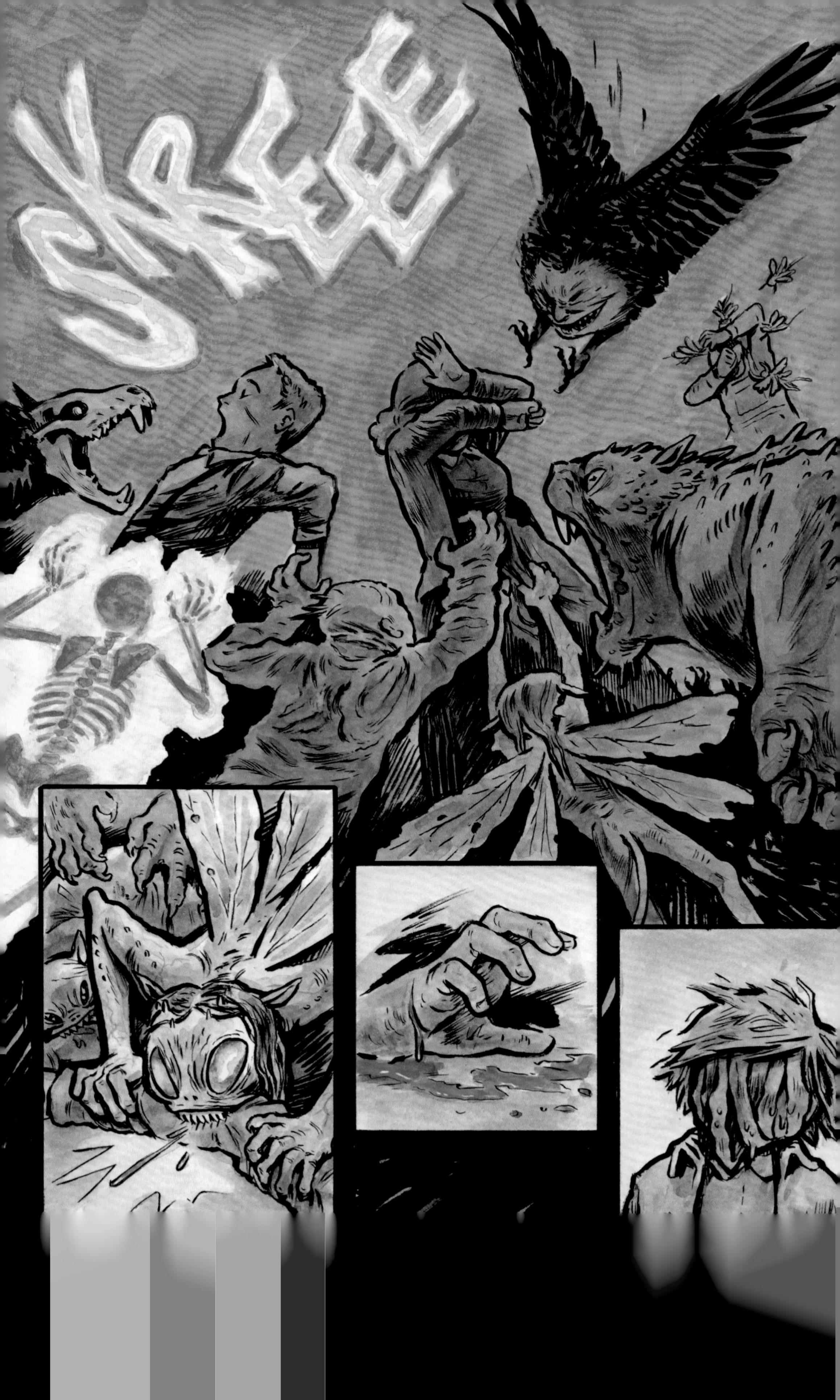
SKREE

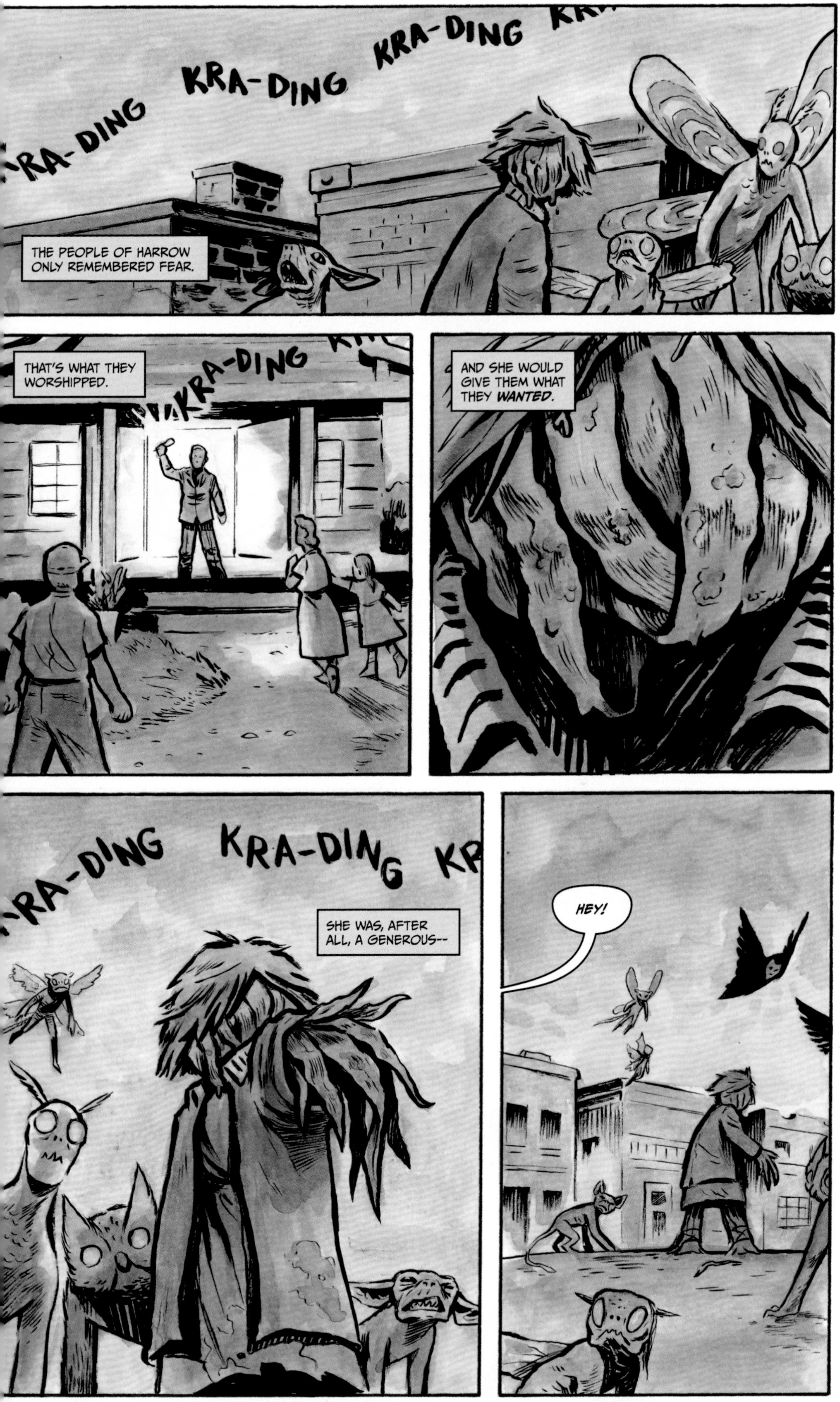

-RA-DING
KRA-DING
KRA-DING
KR
THE PEOPLE OF HARROW ONLY REMEMBERED FEAR.
THAT'S WHAT THEY WORSHIPPED.
KRA-DING
KR
AND SHE WOULD GIVE THEM WHAT THEY *WANTED.*
-RA-DING
KRA-DING
KR
SHE WAS, AFTER ALL, A GENEROUS--
HEY!

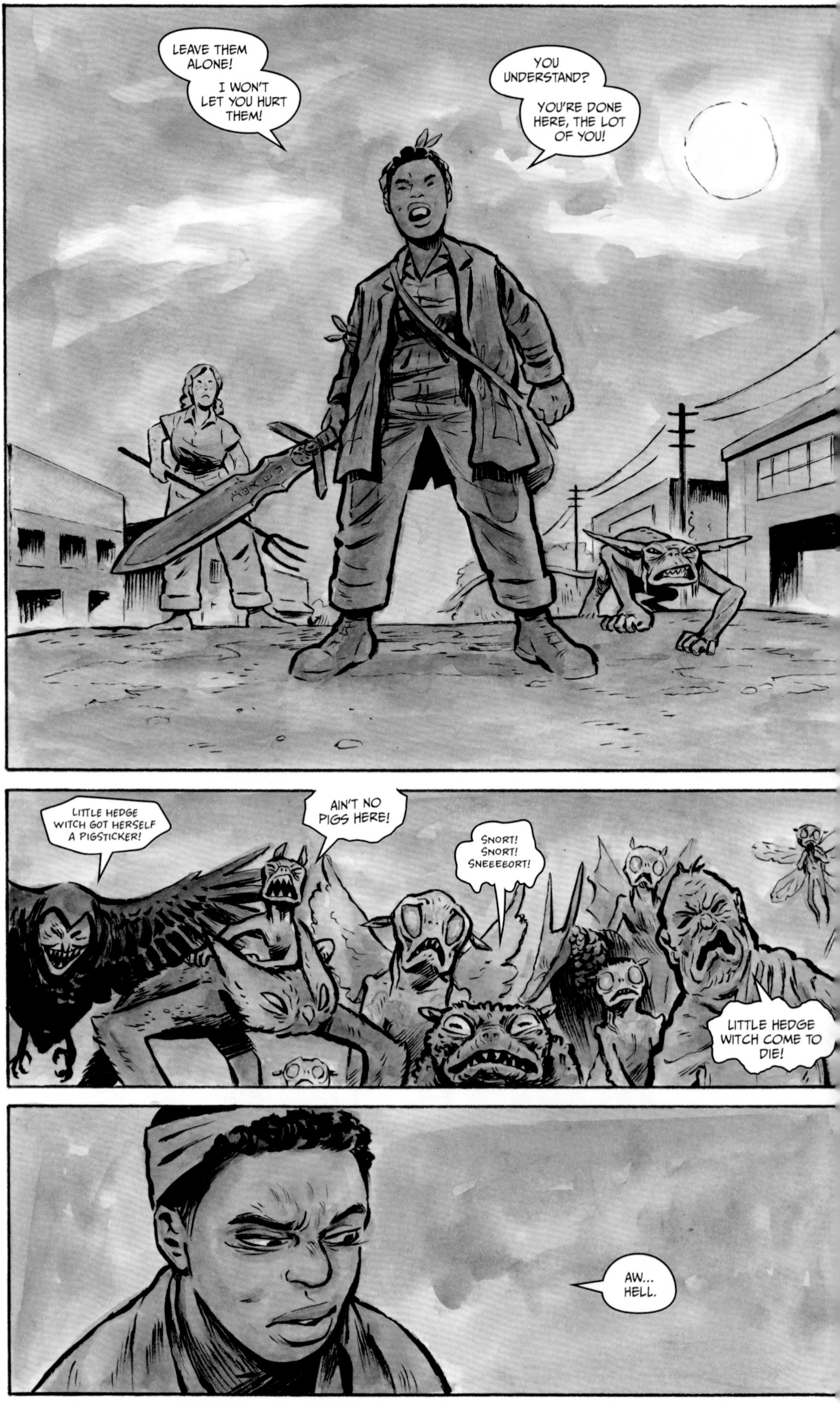
LEAVE THEM ALONE!
I WON'T LET YOU HURT THEM!
YOU UNDERSTAND?
YOU'RE DONE HERE, THE LOT OF YOU!
LITTLE HEDGE WITCH GOT HERSELF A PIGSTICKER!
AIN'T NO PIGS HERE!
SNORT! SNORT! SNEEEEORT!
LITTLE HEDGE WITCH COME TO DIE!
AW... HELL.

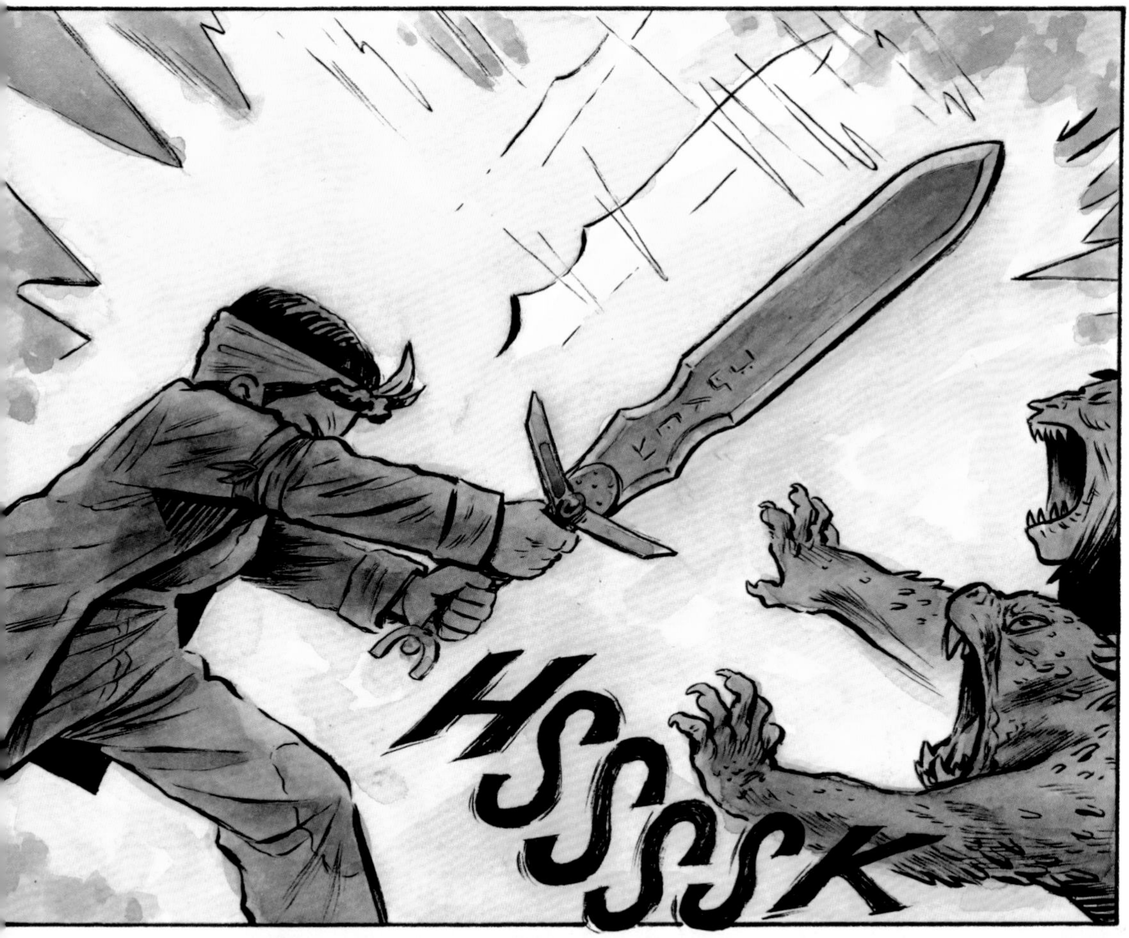
HSSSSK

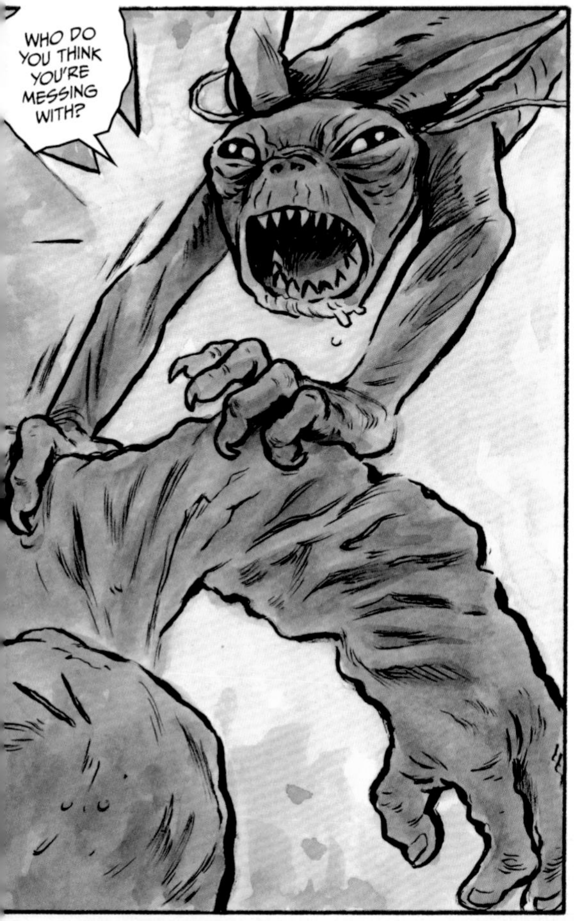
WHO DO YOU THINK YOU'RE MESSING WITH?

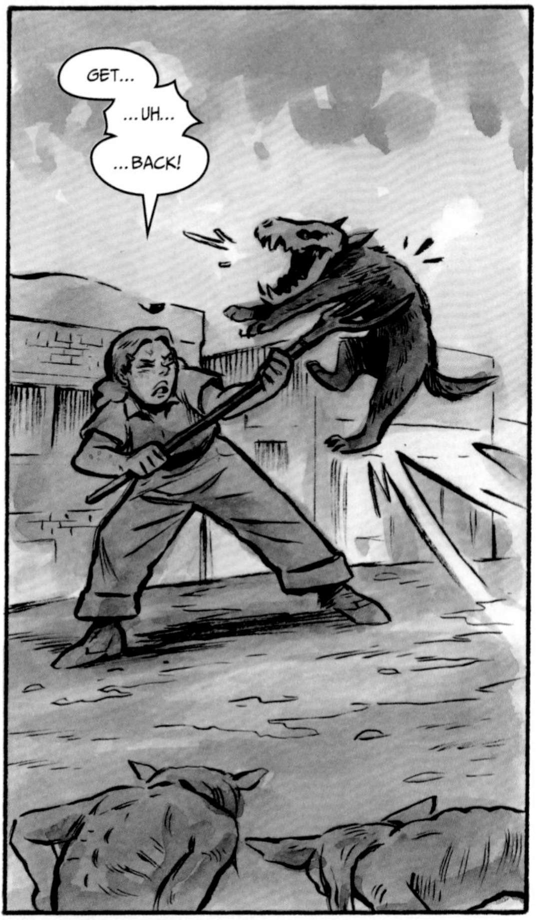
GET...
...UH...
...BACK!

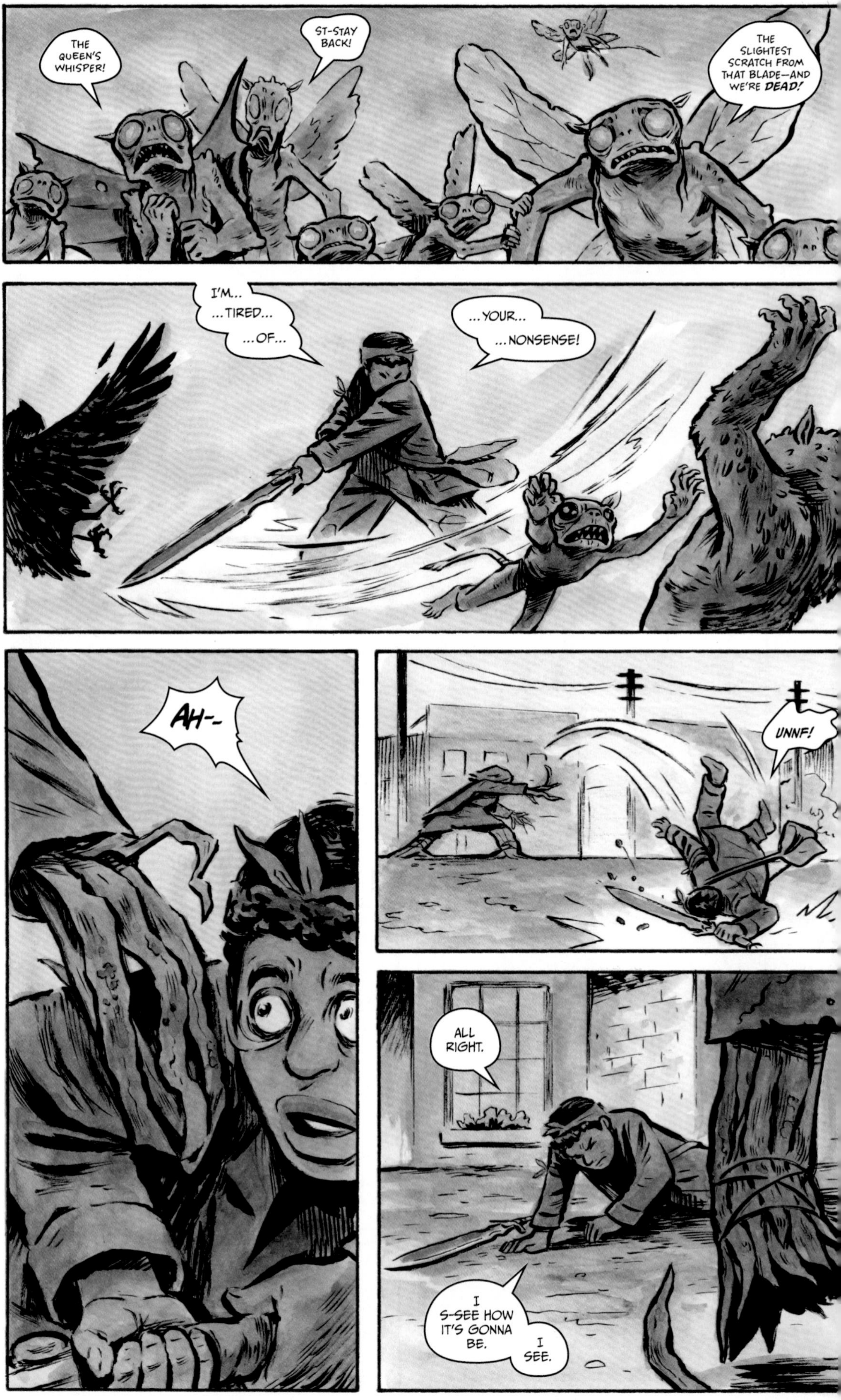
THE QUEEN'S WHISPER!
ST-STAY BACK!
THE SLIGHTEST SCRATCH FROM THAT BLADE—AND WE'RE DEAD!
I'M... ...TIRED... ...OF...
...YOUR... ...NONSENSE!
AH-
UNNF!
ALL RIGHT.
I S-SEE HOW IT'S GONNA BE.
I SEE.

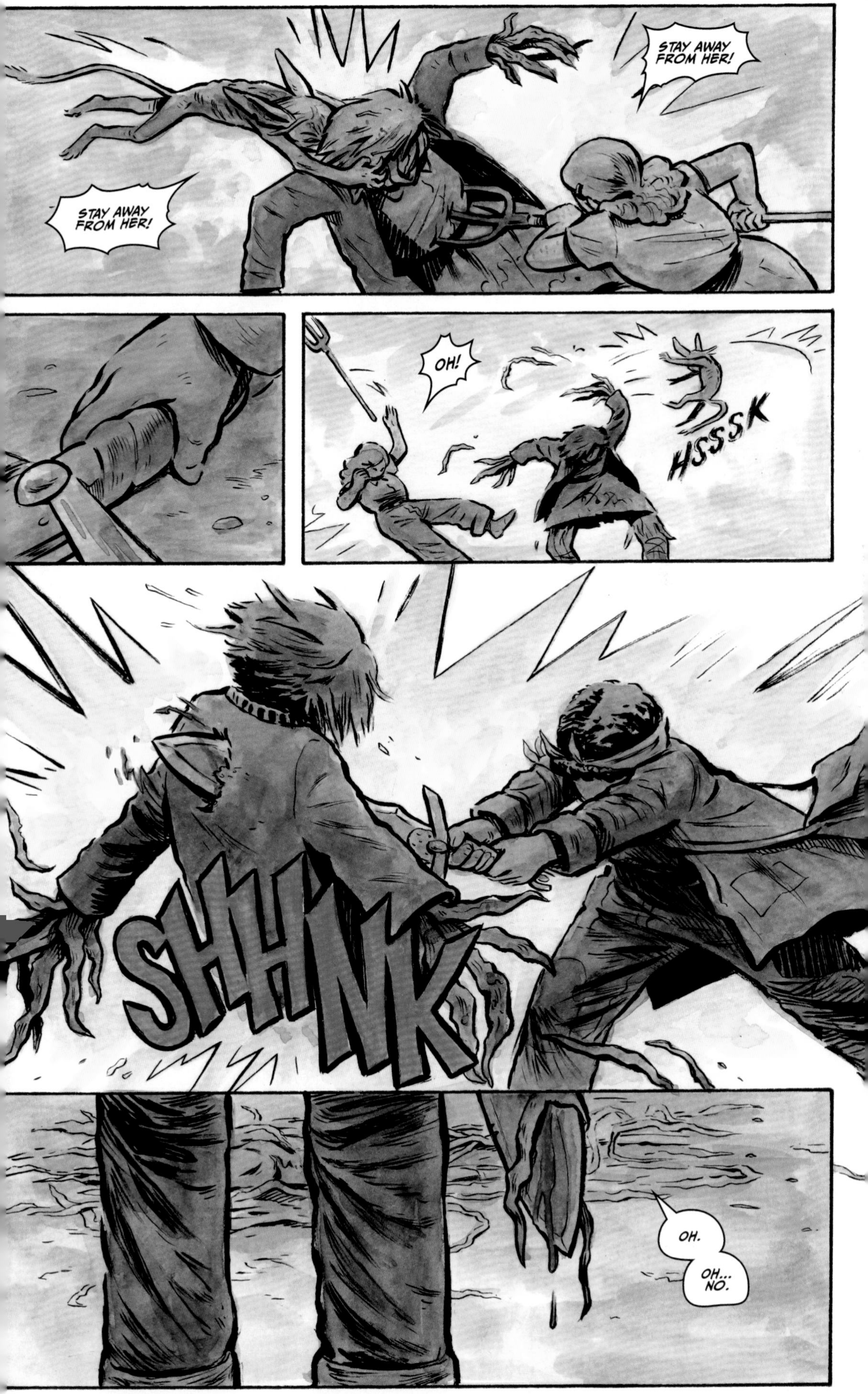
STAY AWAY FROM HER!
STAY AWAY FROM HER!
OH!
HSSSK
SHHNK
OH.
OH... NO.

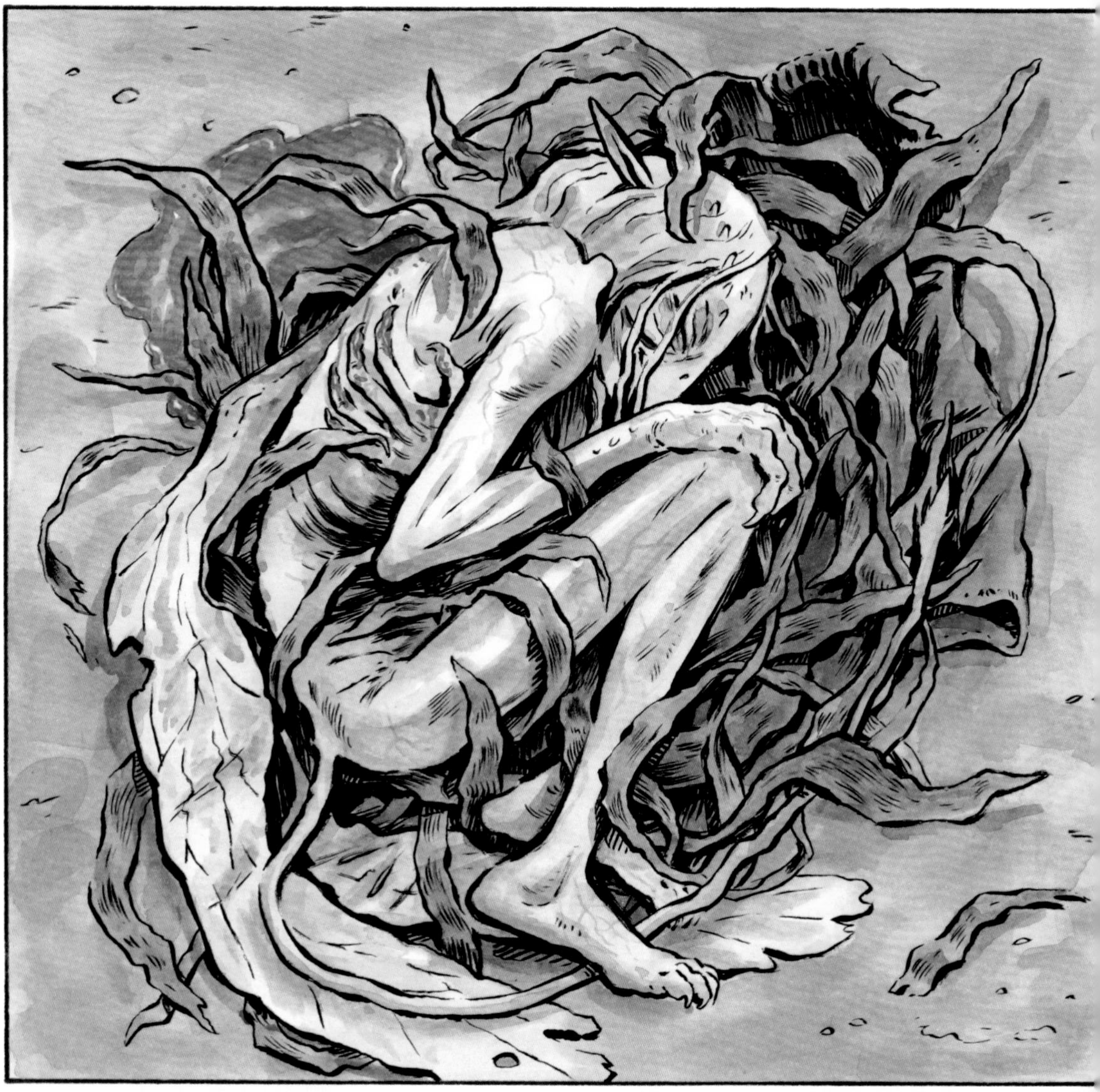

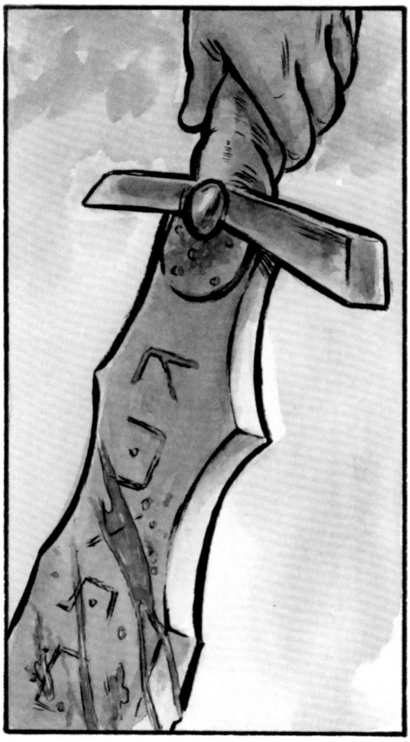

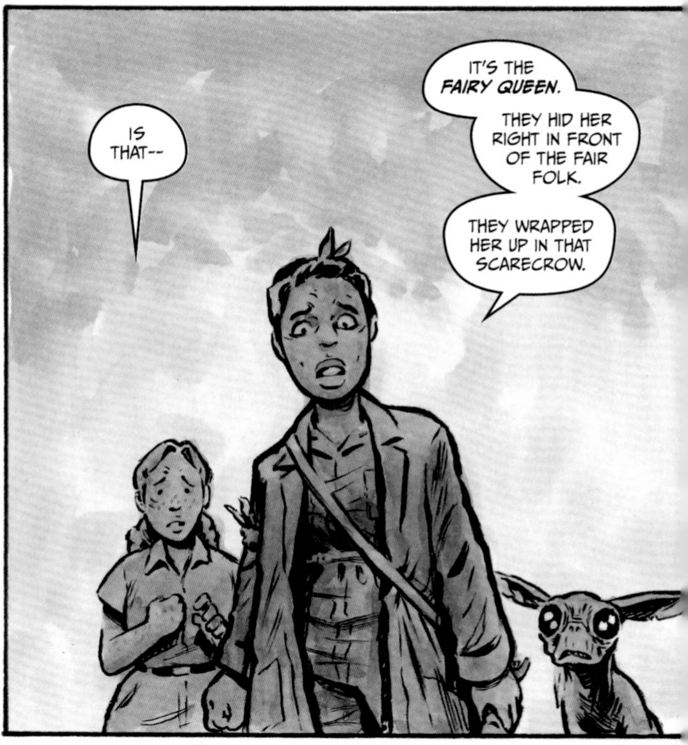
IS THAT--
IT'S THE *FAIRY QUEEN.*
THEY HID HER RIGHT IN FRONT OF THE FAIR FOLK.
THEY WRAPPED HER UP IN THAT SCARECROW.

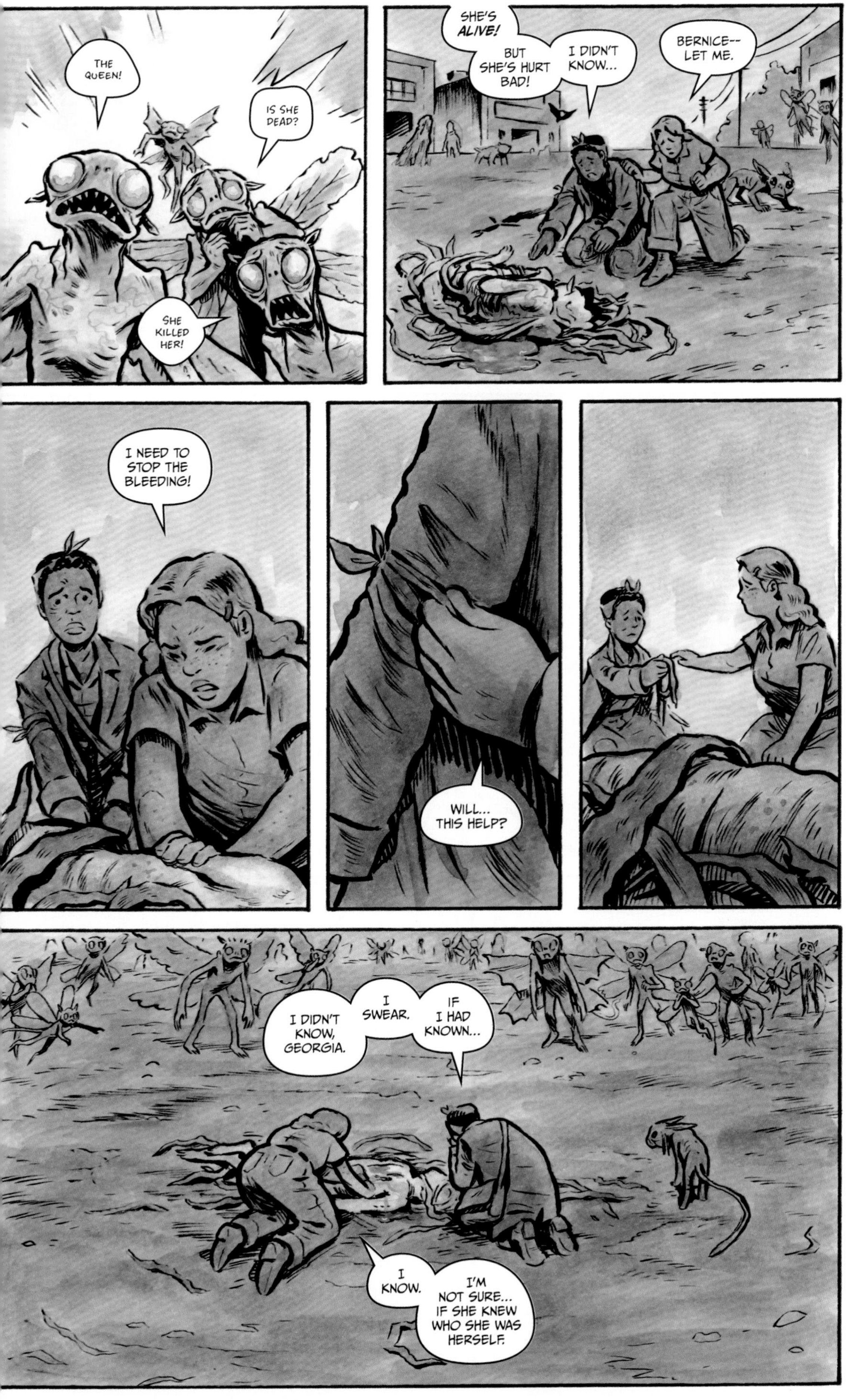
THE QUEEN!
IS SHE DEAD?
SHE KILLED HER!
SHE'S *ALIVE!*
BUT SHE'S HURT BAD!
I DIDN'T KNOW...
BERNICE-- LET ME.
I NEED TO STOP THE BLEEDING!
WILL... THIS HELP?
I DIDN'T KNOW, GEORGIA.
I SWEAR.
IF I HAD KNOWN...
I KNOW.
I'M NOT SURE... IF SHE KNEW WHO SHE WAS HERSELF.

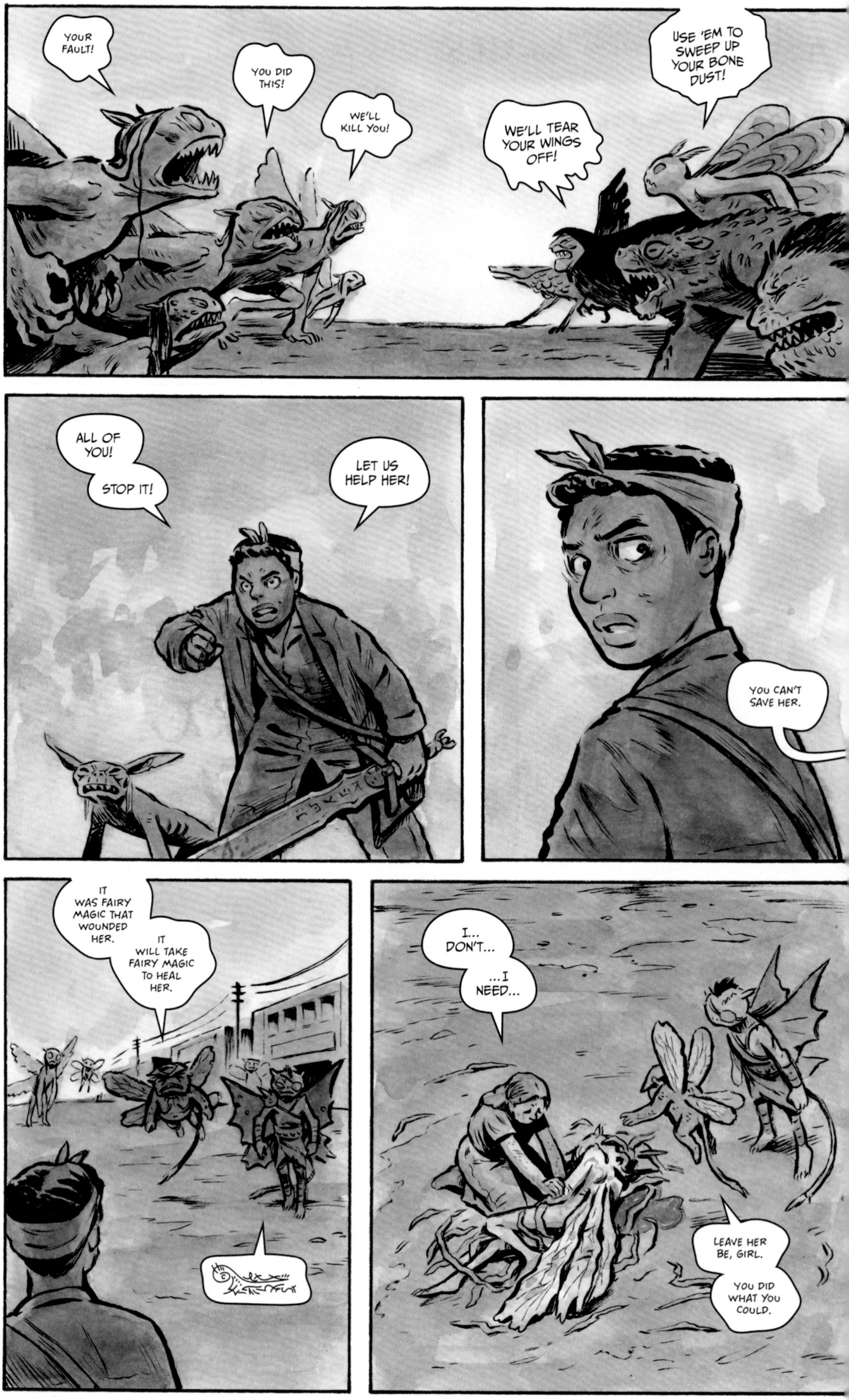
YOUR FAULT!
YOU DID THIS!
WE'LL KILL YOU!
WE'LL TEAR YOUR WINGS OFF!
USE 'EM TO SWEEP UP YOUR BONE DUST!
ALL OF YOU!
STOP IT!
LET US HELP HER!
YOU CAN'T SAVE HER.
IT WAS FAIRY MAGIC THAT WOUNDED HER.
IT WILL TAKE FAIRY MAGIC TO HEAL HER.
I... DON'T...
...I NEED...
LEAVE HER BE, GIRL.
YOU DID WHAT YOU COULD.

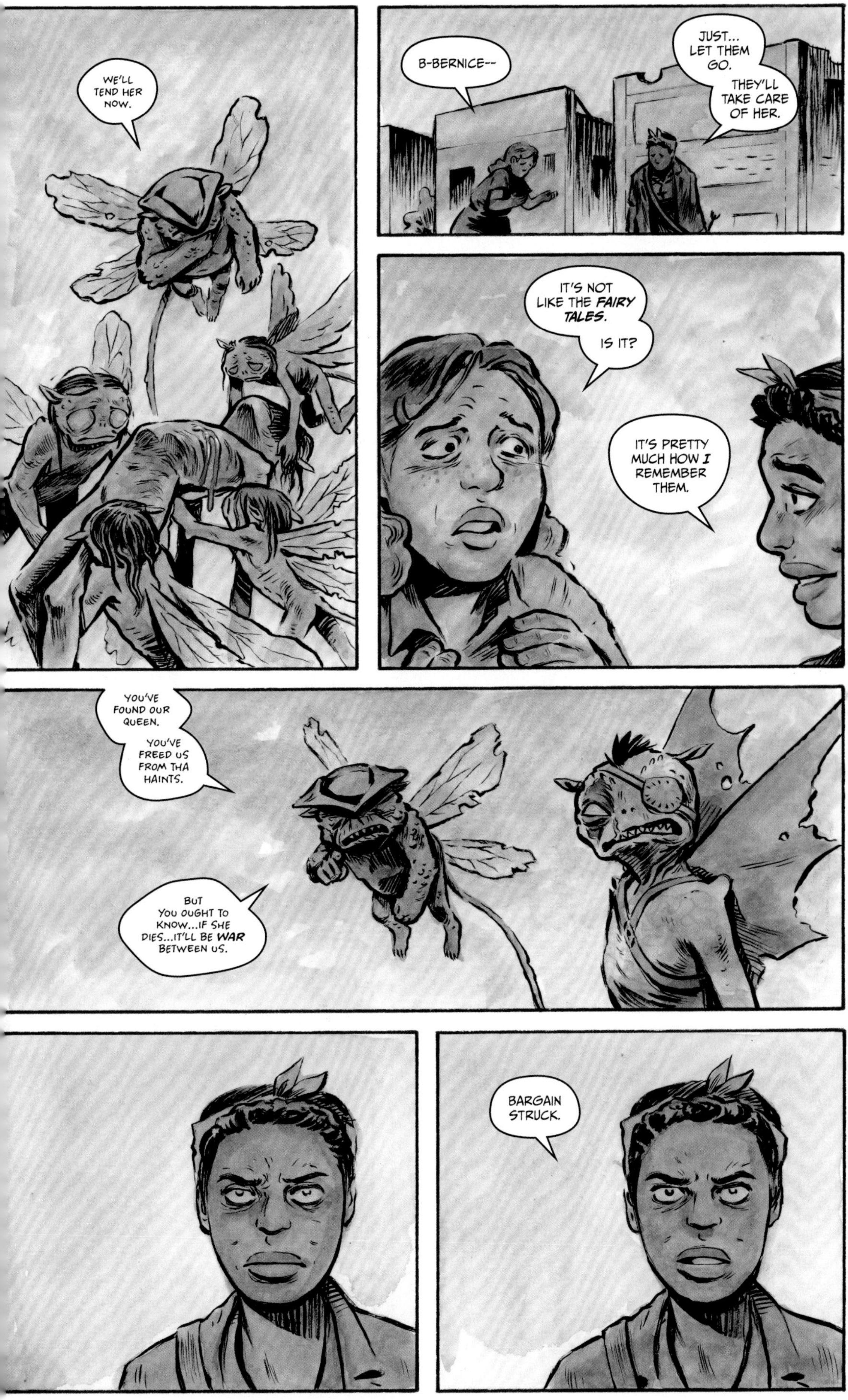

WE'LL TEND HER NOW.
B-BERNICE--
JUST... LET THEM GO.
THEY'LL TAKE CARE OF HER.
IT'S NOT LIKE THE *FAIRY TALES.*
IS IT?
IT'S PRETTY MUCH HOW *I* REMEMBER THEM.
YOU'VE FOUND OUR QUEEN.
YOU'VE FREED US FROM THA HAINTS.
BUT YOU OUGHT TO KNOW...IF SHE DIES...IT'LL BE *WAR* BETWEEN US.
BARGAIN STRUCK.

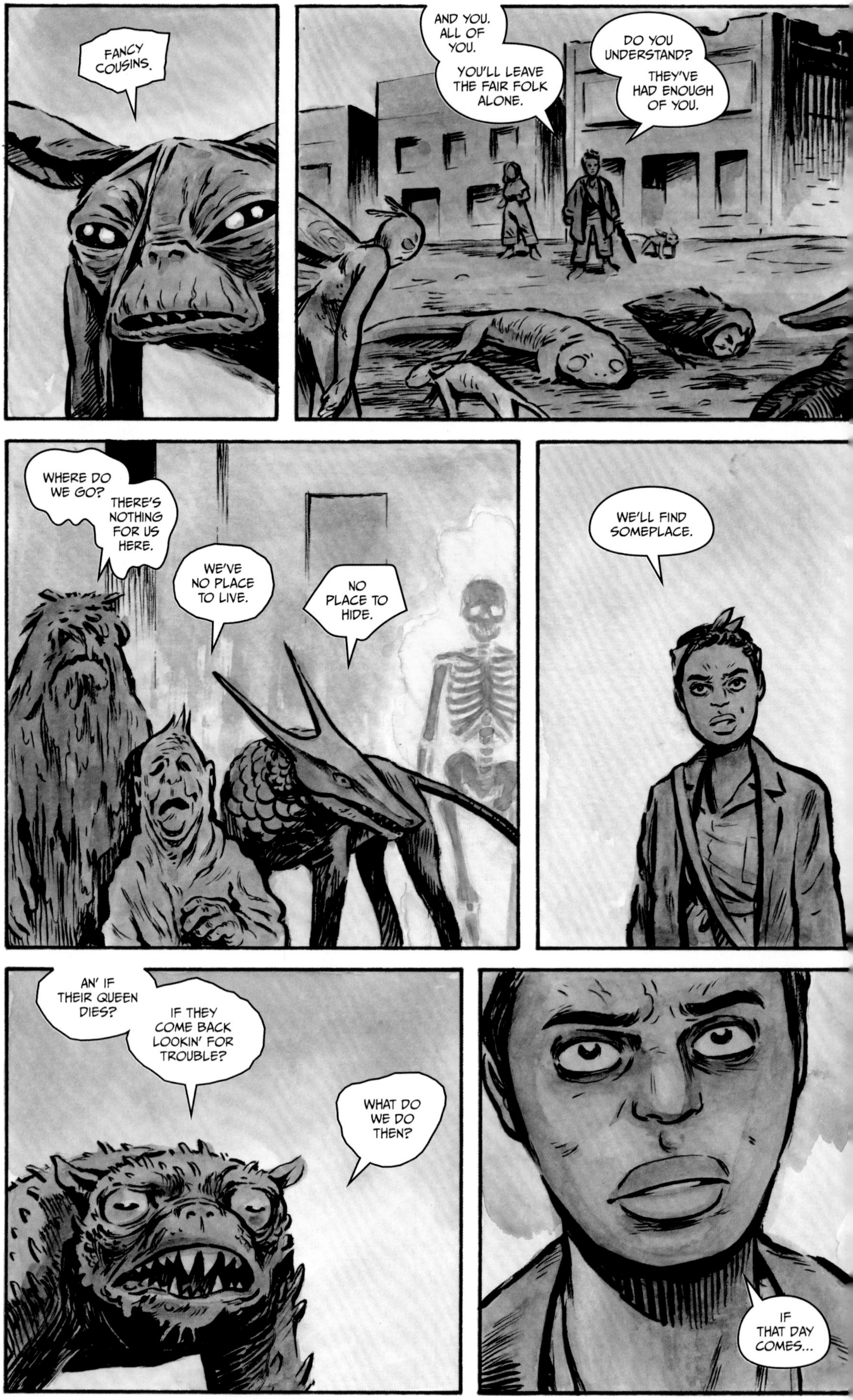
FANCY COUSINS.
AND YOU. ALL OF YOU.
YOU'LL LEAVE THE FAIR FOLK ALONE.
DO YOU UNDERSTAND?
THEY'VE HAD ENOUGH OF YOU.
WHERE DO WE GO?
THERE'S NOTHING FOR US HERE.
WE'VE NO PLACE TO LIVE.
NO PLACE TO HIDE.
WE'LL FIND SOMEPLACE.
AN' IF THEIR QUEEN DIES?
IF THEY COME BACK LOOKIN' FOR TROUBLE?
WHAT DO WE DO THEN?
IF THAT DAY COMES...

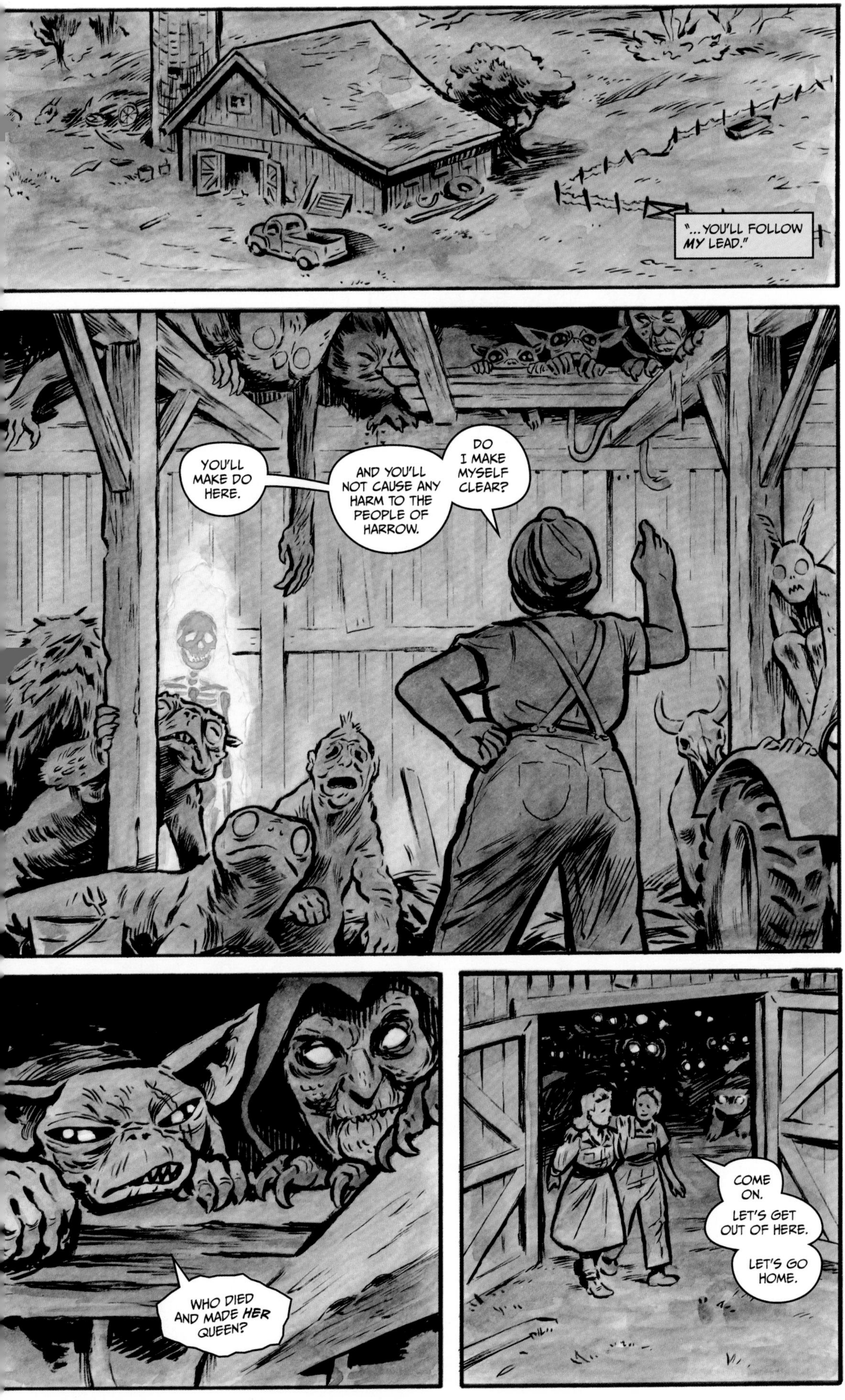
"...YOU'LL FOLLOW MY LEAD."
YOU'LL MAKE DO HERE.
AND YOU'LL NOT CAUSE ANY HARM TO THE PEOPLE OF HARROW.
DO I MAKE MYSELF CLEAR?
WHO DIED AND MADE HER QUEEN?
COME ON.
LET'S GET OUT OF HERE.
LET'S GO HOME.

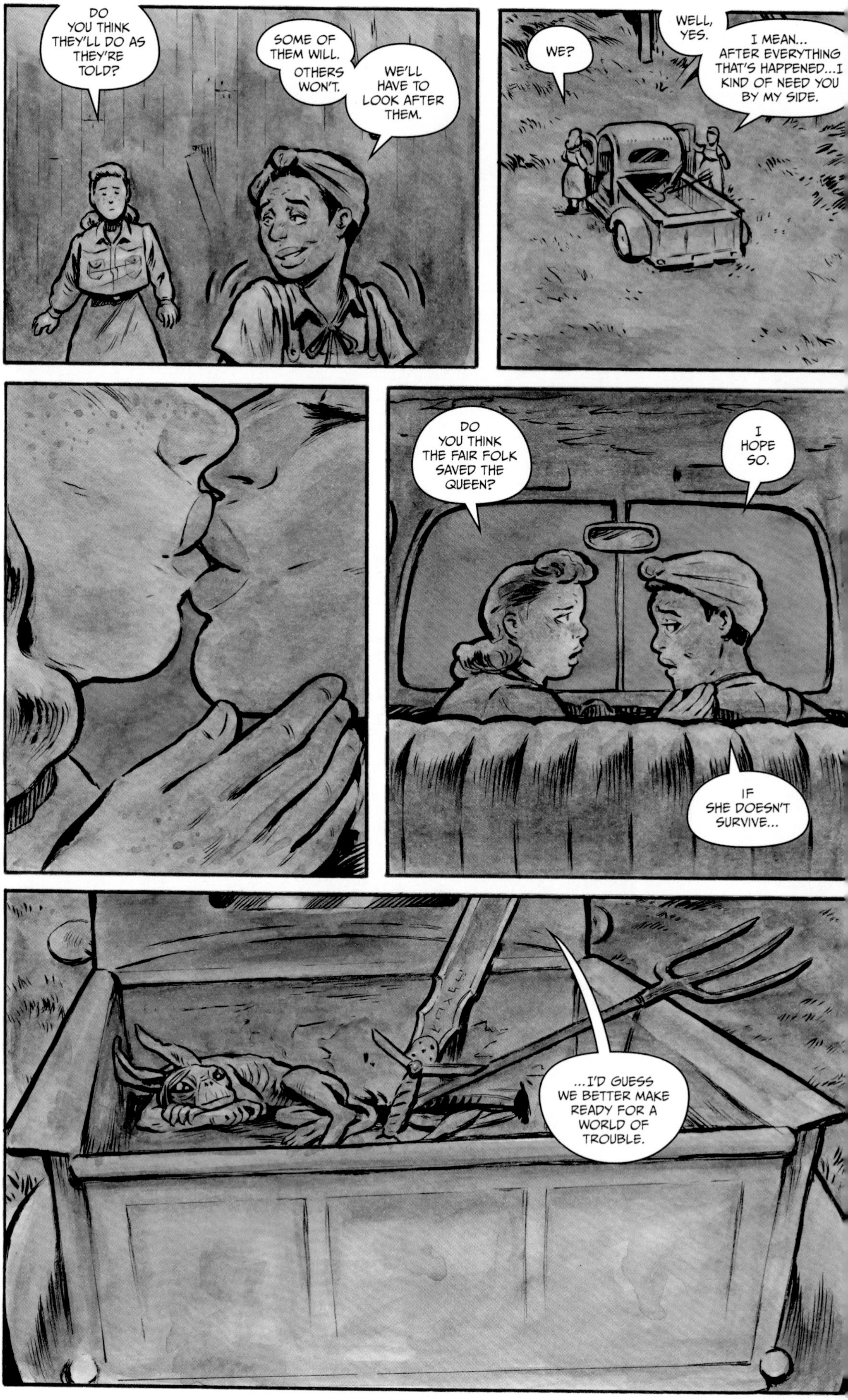
DO YOU THINK THEY'LL DO AS THEY'RE TOLD?
SOME OF THEM WILL.
OTHERS WON'T.
WE'LL HAVE TO LOOK AFTER THEM.
WE?
WELL, YES.
I MEAN... AFTER EVERYTHING THAT'S HAPPENED...I KIND OF NEED YOU BY MY SIDE.
DO YOU THINK THE FAIR FOLK SAVED THE QUEEN?
I HOPE SO.
IF SHE DOESN'T SURVIVE...
...I'D GUESS WE BETTER MAKE READY FOR A WORLD OF TROUBLE.

TALES FROM HARROW COUNTY™ SKETCHBOOK

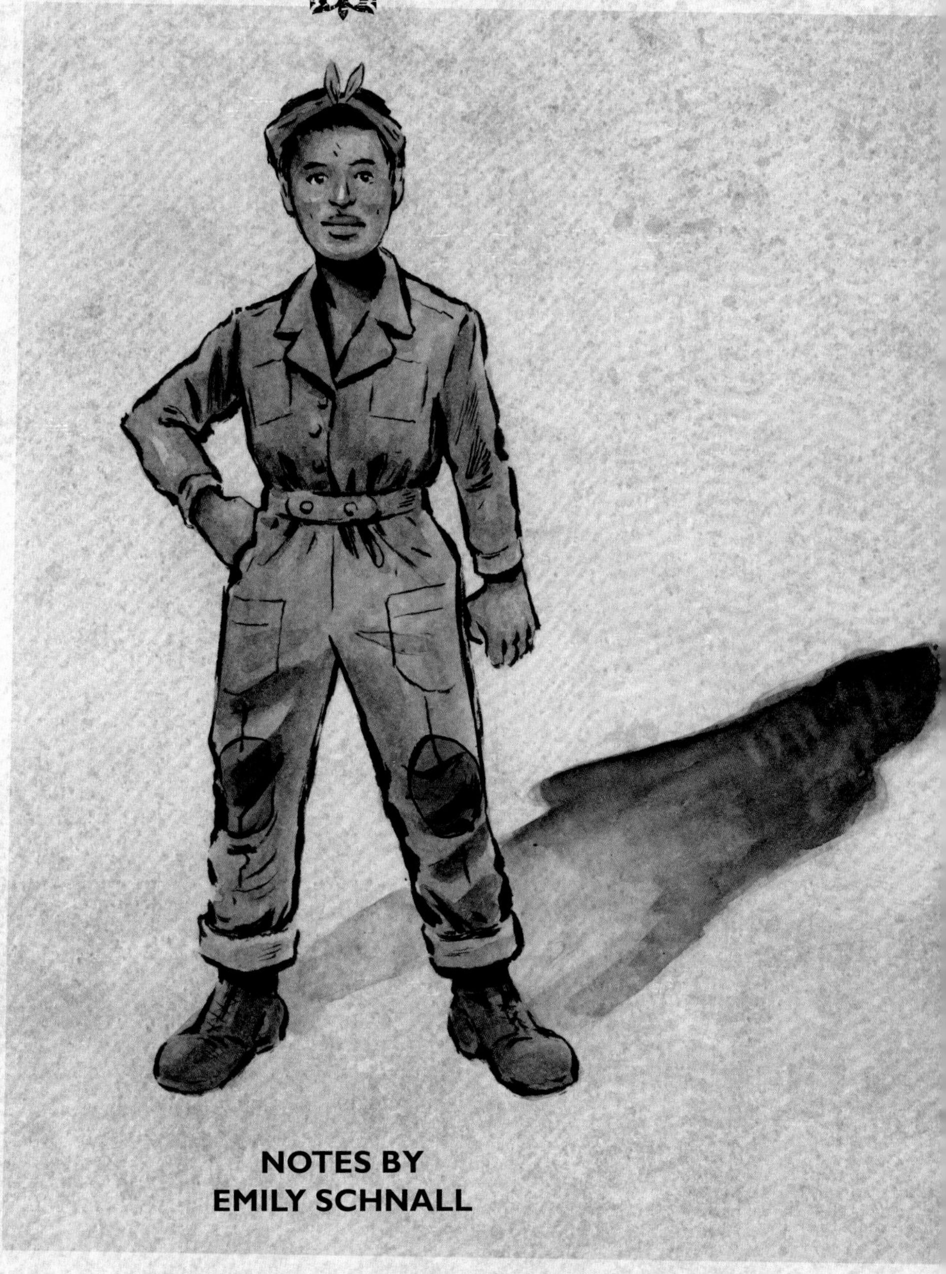

NOTES BY
EMILY SCHNALL

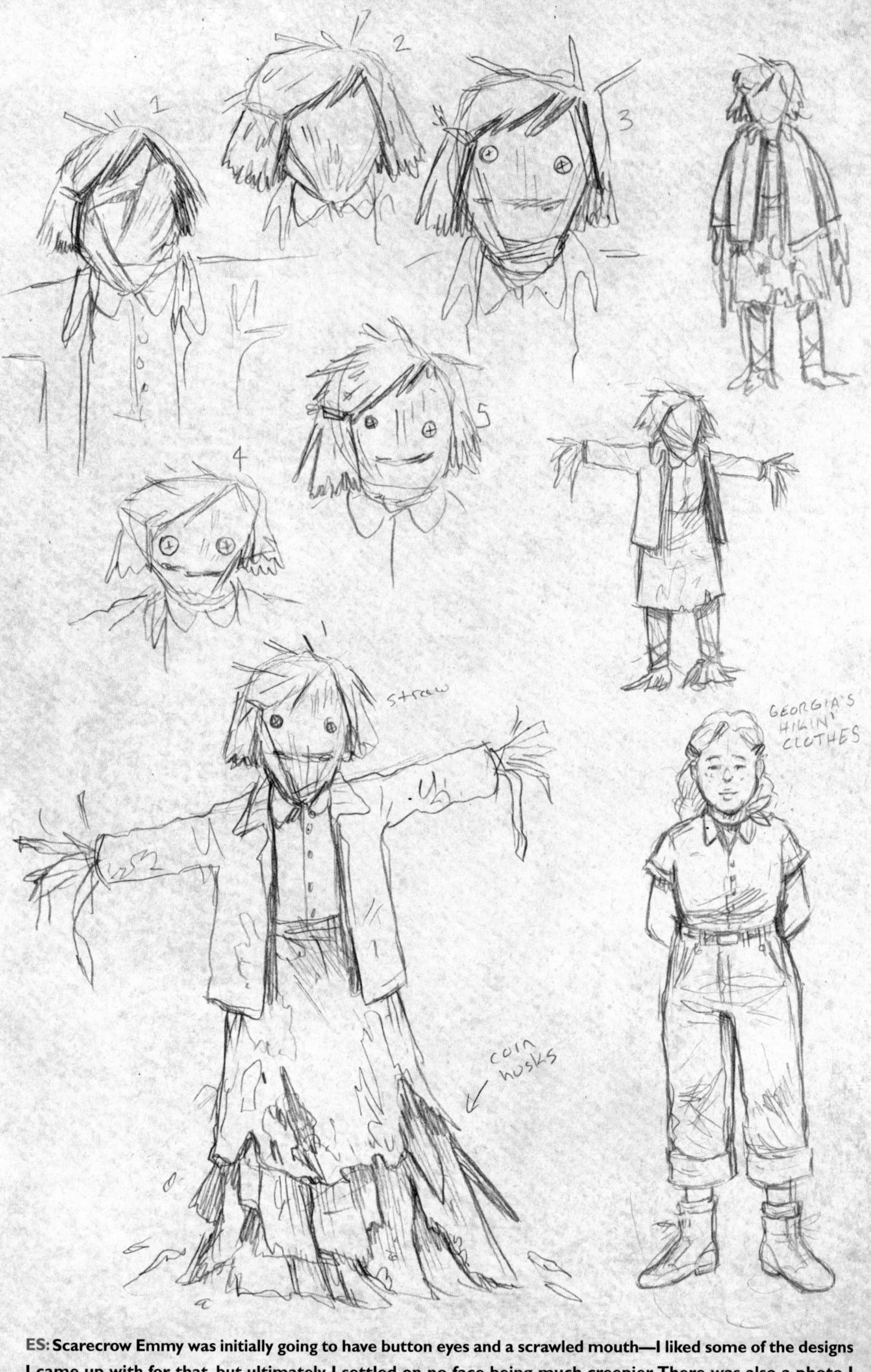
1
2
3
5
4
1
straw
GEORGIA'S HIKIN' CLOTHES
corn husks

ES: **Scarecrow Emmy was initially going to have button eyes and a scrawled mouth—I liked some of the designs I came up with for that, but ultimately I settled on no face being much creepier. There was also a photo I found of a corn husk doll with a skirt made from these overlapping bits of husk; I was very into Scarecrow Emmy having a scaled up, tattered version of that. While I still like that image of her just gliding around, I think it's for the best that we decided on legs. They became very helpful for conveying her movement and emotion on the page.**

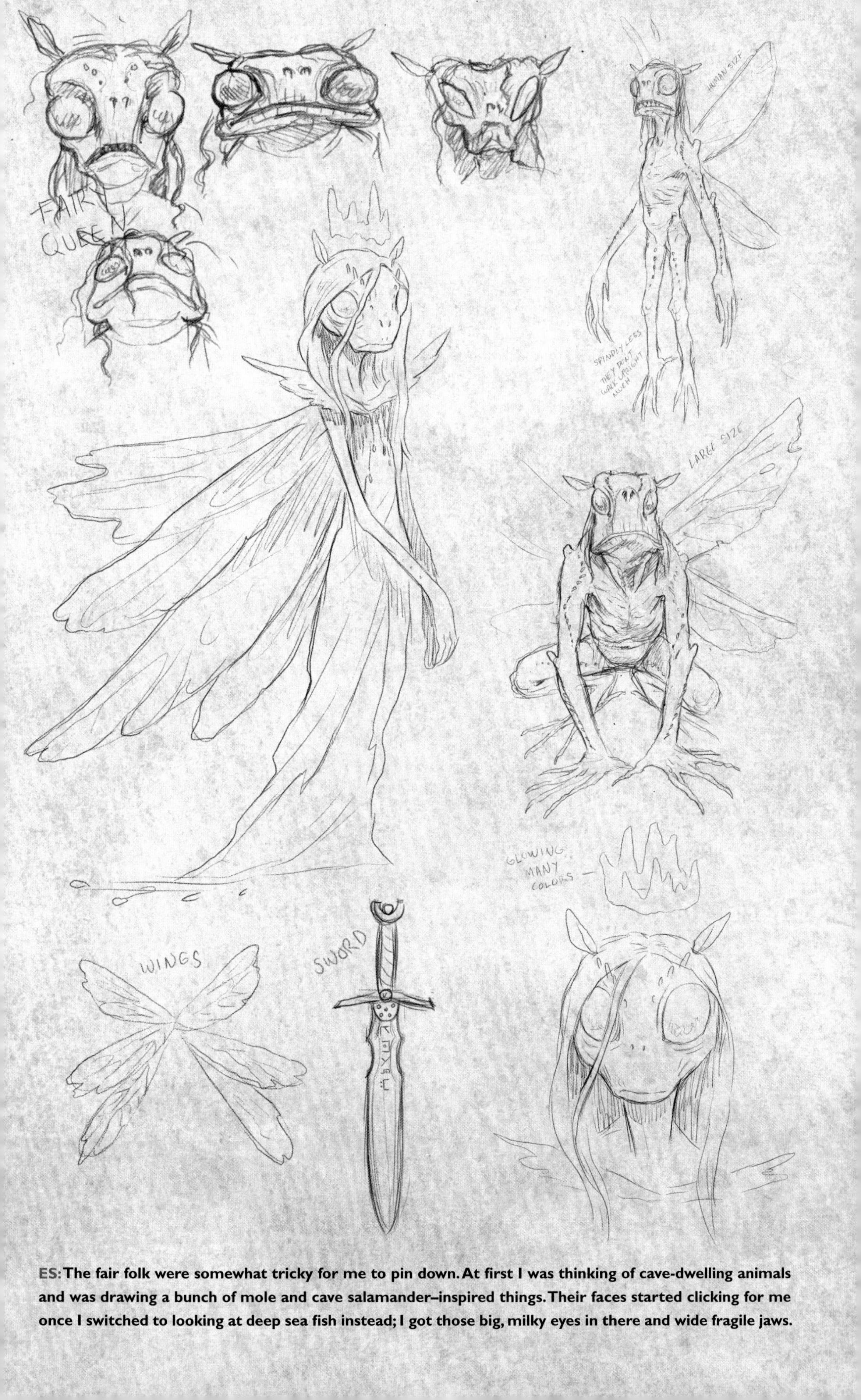

FAIRY QUEEN
HUMAN SIZE
SPINDLY LEGS THEY DON'T WALK UPRIGHT MUCH
LARGE SIZE
GLOWING MANY COLORS
WINGS
SWORD

ES: The fair folk were somewhat tricky for me to pin down. At first I was thinking of cave-dwelling animals and was drawing a bunch of mole and cave salamander–inspired things. Their faces started clicking for me once I switched to looking at deep sea fish instead; I got those big, milky eyes in there and wide fragile jaws.

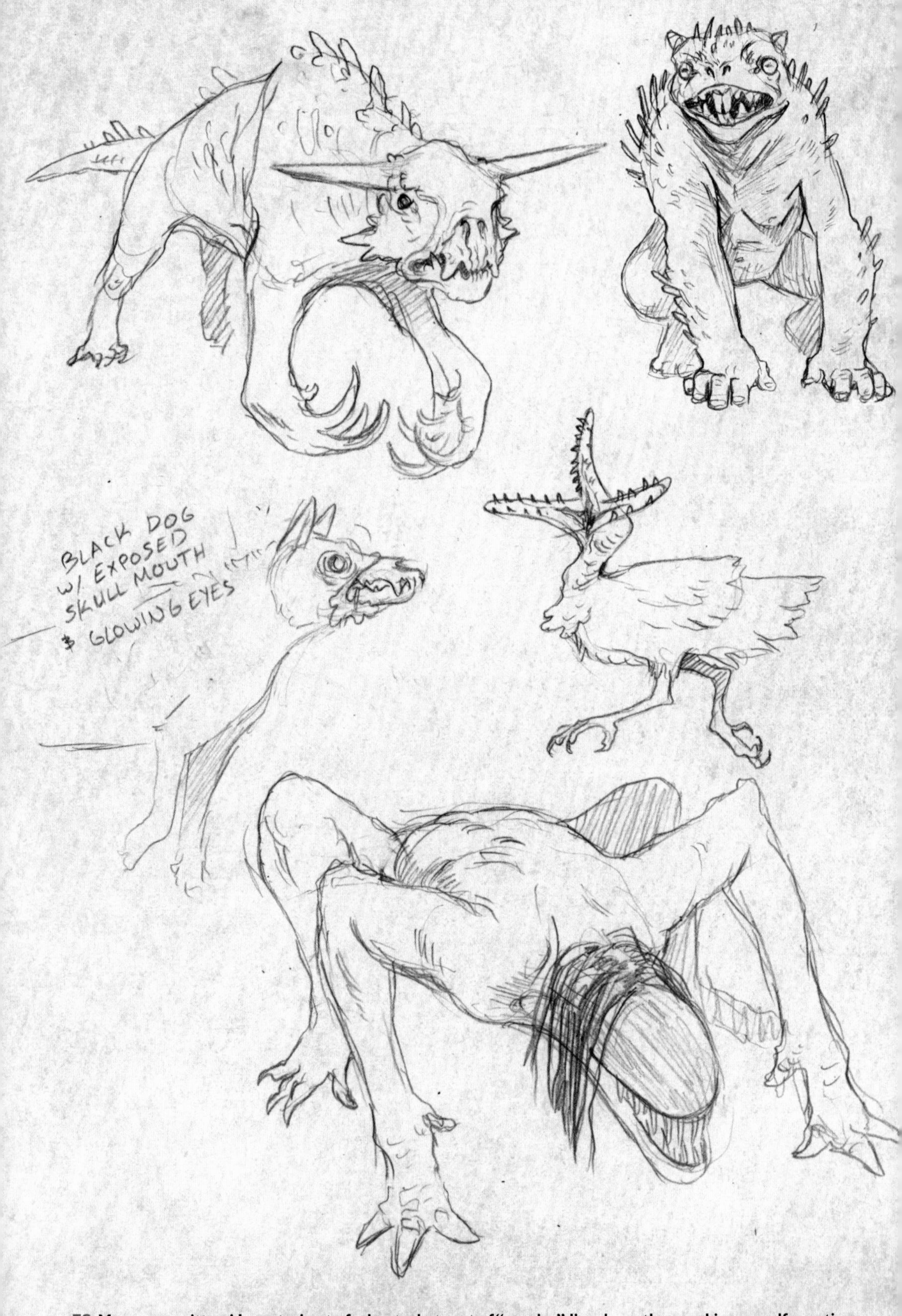
BLACK DOG
w/ EXPOSED
SKULL MOUTH
$ GLOWING EYES

ES: More cave critters! I was trying to feel out what sort of "species" live down there, asking myself questions like how adapted they should feel to digging and living subterranean lives, or if they should simply feel supernatural. I'm really fond of that eyeless guy on the bottom, I wish I threw him into more pages.

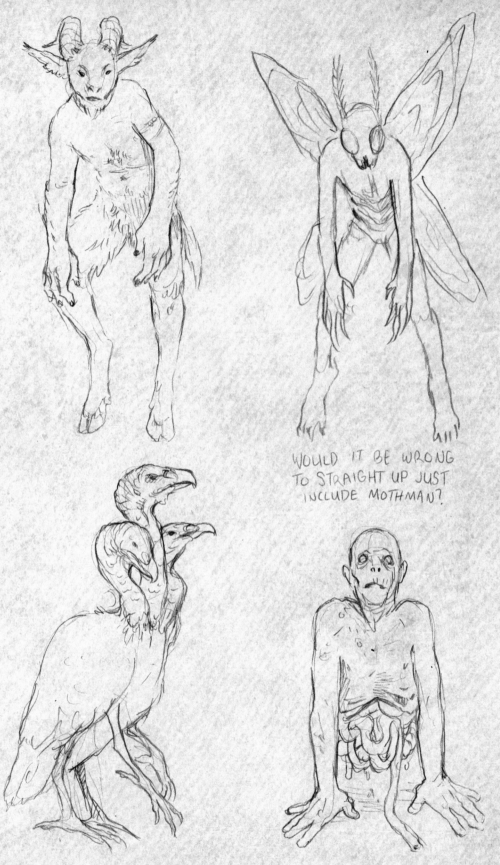

WOULD IT BE WRONG TO STRAIGHT UP JUST INCLUDE MOTHMAN?

ES: Designing more haints was a fun exercise because I wanted everyone to feel like they belonged to the same family as Tyler's creatures. Working within parameters like that is often oddly freeing creatively, plus I got to throw in Mothman!

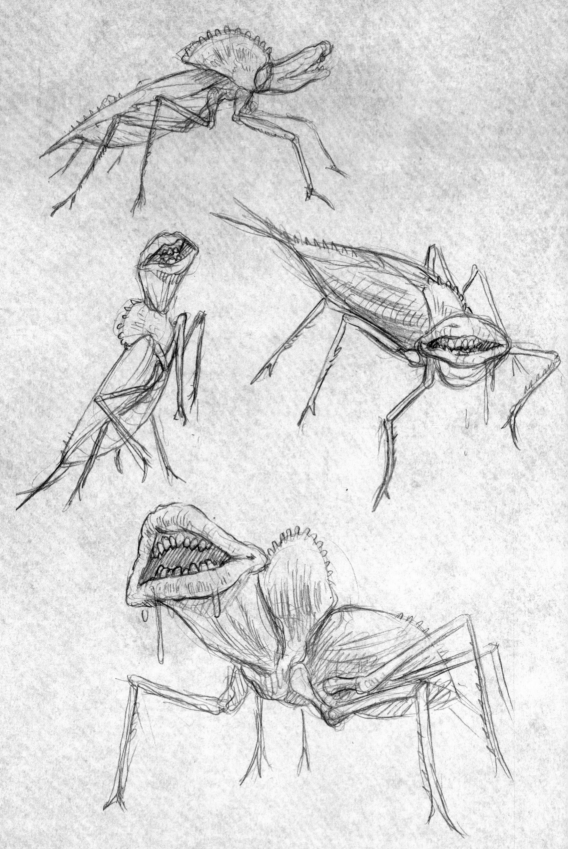

ES: When I read the description of an insect with a human mouth in Cullen's script, I couldn't wait to get this guy on paper. There's something about it that still makes me laugh; I love it so much. I did my best to make the Speaker Haint come off looking gross and creepy rather than comical, and I'm pretty happy with the results. Drool and crooked, little teeth can work wonders.

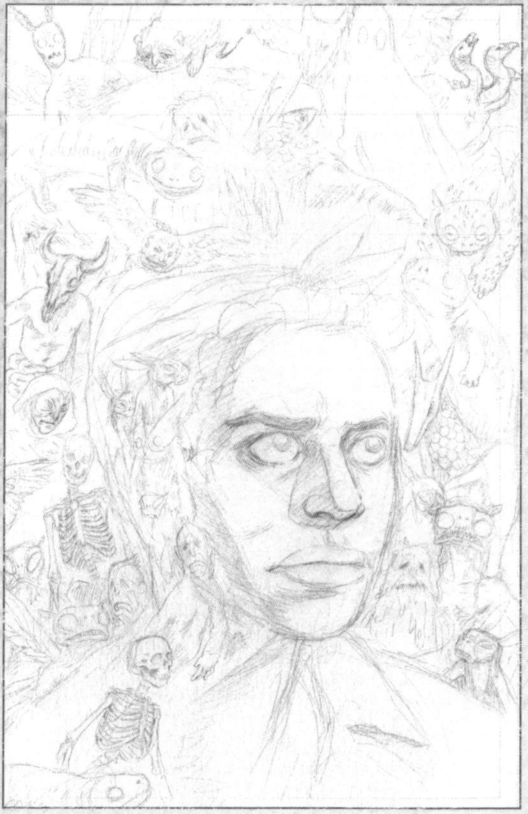
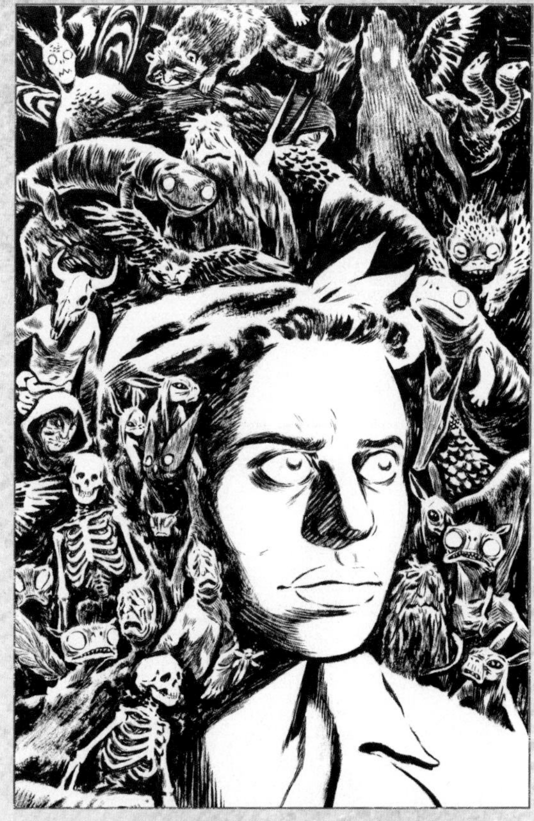
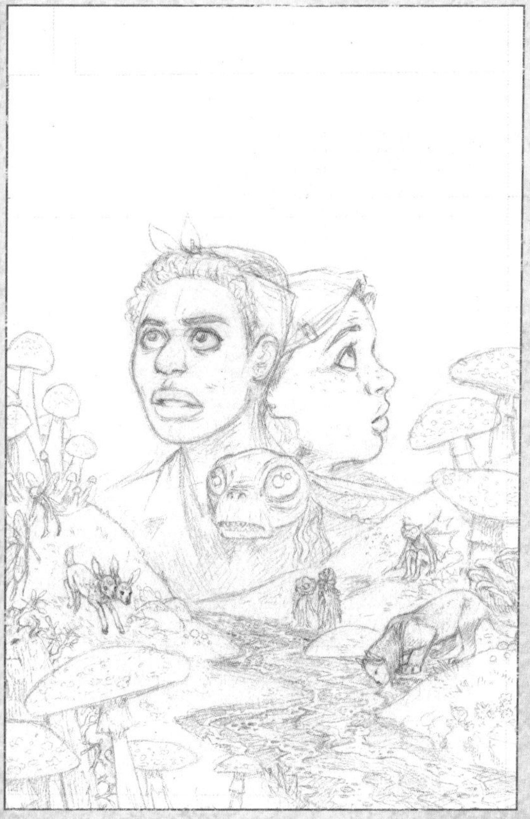
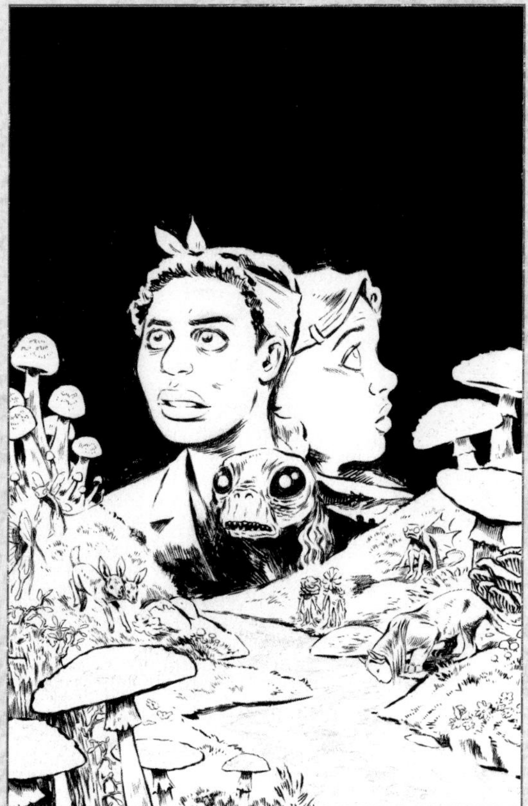

COVER PENCILS AND INKS FOR ISSUES #2 AND #3 BY
EMILY SCHNALL

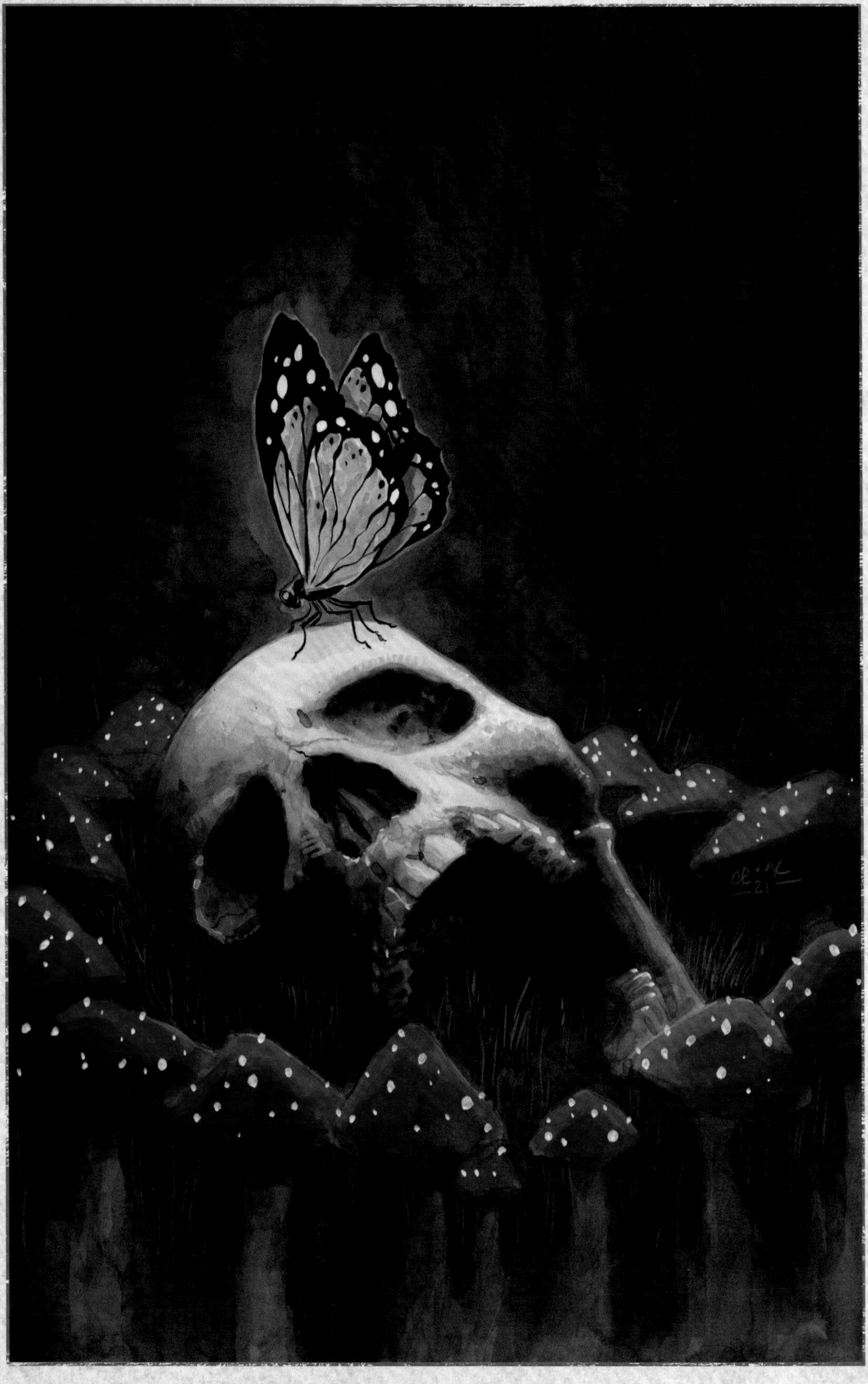

ISSUE #1 COVER VARIANT ARTWORK BY
TYLER CROOK

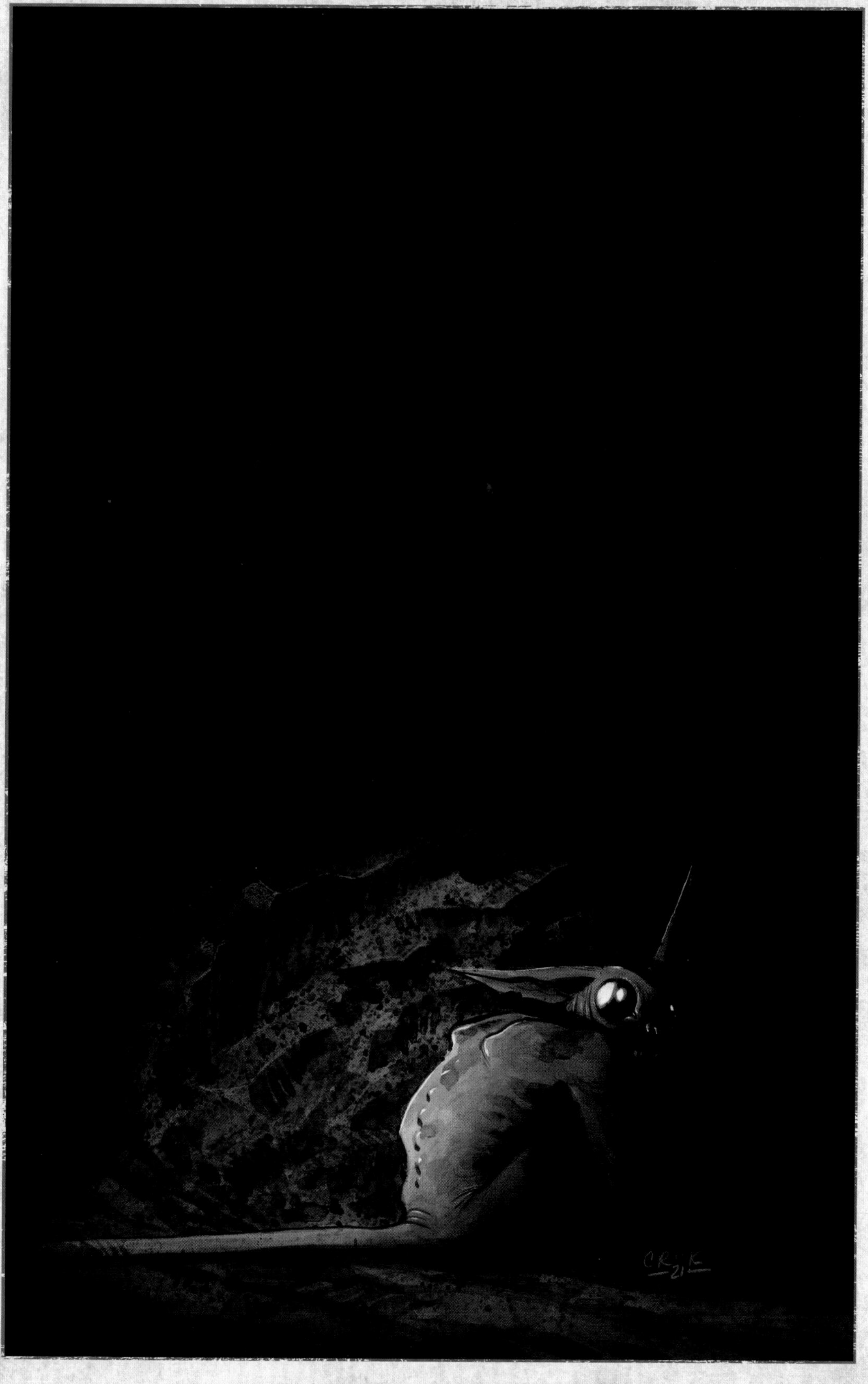

ISSUE #2 COVER VARIANT ARTWORK BY

TYLER CROOK

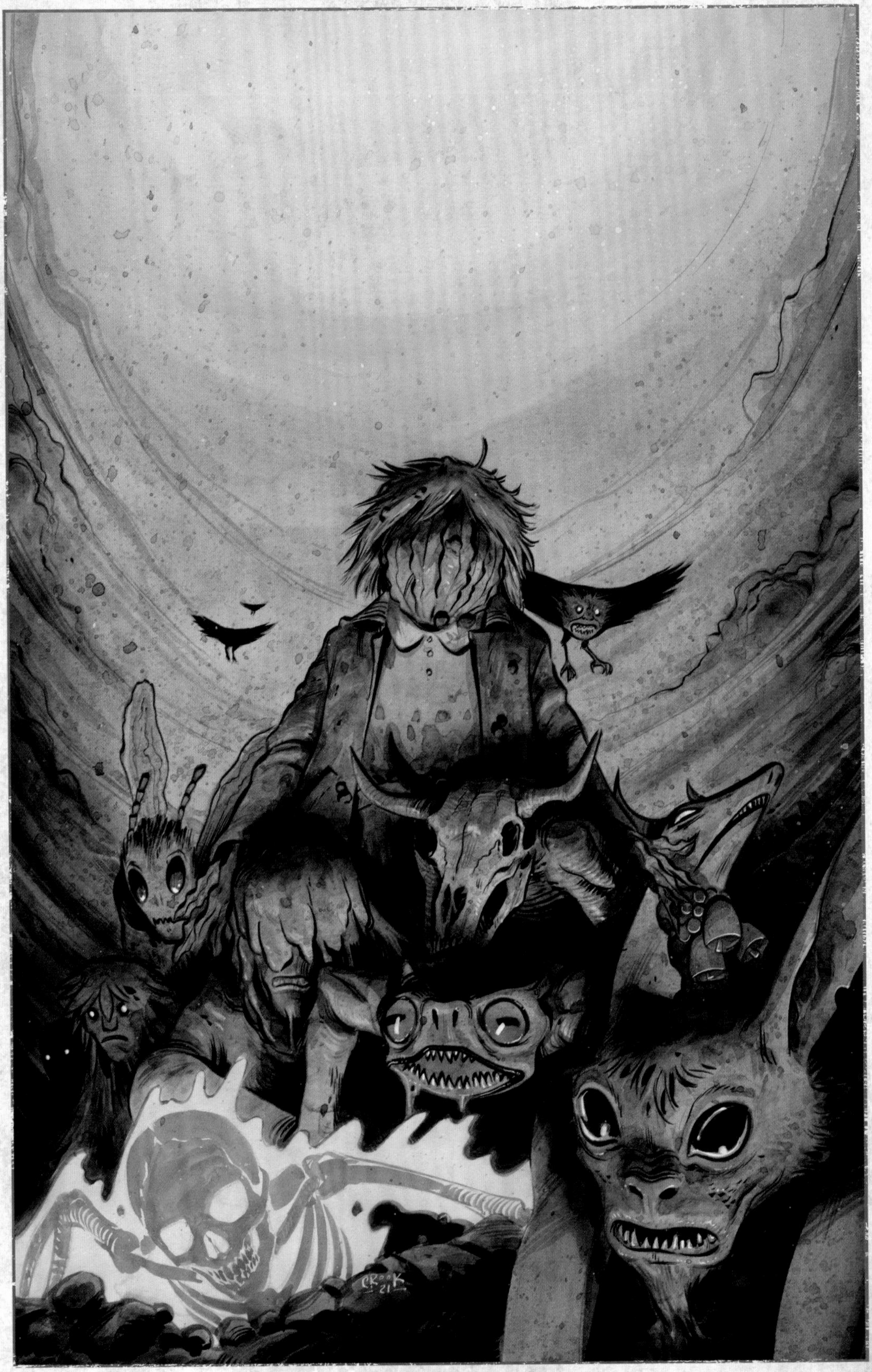
CROOK '21

ISSUE #3 COVER VARIANT ARTWORK BY
TYLER CROOK

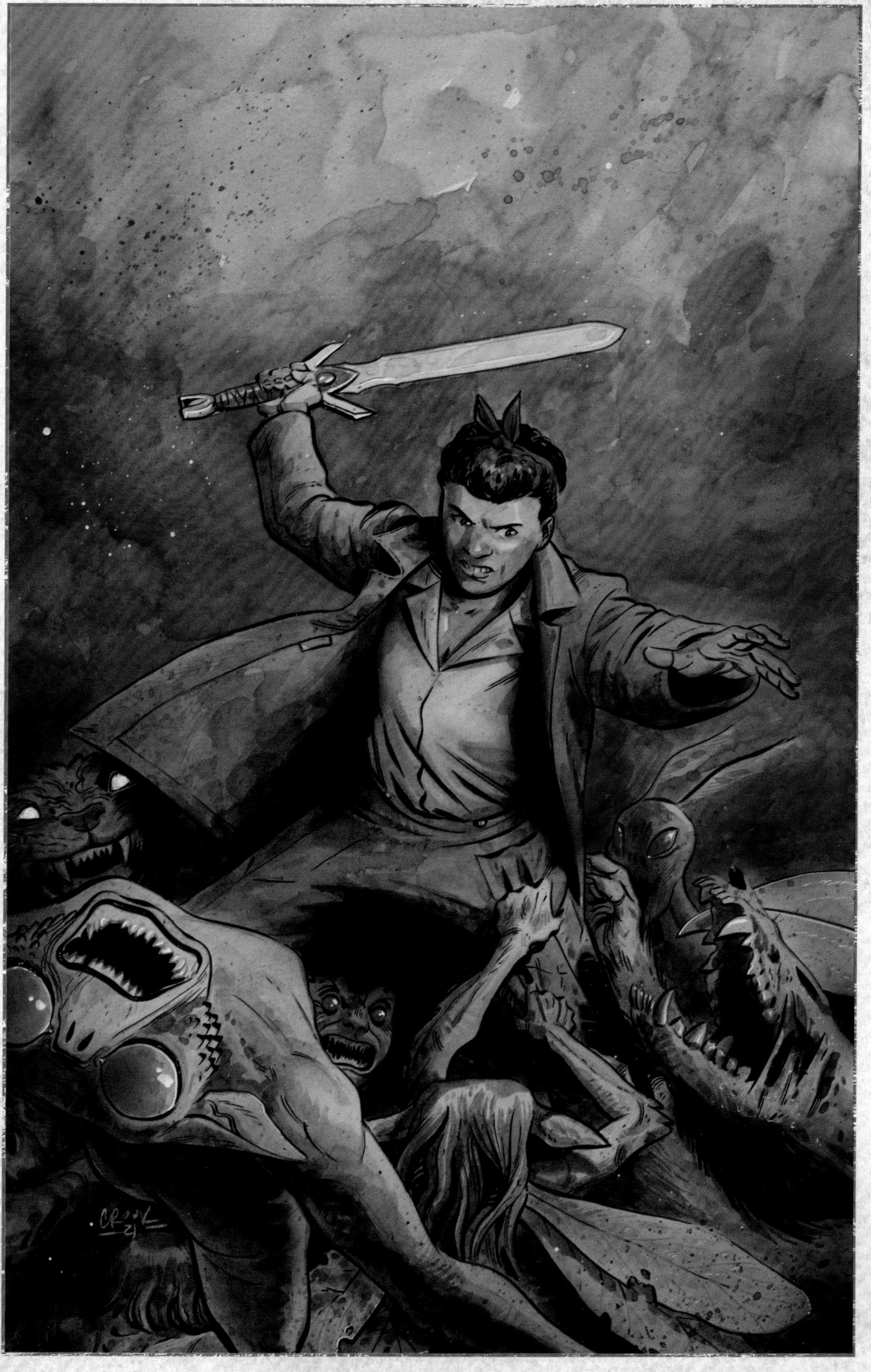
CROOK
21

ISSUE #4 COVER VARIANT ARTWORK BY
TYLER CROOK

DARK HORSE HORROR

drawing on your nightmares

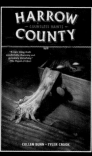

HELLBOY IN HELL VOLUME 1: THE DESCENT
Mike Mignola
ISBN 978-1-61655-444-6 | $17.99

HARROW COUNTY VOLUME 1: COUNTLESS HAINTS
Tyler Crook and Cullen Bunn
ISBN 978-1-61655-780-5 | $14.99

DEATH FOLLOWS
Cullen Bunn, A. C. Zamudio, and Carlos Nicolas Zamudio
ISBN 978-1-61655-951-9 | $17.99

JOE GOLEM: OCCULT DETECTIVE - THE RAT CATCHER & THE SUNKEN DEAD
Mike Mignola, Christopher Golden, and Patric Reynolds
ISBN 978-1-61655-964-9 | $24.99

H.P. LOVECRAFT'S THE HOUND AND OTHER STORIES
Gou Tanabe
ISBN 978-1-50670-312-1 | $12.99

ALABASTER: THE GOOD, THE BAD, AND THE BIRD
Caitlin R. Kiernan, Daniel Warren Johnson, Greg Ruth
ISBN 978-1-61655-796-6 | $19.99

BLACKWOOD VOLUME 1
Evan Dorkin, Andy Fish, Veronica Fish
ISBN 978-1-50670-742-6 | $17.99

STRANGER THINGS V1: THE OTHER SIDE
Jody Houser, Keith Champagne
ISBN 978-1-50670-976-5 | $17.99